MW00635662

DURAND'S CURSE

DURAND'S CURSE

A LINE ACROSS THE PATHAN HEART

RAJIV DOGRA

RUPA

Published by
Rupa Publications India Pvt. Ltd 2017
7/16, Ansari Road, Daryaganj
New Delhi 110002

Sales Centres:

Allahabad Bengaluru Chennai
Hyderabad Jaipur Kathmandu
Kolkata Mumbai

ISBN: 978-81-291-4864-3

Second impression 2019

10 9 8 7 6 5 4 3 2

Printed at Parksons Graphics Pvt. Ltd, Mumbai

For

Maanas and Anaia

May their wisdom enrich the world

Contents

1

Zan, Zar, Zameen

IT MUST HAVE BEEN THE lucky stars, otherwise the 'strongest man from Europe' was not expecting the 'Iron Amir of Afghanistan' to wilt so readily.

To the surprise of Mortimer Durand that is exactly what Amir Abdur Rahman did. He signed on the dotted line and with that single signature on a document written in a language that he did not know, Amir Abdur Rahman gifted away much of southern Afghanistan to the British Empire. Pathans in the distant frontier did not protest immediately because news travelled leisurely through the high mountains.

As for the British, the Durand Agreement was welcome news. With the frontier area in British control, there was no longer any need for humiliating wars with the Afghans. Durand was in seventh heaven. But Abdur Rahman was a wounded man.

Durand's seven-week stay in Kabul was a contest between two strong-willed personalities; one an ambitious diplomat and the other a cruel ruler. The wily Durand was pleased to absorb a territory that Abdur Rahman was finding tiresome. The British official wanted to have his name on the arrangement; the Afghan Amir believed the deal was temporary. But even as they were signing the one-page document, they both knew they were writing history with blurred lines.

On the morning of 12 November 1893, the foreign secretary of India, Sir Mortimer Durand, also drew a line across a small map. It is said that the Amir of Afghanistan, Abdur Rahman, nodded in approval. No Afghan aide was present in that room so there was no witness to the Amir's approval. There are no Afghan accounts either of the event so we have to rely on the version given by British writers. These writings are available in plenty, and they have all been self-laudatory.

This is only natural because it is the privilege of conquerors to tell stories that flatter their past. It is rare to find a historian of an imperial power exposing its misdeeds and describing its faults. Even the ugly business of gobbled frontiers is glossed over or passed off as unfortunate exception to an otherwise honourable enterprise. Britain is no exception to this rule. From the Victorians until the 1950s, its historians saw in the British Empire a great engine for spreading liberty and civilization around the world.

It is on this condescending note that at the end of the nineteenth century, the official *Imperial Gazetteer of India* chose to describe the animals of Afghanistan before it reported on its people, who, it said, are 'inured to bloodshed from childhood...treacherous and passionate in revenge...'

This judgement of the Afghan people was harsh, perhaps unfair as well. But it is strange that the opinion of the conquerors should not have changed over the millennia. In the fourth century BC, one of the first conquerors of Afghanistan, Alexander the Great, said, 'May God keep you away from the venom of the cobra, the teeth of the tiger and the revenge of the Afghans.'

He had reason to be wary because he fell afoul of the Pashtun tribesmen in today's Malakand Agency, where he took an arrow in the leg and almost lost his life.

Centuries later, a Hollywood movie echoed similar sentiments in this dialogue between Rambo and his Afghan interlocutor:

Mousa: This is Afghanistan...Alexander the Great try to conquer this country...then Genghis Khan, then the British. Now Russia. But Afghan people fight hard, they never be defeated. Ancient enemy make prayer about these people...you wish to hear?

Rambo: Um-hum.

Mousa: Very good. It says, 'May God deliver us from the venom of the cobra, teeth of the tiger and the vengeance of the Afghan.' Understand what this means?

Rambo: That you guys don't take any shit?

Mousa: Yes...something like this.

That indeed is the irony of Afghanistan where life imitates fiction, and facts sometimes are hard to believe. Who, for instance, would have thought that a strong-willed Amir, who had expanded and unified

Afghanistan, would whimsically gift away a major portion of Afghan land? This smoke-and-mirrors quality of the country makes it so mysterious and difficult for a foreigner to understand. In fact, history has proved over and over again that if Afghans are stoic fighters, they are also gullible. If that first characteristic keeps the Afghans busy, that latter trait is a weakness which foreigners have exploited over and over again. Afghans were especially miserable in this regard during the nineteenth century.

Let us then start from the beginning of the nineteenth century when the Great Game began. As a prelude to that, a brief primer about the land and its people may be in order.

Myths, Legends and Anatomy

If Afghans were given just one wish they would say, leave us unfettered. Yet this land has been ravaged repeatedly. Why has this unfortunate country been the chessboard of empires? What is it that fascinates them to play their games here? Or is it that the soil of Afghanistan sponsors strife? A legend maintains that Alexander the Great's mother sent him a letter taunting him for being stuck in Afghanistan for three years after conquering Anatolia, Mesopotamia and Persia in a year. Alexander sent her back a sack full of Afghan soil, asking her to spread it around her palace. She did as her son had told her to do. But when the Macedonian nobles walked over the Afghan soil they began to bicker and fight amongst themselves.

Alas, that peculiar quality of its soil continues to haunt the land. Many have written about Afghanistan, but that crafty conjurer of the written word, Winston Churchill, describes it pithily. He was just 23 years old in 1897 when he was embedded on behalf of *The Telegraph* with the British army. It was then fighting a bloody rebellion in the North-West Frontier.

In one of his reports for *The Telegraph* he describes Afghanistan thus,

> All along the north and north-west frontiers of India lie the Himalayas… Nearly four hundred miles in breadth and more than sixteen hundred in length, this mountainous region divides the great plains of the south from those of Central Asia, and parts as a channel separates opposing shores, the Eastern Empire of Great Britain from that of Russia. The western end of this tumult of ground is formed

> by the peaks of the Hindu Kush... The Himalayas are not a line, but a great country of mountains. By one who stands on some lofty pass or commanding point in Dir, Swat or Bajaur, range after range is seen as the long surges of an Atlantic swell... The drenching rains...have washed the soil from the sides of the hills until they have become strangely grooved by numberless water-courses...rain has cut wide, deep and constantly-changing channels through this soft deposit; great gutters, which are sometimes seventy feet deep and two or three hundred yards across.

Now that we have a rough idea of its anatomy, let us try and get a fix on its location. Where is Afghanistan, the cause of many myths, and more specifically where is the frontier, the subject of even greater legends? But let us first begin with the geographical limits, or the 'Hud-e-Sikandar', as many have called it through the ages.

The Indus River has for long fascinated people. Would-be conquerors have paused at its banks wondering how and where to ford its depths. Historians have considered it as a divide between the riches of India and the beginning of the tribal world. In the beginning of recorded history, it was called Sindhu, the Persians called it Hindu and the Greeks preferred the shorter Indu for its rhyming convenience with the land. The rolling plains to its west right up to the foothills have been linked to India and its people. There have been periods when the Indian civilization stretched far beyond the river to include Mohenjo-Daro and Harappa. But that was four to five thousand years ago.

Since then, and for most part of recorded history, Indus has formed a natural boundary conveniently dividing kingdoms. Sometimes though, the Afghan reach has stretched right up to its banks in Punjab. On some occasions, one or the other of the Indian empires have absorbed land up to the foothills of the Himalayas as theirs. At times, the boundary was in the trans-Indus lands, just to the west of the river, rather than to the cis-Indus territories, just to the east of the river. But seldom did they stray too many miles from the river. In essence, Indus divided two essentially distinct territories; marking them as geographically separate, socially distinct and differing from each other in their material configuration and popular institutions.

There has been an attempt in the recent past to claim that Pakistan is centred on the Indus. But it is not. The cis-Indus provinces of Sind and

Punjab have little in common with trans-Indus Balochistan and the North-West Frontier Province (NWFP).

Further up, almost 200 miles northwest of the Indus is the Hindu Kush mountain range. They are the real barriers between Central and South Asia. The name itself is significant; Hindu Kush means the killer of Hindus, as thousands of Hindu and Sikh soldiers and slaves have perished in its snow-covered passes. About 600 miles long, its mountains reach up to 20,000 feet, and some of its passes are at heights of 14,000 feet. It is through such formidable passes that armies of Alexander, Tamerlane and Babur marched down to India.

The Hindu Kush, however, are not the only barriers for invaders into India. Further down, between the Hindu Kush and the Indus is another set of mountains. The Safed Koh and Sulaiman ranges are not high mountains and their passes are at lower heights. But they are strategically located for hit-and-run tactics and to control the flow of trade caravans.

Fearless Tribes

Sometimes, it is said uncharitably that the tribal communities living there depend on this loot for their sustenance and that every stone lying on these passes is soaked in blood. Across these mountain ranges lies the area where people known as Pathans* have lived with a code of honour that had long recognized *zan, zar* and *zameen* (woman, gold and land) as their only lode stars. The Pathans scattered over these largely wild lands are divided into various tribes, and though their physical features differ, they all share the same lust for honour and independence.

Beginning with the little Pamir in the north, this common area classified by the British as the frontier runs through Chitral, Kohistan, Bajaur, Khyber, Tirah, Waziristan and parts of Balochistan. This ruggedly picturesque expanse of almost 40,000 square miles had once belonged to Afghanistan. This region, where geography defines the way of life and where strategy jostles with survival, hosts perhaps the most fearless, ferocious and warlike people in the world.

---

*Pathan, Pashtun and Pakhtoon have been used interchangeably in the text in line with the response given by Khan Abdul Ghaffar Khan in Pakistan's National Assembly on 5 March 1948 and that given by his son, Wali Khan, to a journalist in 1975.

Rudyard Kipling had written about them in an introduction to his short story, 'The Amir's Homily'. With his unique gift for words, Kipling draws this portrait of Afghans,

> To the Afghan neither life, property, law, nor kingship are sacred when his own lusts prompt him to rebel. He is a thief by instinct, a murderer by heredity and training, and frankly bestially immoral by all three. None the less he has his own crooked notions of honour, and his character is fascinating to study. On occasion he will fight without reason till he is hacked in pieces; on other occasions he will refuse to show fight till he is driven into a corner. Herein he is as unaccountable as the graywolf, who is his blood-brother. And these men His Highness rules by the only weapon that they understand—the fear of death, which among some Orientals is the beginning of wisdom.

John Masters too had a view to share. He distilled the spirit of what he observed in these lines, 'Across the scrub covered plain approached men with camels. The men had faces of eagles and walked with a long, slow lifting stride. One of them looked up as he passed by. Anne smiled at him, expecting the salaam and the answering smile of an ordinary Indian wayfarer. But this was not India. The man stared her down from pale green kohl rimmed eyes. He carried a long rifle slung across his shoulders; a woman shapelessly swathed in red and black cotton swayed on top of the camel that he led; a lad of fourteen walked behind the camel; the lad had no beard, but his stride was an exact imitation of his father's lilt, and he too carried a rifle…'

'He [the son] too carried a rifle…' This faith in gun defines the frontier and its people.

Alas, this land has seen more wars than its due. Its people deserve better, yet Pathans have suffered enormously. It is not just in the battlefield that they have been targeted. Almost all British accounts of the second half of the nineteenth century describe them negatively as brutal, untrustworthy and worse. I have read almost everything that was written then about Afghanistan's wars and its foreign relations. But it is odd that after the First Anglo–Afghan War, all British references to Afghans should have been in negative terms. If at all there is a positive word somewhere, it must have escaped me and I readily admit to that as mea culpa.

The question that I have asked myself over and over again is this—don't writers and historians have a moral responsibility to reflect the truth? How can they let a slight or national prejudice colour their views, and distort their writing? The Pathan, who was projected as a wild beast in the British writing of the late nineteenth century, has an entirely different image in India. Here he is seen as a large-hearted man with a beard who hawks dry fruits from Afghanistan. It was one such kind old man who longs for his land and his child in Rabindranath Tagore's 'Kabuliwala'.

Incidentally, the story of 'Kabuliwala' was written in 1892, just a year before Mortimer Durand divided the Pathan heartland into two. Having read that poignant story and having heard the folklore about the brave and perhaps simple-minded Pathans, most Indians wonder why and how they could became so wretched in the English eye? Was it because like Amir Abdur Rahman, the Pathans care for their nam (name)?

But Afghanistan is not just about Pathans. It is an ethnological jigsaw of considerable complexity. Ghilzais, Tajiks, Turkmen, Uzbeks, Hazaras, Kazaks and Chagtai Turks are all found here in greater and smaller numbers. While a theory links the original Afghan settlers to Jewish origin, it is acknowledged widely that this diversity of races has a connection with the passage of conquerors through different phases of its history. Yet it will be simplistic to relate its people and their culture to the passage of different armies through these lands.

Afghanistan may be a wounded land, but it was not always conquered by the sword. In the distant past, at least, many other religions and cultures were embraced by the Afghans. Both the Ramayana and the Mahabharata have references to Gandhar, which probably is the area around today's Kandahar and Peshawar. Buddhism, too, had cast its spell on Afghans. Some of the finest specimens of Buddhist art, particularly the statues of Buddha, were seen in Afghanistan, before the Taliban destroyed them.

Let's turn to the final, and indeed the most fascinating question—who are the people who inhabit the frontier part of this land?

Proud Pashtuns

On 5 March 1948, Pakistan's Prime Minister Liaquat Ali Khan asked precisely this question in its Constituent Assembly, 'Is Pathan the name of a country or that of a community?'

Liaquat Ali's question had considerable political significance, especially because it was directed at the great Pakhtoon leader, Khan Abdul Ghaffar Khan.

The reply given by Ghaffar Khan should clear up all etymological doubts on the subject, 'Pathan is the name of the community and we will name the country as Pakhtoonistan.' He added, 'I may also explain that the people of India used to call us Pathans and we are called Afghans by the Persians. Our real name is Pakhtoon. We want Pakhtoonistan and want to see all the Pathans on this side of the Durand Line joined and united together in Pakhtoonistan.'

Later, in 1975, an acerbic Punjabi journalist confronted Ghaffar Khan's son Wali Khan, the National Awami Party leader, on the issue and asked whether he was 'a Muslim, a Pakistani or a Pashtun first'. He gave a much-quoted reply that he was 'a six-thousand-year-old Pashtun, a thousand-year-old Muslim and a twenty-seven-year-old Pakistani.'

Wali Khan's response captured the spirit of Pashtun pride, because despite endemic conflict among different Pashtun groups, the notion of the ethnic and cultural unity of all Pashtuns has long been a familiar note.

Young Churchill, however, had this to say about the Pathans, 'This state of continual tumult has produced a habit of mind which recks little of injuries, holds life cheap and embarks on war with careless levity, and the tribesmen of the Afghan border afford the spectacle of a people, who fight without passion, and kill one another without loss of temper. Such a disposition, combined with an absolute lack of reverence for all forms of law and authority, and a complete assurance of equality, is the cause of their frequent quarrels with the British power. A trifle rouses their animosity. They make a sudden attack on some frontier post. They are repulsed. From their point of view the incident is closed. There has been a fair fight in which they have had the worst fortune. What puzzles them is that "the Sirkar" should regard so small an affair in a serious light.'

Alas, the simple Pashtuns could never fathom the British Sirkar's mind.

It wasn't always this bad. For a while in the mid-eighteenth century, the situation looked promising. Afghanistan, as an independent state more or less in the form that we know it today, came into being in 1747 with the assassination of the Persian king, Nadir Shah. In the confusion following the assassination, one of his favourite generals, Ahmad Khan, managed to get hold of the bulk of treasure that Nadir Shah had looted in Delhi.

With that under his control, he broke off from the main convoy with a group of soldiers loyal to him. He decided then to settle down in Afghanistan. Eventually, he extended his kingdom to Punjab and parts of Sind besides annexing the Persian province of Khorasan. As king, he felt the need to have a name and title with the gravitas appropriate to his position. That's why he proclaimed himself Ahmad Shah and for good measure assumed the title Durr-i-Durrani, the Pearl of Pearls.

The group that had been loyal to him called themselves Durranis while those from the royal house were Sadozi branch of the tribe. His prime minister was the head of the rival Barakzai tribe.

Ahmad Shah Durrani and his son Timur Shah Durrani expanded their domain, conquering territories from Kashmir to the Arabian Sea and from the Amu River to the Indus River. This Durrani Empire at the end of the eighteenth century included modern-day Afghanistan and most of Pakistan, making it the second-largest Muslim empire of its day.

Ahmad Shah Durrani, poet, warrior and king that he was, wrote of his nostalgia for Afghanistan during ten campaigns to expand his rule over Kashmir, Punjab and Sind, 'Whatever countries I conquer in the world, I would never forget your beautiful gardens. When I remember the summits of your beautiful mountains I forget the greatness of the Delhi throne.'

Ahmad Shah was not exaggerating.

A latter-day traveller to Kabul, Alexander Burnes, compared the city to paradise, 'There were peaches, plums, apricots, pears, apples, quinces, cherries, walnuts, mulberries, pomegranates, and vines, all growing in one garden. There were also nightingales, blackbirds, thrushes and doves...and chattering magpies on almost every tree.'

Today, that paradise-like city is unrecognizable; so complete has been its destruction over the years. The desolate patchwork that greets the visitor now bears hardly any fruit and hosts almost no bird. But even back then, the glory did not last long. After Ahmad Shah, his Afghan homeland was to provide a lasting challenge to his heirs.

According to Thomas J. Barfield, this Durrani Empire was 'a coat worn inside out', because Kandahar, Kabul and Peshawar were poor and sparsely populated compared to the rest of the country. The wealthiest territories remained on frontiers in every direction. However, this glory did not last long. After the death of Ahmad Shah, Afghanistan became an 'orgy of intrigue, treachery, murder…and betrayal'.

Even if it was so and the tribes were in strife, isn't that description of Afghanistan a bit extreme? Let us, therefore, give the final word to a Pashtun perspective. This is what a Pakhtoon leader told Lord Elphinstone, 'We are content with discord; we are content with alarms; we are content with blood; but we never will be content with a master.'

This, therefore, is the question that must be asked. Pashtuns may have been conquered many times, but have they ever been vanquished?

2

The India Campaign

AFGHANISTAN'S VAST TERRITORIAL SPREAD STARTED to fray during the final years of the eighteenth century. It wasn't just in this part of Asia that changes were taking place. As the eighteenth century was folding into the nineteenth, it brought in a series of new developments in Europe. The two events seemed to be unrelated at first, but over time they were to have profound consequences.

Until then, Afghanistan did not figure in the East India Company's order of priorities. As an essentially commercial company, its focus was mercantile. But when the Afghan king, Shah Zaman, reached up to Lahore and received the allegiance of the Sikh rulers there, it set the alarm bells ringing in the Company headquarters in Calcutta. As it is they were getting reports from their agents that Tipu Sultan, the rulers of Oudh and many rajas were in touch with Shah Zaman.

Separately, and more worryingly, they received the news that Napoleon was showing increasing interest in India. He had been hearing exaggerated accounts of India's riches. This, and the possibility of snatching the Crown jewel of the British Empire, excited him greatly. 'I was full of dreams,' Napoleon explained, 'I saw myself founding a new religion, marching into Asia riding an elephant, a turban on my head...'

His plan was to co-opt Russia in this venture and use the route via Persia and Afghanistan to reach India. It was an ambitious venture and, typically for Napoleon, audacious in nature. The British should have realized the impracticality of it given his fluctuating fortunes in the European battles, but they were so dazzled by Napoleon's military genius that they were willing to believe anything.

Up until then the British had only a passing interest in Afghanistan as an unruly neighbour. But this did not bother them much because Afghanistan was a safe distance away from India. Moreover, there were the buffers of Punjab and Sind between them. Besides, the British ingress into India had been through the sea route. Its trade links were also by the sea. And after Nelson had defeated Napoleon's fleet in Egypt, the British navy commanded the seas right up to India. So its preference was to use the familiar sea route rather than the long and treacherous land route. Therefore, rugged Afghanistan had not entered into its strategic picture so far.

But the twin developments of Shah Zaman's foray into Punjab and Napoleon's interest in India alarmed the British. Academically, though, it is worth wondering whether the wars, bloodshed and the grab of Afghan territories by the British would have happened had these two events not taken place or not happened almost simultaneously.

The British paranoia did not stop there. A little prior to these developments, there had been troubling news from Afghanistan as well. In 1798, Richard Wellesley, the Governor General of India, received a letter from Afghan Amir, Shah Zaman. This unexpected letter informed him of the Shah's proposed military expedition into northern India, and in that enterprise, he sought Wellesley's help in driving out the Marathas. This was enough to frighten the British Governor General. Wellesley started having visions of wild Afghans pouring down from their mountains and causing mayhem in India.

So while the rest of the world was preparing for the new century, the British in India were worried about the fate of their empire. In order to check the Afghan Amir, Wellesley approached the Iranian ruler Fath Ali Shah, requesting him 'to take measures to keep Shah Zaman in perpetual check to preclude him from returning to India...'

The British response to the threat from Europe was also quick. There was no way it would let the Franco–Russian combination reach anywhere within sniffing distance of India. It had to try and stop their aggression at its first entry point. Accordingly, Captain John Malcolm was dispatched to Persia to come to an agreement with King Fath Ali Shah. They signed a treaty by which Fath Ali committed himself to the British bidding. He agreed that there would be no peace between Persia and Afghanistan till the Afghan Amir gave up his designs on India. He also conceded to the British demand for expulsion of French nationals from Persia.

Napoleon was not deterred by this treaty. He first tried to woo the Persian king by offering to help him recover his territories of Georgia and Armenia, which had been seized by Russia. But Fath Ali rejected that because he did not want to ally with a country which had beheaded its monarch. Moreover, British India was closer physically to Persia and their trade and political interests were complementary.

At any rate, Napoleon proved to be a fickle suitor because he was soon seen engaging with Russia for his enterprise towards India. After they had signed the Treaty of Tilsit, the Russo–French plan seemed to be a real possibility. But once again, Napoleon changed course. The result was a war between France and Russia.

British Phobia

The British were relieved that the French monster had shifted his attention elsewhere. But there was the Russian bear still to contend with and it was making ominous moves towards Central Asia. As an essentially sea power, Britain decided that it was time to build up its military resources to protect its land flanks. So the seed of suspicion that the short-lived Russo–French move had sown in the beginning of the nineteenth century was going to last throughout that century. Russia began to dominate British India's strategic thinking and its military plans.

In retrospect, it is good to ask if the situation was really that serious for the British. Realistically speaking, it was more the work of some over enthusiastic and feverish British minds because at the beginning of the nineteenth century, Russia was far away, beyond the Afghan mountains and the Central Asian deserts. Its boundary in that period ran along the northeast of the Caspian Sea and by the Ural River up towards Orenburg. Until then, British India was geographically safe on the east side of the Sutlej River. Between the two, lay deserts, mountains and barren lands full of murderous tribes and tricking thieves. In fact, the situation on the ground right up to 1838 was such that there was a physical distance of almost 2,000 miles between the two.

What then was the cause of British paranoia? Naturally, there cannot be a simple, single answer to so complex an issue. However, if one is looking only for a straightforward and simple answer then the term 'Great Game' is the most appropriate explanation; because essentially it was a game between two great powers at the cost of many ordinary people.

In this game the Afghan people were the pawns; their apprehensions were of no concern to the big two, nor was their fate of any consequence. As the game progressed, so did Afghan troubles. The colonial powers of Europe started to view Afghanistan as an essential first step before they hopped on to the riches of India.

'Indian Campaign' had been Napoleon Bonaparte's idea. He was supported by Paul I of Russia who was disappointed with the fiasco of the Russian–British invasion of the Netherlands. He was also infuriated by the British occupation of Malta because, at that time, he bore the title of the Grand Master of the Order of Malta and took the British attack as a personal affront. As a result of his pique, Paul I cut off relations with Great Britain and made a deal with Napoleon.

Since the attempt to reach India via Egypt had been stymied by Lord Nelson, Napoleon came up with the idea of a land operation. According to Napoleon's plan, a Russian corps of 35,000 soldiers was to set out from Astrakhan and, after crossing the Caspian Sea, this force was to land in the Persian city of Astrabad. A similar French corps led by French General Jean Victor Marie Moreau of the Rhine was to go down to the Danube estuary, cross over to Taganrog and then march through Tsaritsyn to Astrabad. In Persia, the French troops were to join the Russian corps for a march towards India.

The scale of this plan measured up to the campaigns of Alexander the Great. A total of 22,000 Cossacks were conscripted by Paul I. The Russian treasury earmarked a large sum of over 1.5 million roubles for the operation. All this was quickly arranged because his courtiers were conscious of Paul I's whims and eccentricities. They had borne with a straight face many of his bizarre ideas like his plan to paint St Michael's Castle the colour of his mistress's gloves.

To cross Central Asia in just two months, then to cross the mountain ranges of Afghanistan and come crashing down on the British as a bolt from the blue was exactly the kind of idea that the Russian emperor could get carried away with. But he had absolutely no inkling of the ordeal he was going to put the Cossacks through. Or where in the world he was sending them because back then the Russian maps did not show anything beyond Khiva in Central Asia!

According to the preliminary plans, Napoleon was to simultaneously open up a second front. But Paul I did not trust Napoleon, so he opted to strike out on his own. On 12 January 1801, he ordered the commander of the Cossacks to set out for India.

Mid-January is the coldest time of the year—the time when horses can walk over frozen rivers. But by the time the Cossacks reached Volga River, it was early spring. The soft sun had begun to thaw the ice. The sheet of ice over the Volga had become so fragile that the horses fell into the river. But that was not the end of their troubles. Their going got even more difficult after crossing the river—the spring sun had melted the snow on land too, turning the road into a swamp. Horses tripped to fall into it and the route was marked with hundreds of their corpses. Artillery men were an anguished lot too; they had a harrowing time trying to pull their cannons through the mud.

To top it all, a new trouble awaited the Cossacks on the other side of the Volga as they marched through the Saratov region. This was largely a barren land with very little vegetation and they had to go without food or fodder for days on end.

Their ordeal, however, ended unexpectedly. Word reached them of the demise of Paul I on 23 March 1801. Alexander I, the emperor's son who succeeded him to the throne, did not fancy the idea of waging war in faraway lands. He decided to call back the campaign. When the commander of Cossack troops, General Vasily Orlov, received the order to return, he addressed the soldiers saying, 'God and the Emperor bestow upon you your fathers' homes.'

This was the end of their Indian crusade.

There are many conspiracy theories about the assassination of Emperor Paul I. The most prevalent in Russia blames the British. According to this, the killers were financed by British Ambassador Lord Whitworth in an attempt to save India from the Cossack attack.

The British may have been relieved at the news, but their phobia of the Russian invasion of India, via Afghanistan, was to last a full century. In those almost one hundred years, there were mistakes galore; human lives were wasted and fortunes squandered. The world may have been spared of this trauma if only the British had paid heed to Rumi,

Whoever travels without a guide
Needs two hundred years for a two-day journey

After the death of Paul I and the defeat of Napoleon at Waterloo, the dice had fallen in Britain's favour. The British should have rested easy. But did they?

A New Arrangement

When France was rolled back from its dominant position after the Napoleonic Wars, a new order emerged with the aim of restoring calm in Europe. Consequently, the first few years after 1815 were an 'Age of Recuperation', in which governments were trying to heal the wounds of war and resume normal life through economic recovery and development. Ideology too played an important role. A prominent example was the Holy Alliance formed in September 1815, bonding the monarchs of Russia, Austria and Prussia, and later the rulers of almost all the Christian states of Europe. This fraternal union was to deal with each other on the basis of their common religion. It did not mean the end of their rivalries, but it certainly resulted in the end of the type of wars that Napoleon had forced upon Europe.

Essentially, the European system was a five-power polarity. There were two world powers, Britain and Russia, and three major Continental powers, Austria, France and Prussia, which were distinctly weaker and more vulnerable. This European 'balance of power' was conducted via an equitable distribution, at least as far as the geographical domination was concerned.

But in Asia, especially in Central and South Asia, it became a contest for 'areas of influence', between Russia and Britain. It was this hunger for more geographical space that led Russia eastwards through the inhospitable Central Asia. But every new town captured by it added to the British anxiety. It feared that the Russian advance was aimed at snatching India and its riches out of the British hands. To safeguard that prized possession, Britain kept pushing in the northwesterly direction, capturing new territories in Punjab and Sind. Finally, there was just Afghanistan which separated them.

So even as the European powers were engaged in keeping peace in their continent and pushing it into the industrial age, the nineteenth century was a long and sorry saga of wars, suppression and colonial domination for this Asian part of the world.

This contest was termed the 'Great Game'. It was first used by Arthur Conolly, an intelligence officer of the 6th Bengal Light Cavalry. In a letter of July 1840 to Major Henry Rawlinson, who had been recently appointed as the political agent in Kandahar, Conolly wrote: 'You've a great game, a noble game, before you.'

Kipling borrowed this phrase to make it immortal, 'Now I shall go far and far into the North, playing the Great Game.'

Like the Cold War of the twentieth century, the Great Game was a proxy battle whose protagonists rarely confronted each other. Britain's principal aim was to keep Russia from crossing the Oxus River on Afghanistan's north, to keep it away from India. It was largely this pursuit that led to unending suspicion of every Russian move in the easterly direction. It did not lead to a war between them, but unfortunately it led to the Anglo–Afghan wars. It was a story of British aggression and the heroic Afghan resistance to it. This was certainly a period of valour, sacrifice and brutality, but one with sorry consequences for the Afghan people. The wounds they suffered then continue to bleed their land even now.

With the benefit of hindsight, historians have questioned whether there was ever any *real* Russian threat to India, considering the immense obstacles that an invasion force would first have had to overcome.

Yet generations of British statesmen and army officers thought the danger was real. Their Russian counterparts were similarly plagued by fears of British designs on Russian territory.

'They will attempt to extend their influence to Kashgar, Persia, and all the Central Asian States bordering on us,' a Russian newspaper warned, 'and then will pose a direct threat to our interests in Asia.'

Finally, Russia's defeat by Japan in 1907 brought this Great Game to a close. If the end of the Napoleonic Wars had signalled the beginning of the Great Game, its curtain call was the sign that the Great War was not far.

In the interim, a drama of Greek proportions was being staged in and around Afghanistan.

In one of the first of many impulsive British reactions during this century, Mountstuart Elphinstone was dispatched in June 1809 to Afghanistan. He found the scene at Amir Shah Shuja's durbar to be one of great opulence, 'In the centre of the arch sat the King on a very large throne of gold or gilding. His appearance was magnificent and royal: his crown and all his dress were one blaze of jewels...'

Elphinstone's mission was a success. He was able to easily conclude a treaty with the Amir whereby no Frenchman or any other European was to be allowed entry into Afghanistan. But as was to happen repeatedly over the next decades, every Afghan interaction with the British was either in nature of a concession to British India, or a signal for internal strife.

In this case, bad news for the Afghan Amir started to pour in even as they were signing the treaty.

First came the news of the seizure of Kandahar by a Durrani prince, Shah Mehmud. This was followed by the information that Shah Shuja's forces had been routed in Kashmir. As if this wasn't bad enough, yet another courier brought in the news that Shah Mehmud and Shah Fath Khan had conquered Kabul and were now marching towards Peshawar! The two armies met at Gandamak, yet another harbinger of misfortunes for Afghan rulers over the years. Shah Shuja's forces were defeated and he fled leaving behind a treasure chest of two million pounds, about £200 million now.

Elphinstone and his mission were fortunate that they had already packed their bags and departed from Peshawar. But this first contact with the British was to set a pattern of strife, intrigue and penury for the Afghan royals. The Afghan durbar was never this grand again.

How much of that decline was due to the wars that followed will become clear as we move on. But one thing was clear all along, that for one reason or the other the British were not willing to give the benefit of doubt to Russia. The slightest transgression was enough to conjure up the demons that Russia was about to gobble up Afghanistan. Once it was secure in Kabul, all it needed to do was to step down from the high mountains and chase the British out of rich India.

Occasionally, however, there was genuine cause for concern. Britain needed to be on its guard then. But what should have been only a minor blip on its worry radar got magnified as diplomats and army men got into the act. John MacNeill, the British ambassador in Tehran, was one such. This conspiracy-minded ambassador heard in 1837 that his Russian counterpart,

Count Ivan Simonitch, had made the offer to the Shah of Iran of 50,000 gold tomans and offered to write off the Iranian debt in return for letting Russians set up a mission in Herat once the Shah had conquered it. Now, Ambassador MacNeill was the kind of person who firmly believed that Russia was waiting for a chance to attack India. Accordingly, his reports were uniformly alarmist.

However, he was not alone in sending such reports. British India was receiving alarms of this nature from other quarters as well.

3

The Great Game Begins

STILL, THE BRITISH ATTITUDE UP to the mid 1830s was one of benign neglect. There were many reasons for this, the foremost being the consolidation of territories they had acquired in India. Moreover, the Afghans themselves were going through a fractious and troubled transition; therefore, they were unlikely to pose a threat to India. There was also assurance in the fact that in the event of an invasion on India, the formidable Sikh Empire was the first hurdle the invader would have to cross.

Gradually, however, the desire to trade with Punjab and beyond with Central Asia took hold. It was not an impracticable wish, because for the last 2,000 years trade caravans had used the Silk Route successfully to carry goods to and from Europe. But the British idea was not a simple carriage of goods across the mountain passes. Their objective was to combine trade with the flag; commerce and political power was to be projected together. The plan was to put the Indus River to this use.

For this purpose, they needed to find out whether it was navigable all the way through. More importantly still, from the military perspective they needed to know the depth of the river at different points. To do this without raising local suspicions, they devised a ruse; five huge dray horses and a stage coach were to be carried up the Indus all the way to Lahore as royal gifts for Maharaja Ranjit Singh. The man chosen for this mission was 26-year-old Alexander Burnes, a linguist and a talented young officer. He was born in Montrose in 1805 and joined the army of the East India Company at the age of 16. He was witty, with a great ability to spin amusing accounts of his travels. He was also an accomplished Persian speaker and an ambitious opportunist. Moreover, he had a knack of being at the right place at the right time, though this talent failed him when he needed it most. He proved his ability to charm and disarm opposition when some tribes in Sind got suspicious about this unusual journey by the boat. In fact, a Hindu holy man on seeing this strange spectacle float by uttered prophetically, 'Alas, Sind is now gone.'

Ranjit Singh, the powerful ruler of Punjab, was not worried. He was pleased to receive his presents, and for the next two months, Alexander Burnes and his delegation were the Maharaja's guests.

'Cunning and conciliation have been two weapons of his diplomacy,' Burnes was to write later in his report in 1831. 'It is probable that the career of this chief (Ranjit Singh) is nearly at an end. His chest is contracted, his back is bent, his limbs withered.' Burnes also felt that his nightly drinking bouts with his favourite tipple, which was stronger than the strongest brandy, would not let him live long. But Maharaja Ranjit Singh was to live for another eight years.

On his way back, Burnes stopped in Ludhiana where he was to meet the exiled Afghan Amir, Shah Shuja. This time, too, Burnes's confident prediction was to prove wrong, 'I do not believe that the Shah possesses sufficient energy to set himself on the throne of Cabool.'

Burnes had barely settled back in Simla, when he got the opportunity to lead a British trade mission to Kabul. This was to be his first visit to Afghanistan, and despite the reports they had heard about bandits along the way, they travelled in a small party. Fortunately for them, their passage to Kabul was trouble-free. There, in 1832, Burnes was received well by Amir Dost Mohammad. His impression of the Amir was of a well-liked ruler of high character who was praised for equity and justice by the peasant and the common citizen.

Burnes's secretary, Mohan Lal, was not so sanguine. He agreed that Dost Mohammad was wise and prudent, but he was of the view that the Amir was adept in the arts of treachery, cruelty, falsehood and murder.

Dost Mohammad had been an attentive and considerate host all through their stay, but he also had an objective in mind which he shared, at last, with these rare visitors from British India. He confided in Burnes towards the end of his stay in Kabul that he wanted to help the British in overthrowing the powerful and arrogant Sikh king whom he hated. Burnes faithfully conveyed this suggestion upon his return to India, but this was not acceptable to the Governor General.

Dashing Mr Burnes

Around this time, another development had taken place regarding the tenure of the East India Company in India. By a Charter Act passed in 1833 and valid for another 20 years, the East India Company was permitted to hold Indian territories in trust for the British Crown. The Company was run by a Court of Directors situated in London which, in turn, was supervised by a Cabinet minister. It was this body which was in charge of the policy. The governor generals may have had the power of life and death in India, but they were treated rather roughly by the Board; and in most cases, they were not considered as being more than regional executives. However, this extension of tenure by 20 years gave the company and the governor generals the confidence to formulate their policies over the longer term. The move towards Afghanistan would now not take long in coming.

The British attitude thus far towards Afghanistan had been passive. But, in June 1836, Governor General George Auckland received instructions from London, advising him 'to watch more closely than had hitherto been attempted the progress of events in Afghanistan, and to counteract the progress of Russian influence.'

This was just the trigger he needed. He interpreted that missive to mean a carte blanche to use whatever means he thought necessary to stop the Russian advance. This marked the end of the benign phase of just keeping an eye on the area. Auckland plunged headlong into what he thought was his assigned task, and from this point on, a series of British blunders followed.

Instead of attempting to keep the Russians out of the area, Auckland became obsessed with gaining territory for the British Empire. To do this, he began to undercut the capable and popular Afghan Amir, Dost Mohammad. His aim was to replace him with the British puppet, Shah Shuja. As a first step, Auckland decided to send a mission to Kabul making it just the opportunity that Alexander Burnes was waiting for.

Alexander Burnes had the right qualifications for the job—he was a smooth talker and rakish looking, precisely the sort who could charm his way out of trouble and inveigle himself in favour with the high and mighty. When he was first sent to Kabul in 1832, he was only 27-years-old. But Amir Dost Mohammad Khan considered him good enough to make the offer that he should take over as the army chief of Afghanistan so that he might destroy the rude Sikh, Ranjit Singh.

Burnes had wisely declined the offer. Though he had missed the chance to conquer Punjab, Burnes soon became a huge literary success. Despite the star status in London society on account of his book, *Travels into Bokhara*, and a knighthood largely because of that book, not all were taken in by his charm. Mortimer Durand's father, Major General Henry Durand, assessed him as, '…credulous, never pausing to weigh events, and not gifted with a comprehensive mind…'

Maud Diver, a writer, said witheringly of Burnes, 'Wisely adopting Mohammedan dress, he unwisely adopted Mohammedan way of life; including the harem.'

Meanwhile, the steady reports of the Russian advance in Central Asia had raised British concern. Information also came in that after Britain had rebuffed Dost Mohammad's efforts to get its aid in taking on Ranjit Singh, he had approached the Russians. This, plus the recent sighting of Russian agents in Kabul, was enough reason to rush Burnes back to Kabul a second time in 1836.

Lord Auckland had not made a bad choice. Young Alexander Burnes or 'Sekundar' (the Pashto version of Alexander) Burnes, as he was to become known in Kabul, was popular in the Afghan circles. It is true that he had a glad eye and kept many Afghan women as mistresses, which would eventually cost him his life, but so long as the going was good he was a great asset for the mission that he had been assigned. One of his many qualities was that he was eager to prove himself and was hardy enough to rough it out if the circumstances so demanded. But for serious matters of state was he not too young? Moreover, this visit too was noted with concern by Russia whose trade with Afghanistan was beginning to suffer.

Burnes's assignment once again was to explore the possibility of opening Central Asia to British trade. But that was a ruse. The real objective of the Governor General was to put Amir Dost Mohammad on notice that Britain wanted to make Afghanistan its protectorate. Moreover, Alexander Burnes was not told that a war with Afghanistan was not a question of if but when.

Even as Burnes made preparation to leave for Kabul, an act of great magnitude was being played out in Afghanistan. Amir Dost Mohammad wrote to Hari Singh, Ranjit Singh's General who had recently occupied Peshawar, offering conciliation. In the alternative, his letter warned, that Hari Singh should be prepared to face his son Akbar Khan.

When the Amir's offer was turned down, a battle seemed inevitable. On 30 April 1837, Akbar Khan led his forces against Hari Singh near the new fort at Jamrud.

The account of the battle in Siraj al-Tawarikh glorifies Akbar Khan,

> In the heat of the furious combat, Akbar Khan encountered Hari Singh. Without recognising each other, they exchanged blows and after much thrusting and parrying, Akbar Khan won out, knocking Hari Singh to the ground, and killing him. With their commander dead and the army of Islam rolling towards them like a tide in flood, the Sikhs abandoned the field…

This was the first great victory of Akbar Khan who was now on course to become a legendary Afghan commander.

These two interesting young men, Akbar Khan from the East and Burnes from the West, were destined to have the first of their encounters soon.

Burnes was camping at Nimla on his way to Kabul when he received a special visitor. Hawk-faced Akbar Khan resembled his father in bravery, charm, ruthlessness and his sense of strategy, all qualities for which he was later celebrated as a heroic figure in Afghan folklore:

> *When Akbar the Brave, Master of the Sword*
> *Conquered and defeated the enemy forces*
> *When he fought the fierce armies of the Punjab*
> *He was but a youth, yet he had the mettle of a Sohrab*
> *He became a legend potent and brave*
> *As famed through the land as the mighty Rustam*
> *When he reached the season of his manhood*
> *He was tall and graceful as a young cypress*
> *He mastered every science*
> *And excelled in every art*
> *His luminous countenance shone with a light divine*
> *Worthy of crown and throne*

This was not a flight of poetic exaggeration. According to most Afghan accounts of the period, Akbar Khan was an Achilles-like hero of Afghans and a sex symbol in Kabul of the 1830s. The effect is described in this manner in *Akbarnama*,

All the world was drawn to his face,
Every eye turned towards him

It is no accident that the diplomatic quarter of Kabul is named after Wazir Akbar Khan, because he was also the General who oversaw the rout of the British in 1842.

Intrigue and Prejudice

Alexander Burnes was seated with Akbar Khan when, on 20 September 1837, their elephant entered Kabul. As during his earlier visit, this time too, Burnes was received well by the Amir. Burnes, in turn, did his best to interpret the Amir's intentions towards India in a favourable light.

His reports were based on sound observation and had they been acted upon, the course of Anglo–Afghan history may have been less violent. But Burnes's reports did not reach the Governor General directly. They were routed via Ludhiana and reached the Governor General only after they had been seen and commented upon by Captain Claude Wade, the British political agent at Ludhiana. Wade, in turn, sent his recommendation via William Macnaghten, secretary to the Secret and Political Department in Calcutta.

Bureaucratic jealousy, rather than sound analysis, took over then. Neither Wade nor Macnaghten had visited Afghanistan. Their theoretical knowledge could not match Burnes's personal experience and his reports from the ground. Yet, since they had the ear of the Governor General, their comments, often dismissive of Burnes's carefully written recommendations, prevailed.

Macnaghten considered Burnes to be naive and a bit of an upstart. In contrast, he valued the recommendations of Wade, the veteran spymaster. 'Where there is a difference of opinion between them,' Macnaghten advised Auckland, 'I should be disposed to concur with Capt Wade, whose arguments and conclusions rest on recorded facts, whereas those of Capt Burnes seem for the most part to be formed from the opinion of others…' This was blatantly unfair, but Burnes had no means of knowing that he was being undercut at every stage.

Unknown also to Burnes was the fact that all this while, Wade was encouraging Auckland to bring Shah Shuja back into play.

Nor was Burnes having the smoothest of times in Kabul. It is true that the Amir gave him the place of honour in his durbar and in his confidence. But there were jealousies at play as well. Maulana Hamid Kashmiri writes in his *Akbarnama,*

The Amir, with his kindness and natural grace
Treated him as a most honoured guest
He elevated him above all others
And bestowed every mark of distinction upon him
But Burnes had mixed poison into the honey
From London, he had requested much gold and silver
With dark magic and deceit he dug a pit
Many a man was seized by the throat and thrown in

Despite these intrigues against Burnes and the sentiment of some of his advisers in Kabul in favour of Russia, Dost Mohammad remained steadfast in his desire to be on good terms with the British. He had told this repeatedly to Alexander Burnes, and he had expressed the same sentiment in his letters to Auckland. He had only one great wish, he longed to recover the possession of Peshawar.

When Peshawar was first taken by Ranjit Singh, a major effort was mounted by Dost Mohammad to regain it. He called for a holy war and the tribesmen flocked to their leader's standard. Despite their enthusiasm, the effort ended in disaster. The Afghans were hurled violently back into their own mountain fastnesses, and Peshawar remained under the 'Lion's' paw.

Then Dost Mohammad turned to his English friends and had hoped the powerful Company would intercede on his behalf with Ranjit Singh. But Lord Auckland was convinced by his advisers that Dost Mohammad was a villain of the darkest shade. Therefore, when Dost Mohammad sought his helping hand, Auckland sent him a curt reply, the substance of which was this:

> Ranjit Singh had long been the firm and ancient ally of the British; his conduct had been generous in the extreme; and the Afghans should consider themselves fortunate to have been let off so lightly.

Meanwhile, a Russian envoy, Ivan Vitkevitch, reached Kabul and made generous promises to Dost Mohammad. But the Amir still kept pressing

Burnes for a positive response from India because that is the relationship he sought, rather than the one that the Russian envoy was so ardently pursuing. Finally, in frustration, Dost Mohammad summoned Vitkevitch on 21 April 1838 and received him in the Bala Hisar fort with full honours.

At the formal durbar, Vitkevitch said Russia did not recognize the Sikh conquests of Afghan territory and as far as Russia was concerned, Peshawar, Multan and Kashmir belonged to Afghanistan. He went on to add that Russia would protect Afghanistan diplomatically as a barrier against British expansion into Central Asia. He admitted that Russia was too far to dispatch troops at short notice, but promised to give Dost Mohammad money to fight Ranjit Singh.

After this, there wasn't much that Burnes could have achieved by extending his stay in Kabul. In any case, the Governor General had already summoned him back to India. Alexander Burnes left Kabul on 26 April after bidding farewell to the Amir. But his departure was seen as a hurried exit by the Afghans. Maulana Kashmiri describes it as so in *Akbarnama*,

He set out from Kabul upon the road to Hind
Like a sheep running away from a roaring lion
Every step of the way he would look back
Lest the falcon should seize him again

By the time he returned to India, Burnes could sense that the formal mission that had been assigned to him about 'opening trade' was not a serious issue. The real objective of that mission was to send a message to the Afghans as well as the Russians. That's why he wrote in his diary, 'I had the satisfaction of being told that I was sent to do "impossible things" at "Cabool" so all my labour that did not succeed was not expected to succeed! Politics are a queer science.'

Auckland's next major step was to issue the Simla Manifesto in October 1838. This showed Dost Mohammad as an unpopular ruler, and praised Shah Shuja as just the man all Afghanistan wanted as its Amir.

Both of these statements were self-serving untruths. Historical record demonstrates that Dost Mohammad served Afghanistan as a visionary ruler, whereas Shah Shuja was almost universally considered to be inept. But the 1838 manifesto had its merits too, at least from the British point of view. With that manifesto, Auckland had planted the seed that would, in course of time, sprout into the ambition of Durand and his compatriots. However, the principal objective remained the same—Russians must be kept out of Afghanistan at all costs by decree or by sheer brute force.

The question that the British should have asked themselves was this—was their fear of Russian advance based on sound intelligence? Even as they kept a watchful eye on Russian expansion, they should have introspected too. They should have considered the fact that by 1800, East India Company controlled 2.43 lakh square kilometres of territory in India and supported an army of two lakh men. But their judgement was clouded by prejudice.

The reasons why Russia was expanding into Central Asia were not related to Afghanistan or India. But a phobia is difficult to cure. Therefore, for the British in India, expanding Russia became the ominous Satan. To make their sense of discomfort complete, the first decades of the nineteenth century saw a great increase of the Russian Empire in every direction, especially towards the East.

All this was being warily watched by the East India Company. It became an overriding priority for them to keep between the sphere of Russian influence in Central Asia and the Company's possessions in India, a state friendly to the British. Afghanistan had to be that buffer state, and it must be ruled by an Amir whose love for the English could only be excelled by his hatred for Russia.

4

Prelude to Disaster

DOST MOHAMMAD WAS JUST SUCH an Amir. He was partial to British India and even in the deepest periods of his frustration when the British Governor General was not reciprocating his call for friendship, he did not ally with Russia. His twin faults were that he was not a lackey, and he was a proud nationalist who wanted to wrest Peshawar back from Ranjit Singh.

But Auckland was looking for a lackey.

In this respect, Shah Shuja fitted the bill perfectly. However, it was not a simple matter of replacing one Amir by another. The British were realistic enough to acknowledge that on their own they could not defeat Dost Mohammad. They were also conscious of the fact that Shah Shuja did not have an independent army of his own, and that when he marched at the head of a column with them, it would be to lead a mercenary force of Indians financed by the British. So it was clear that they needed Ranjit Singh's formidable force to take on the Afghans. The British decided that it was time to recall the Tripartite Treaty that they had signed with Ranjit Singh and Shah Shuja in June 1838 at Lahore.

A Show for Ranjit Singh

With Ranjit Singh's forces by their side, the British were confident that they could install Shah Shuja on the Afghan throne. It was in pursuance of this agenda that Lord Auckland reached Ferozepur on 27 November 1838. At this meeting, the British were keen to impress Ranjit Singh with their military power, just as the shrewd maharaja had prepared to return that compliment with an equally impressive military show.

The infantry, cavalry and artillery of the two sides stretched for miles on open ground providing a grand spectacle. At a pre-arranged time, there was a joint firing of guns by the two armies. This was a signal for the military bands to strike up. While this fanfare was going on, elephants carrying the maharaja and his staff started to move from one side of an avenue created by a long row of soldiers towards the other end.

Lord Auckland and his party, mounted on their elephants, started to move towards Ranjit Singh from the opposite end.

All this was great pageantry with a lot of colour and the constant firing of big guns. This was certainly a thrilling spectacle for people, but the elephants were not accustomed to cacophony on such a large scale. As the two processions neared each other, some elephants collided. For a few dangerous moments, there was confusion with elephants jostling into each other and the howdahs swaying precariously. At one stage, it seemed as if Ranjit Singh was going to be thrown off his howdah. Somehow the mahouts managed to calm their beasts. In this confusion, the elephants of Ranjit Singh and Auckland were brought next to each other and Ranjit Singh being smaller in build was transferred to Auckland's howdah.

Seated together, they proceeded to the durbar tent. There, an even greater melee of people greeted them: The sheet of crowd was so thick that Ranjit Singh's soldiers drew their weapons in case their king was to come to some harm.

Among the many British accounts of the event, let me quote just two. Emily Eden, the sister of the Governor General, wrote in *Up the Country: Letters Written to Her Sister from the Upper Provinces of India*, 'Runjeet [sic] had no jewels on whatever, nothing but the commonest red silk dress. He had two stockings on at first, which was considered an unusual circumstance; but he very soon contrived to slip one off, that he might sit with one foot in his hand comfortably.'

There is also a mention of this meeting by Arthur Swinson in his book *North-West Frontier*,

> …then things went wrong; in the excitement one of the shells which had been knocked over rolled into Ranjit Singh's path, and before anyone could prevent him, he had tripped over it and fallen flat on his face. He was hauled to his feet and proved unhurt, but the incident was looked on as a bad omen by the Sikhs present. The symbolism of their ruler lying prostrate before the British guns was too plain for comfort.

Ranjit Singh was a rare ruler who the British were afraid of in India. They acknowledged his military genius. Yet, it was his physical disabilities that occupied the British descriptive gaze; as if a focus on them might somehow neutralize the advantage he otherwise enjoyed in the military sphere over them.

If Ranjit Singh was short, so was General Frederick Roberts, the greatest British General of the nineteenth century whose victories in Afghanistan had made him the stuff of legends. Almost all British writing about Roberts is adulatory; be it the poems by Rudyard Kipling or dispatches by journalists from the battlefield. No British writer seemed to have noticed that he too was diminutive, almost as short as Ranjit Singh.

Let us contrast this prejudice with the Asian view of Maharaja Ranjit Singh. Mohan Lal Kashmiri's book, *Travels in the Punjab and Afghanistan and Turistan to Balkh, Bikhara and Herat and a Visit to Great Britain, Germany (1846)*, describes what transpired at the court of the Shah of Iran.

It was Eid-ul-Fitr and the Shah was camping at Mashad. Among the multitude that had come to pay their respects was Mohan Lal. After the formalities of this impressive ceremony, the Shah turned towards Mohan Lal and asked, 'You have seen both courts, Ranjit Singh's and mine. Tell me whether Ranjit Singh's court could match in magnificence with what you have seen here? And whether the Sikh army could compare in discipline and courage with my sirbaz (army)?'

Mohan Lal replied modestly, but firmly, that 'Maharajah Ranjit Singh's darbar-tent was made of Kashmir shawls, and that even the floor was composed of the same costly material; and as for his army, if Sardar Hari Singh (Ranjit's commander-in-chief on the Afghan frontier) were to cross the Indus, his highness would soon be glad to make good his retreat to his original government in Tabriz.'

Mohan Lal had conveyed his views in a non-offensive way. Still, it was unusual for anyone to be heard challenging the Shah's opinion. The nobles present in the durbar were apprehensive that the Shah may have got offended. It was, therefore, a fraught moment in the durbar hall.

'Wonderful, wonderful!' said Abbas Mirza, the Shah, drawing the attention of the court towards Mohan Lal. 'How inscrutable are the decrees of Providence which has conferred so much power on a kafir! (infidel); but if Ali, the Lion of God, favour us, we will yet plant our standard in Kashmir, and dress all our sirbazes in shawl pantaloons.'

On his departure from Mashad, Mohan Lal was conferred with the order of the Lion and Sun by the Shah.

The Shah of Iran and Mohan Lal Kashmiri obviously had a more exalted view of Ranjit Singh than the British.

It is indeed a fact widely acknowledged that Ranjit Singh was one of the greatest rulers of his time. He had succeeded in building a magnificent Sikh Empire from a modest beginning. His rule now covered entire Punjab and extended right up to Peshawar. As a strategist, he was forever open to ideas—he travelled in disguise to British military camps to observe their training methods, and then engaged French, Dutch and Italian military experts to train his forces in modern military practices.

Above all, he managed to outwit the British regarding the Afghan expedition. At first, Auckland had hoped that Ranjit Singh would provide the entire force for the military campaign into Kabul. According to this plan, Shah Shuja was to have accompanied them with a token force supplied by the British. But Ranjit Singh had no intention of getting stuck in the Afghan quagmire. He was aware that the Afghans were a formidable fighting force in their hills and that they were deeply resentful of invading armies, which made their resistance even fiercer.

However, he did not want to dissociate himself from the idea of dislodging Dost Mohammad, because he was a constant menace to the Sikh kingdom's precarious hold over Peshawar. So when Auckland's envoy, Macnaghten enquired whether he would like to revive his treaty with Shah Shuja and have the British become a partner to it, Ranjit Singh replied, 'This would be adding sugar to milk.'

While Ranjit Singh was being merely pleasant with words, Macnaghten misunderstood it to mean that Ranjit Singh was with them in the military campaign. However, Auckland realized that the Sikh army would not be available as he had initially hoped. He then decided 'to give direct and powerful assistance of the British government to the enterprise of Shuja-ul-Malik...'

Some historians suggest that the young advisers surrounding the Governor General had misguided him. But that is not correct. Auckland was the Governor General. It was at his desk that the buck stopped, and it was he who was responsible for the consequences of the decisions taken by him or in his name. All actions taken by Auckland at this point suggest that he was a man in a hurry; he wanted to achieve glory fast. He had also miscalculated both the British staying power in Afghanistan and the possibility that wounded Afghans could be even more ferocious.

In fact, the Duke of Wellington had warned that where the military successes ended in this enterprise, the political difficulties would begin. But Auckland was in no mood to reconsider—his Army of the Indus was ready to be launched.

In the summer of 1839, the British army marched up the Khyber Pass into Afghanistan. Its aim was to replace Dost Mohammad, a Khan who had never done the British any harm, with Shah Shuja, a Khan who had never done the British any good.

An Army and the Caravan

British aggression and its constant interference in the internal affairs of Afghanistan was going to be a perpetual puzzle to a succession of Amirs. Some took advantage of this extraordinary and, as many thought, unnecessary interest and kept squeezing the British for more money and more armaments. Others were manipulated relatively easily. At least that is how both parties viewed the situation—each arrangement was temporary, each understanding transient to suit the mood and the need of the moment.

Amir Dost Mohammad expressed Afghan angst best when after he had been dethroned he asked his British interlocutor,

'I have been struck with the magnitude of your resources, your ships, your arsenals, but what I cannot understand is why the rulers of so vast and flourishing an empire should have gone across the Indus to deprive me of my poor and barren country.'

Whether he was given a response that satisfied him has not been recorded. But he may have got satisfaction from the fact that British interference in Afghanistan had provoked a tribal chief in Africa, the Sultan of Ben Walid, to ask a British traveller, Dr Richardson, 'Why do you go so far from home to take other people's country from them?'

'The Turks do the same,' Dr Richardson replied.

'Do you wish to be oppressors like the Turks?' the Sultan asked curtly.

Despite this wonderment of other people, the expedition to Afghanistan was promoted by the hawks in East India Company. They believed that breaching the classic frontiers of British India would send a signal to the Russian Czar and subdue another native state.

This was certainly the biggest military mission launched by the East India Company after the one against Tipu Sultan in 1799. And it was the first time that the Company was sending an army outside India. But unlike in the campaign against Tipu, this time the British generals had hardly any knowledge of the military tactics that the Afghans might employ because the British had not so far faced them in the battlefield. This was a major handicap, but to compound this disadvantage further, they were venturing into a land of which they did not have a proper map.

Still, they went marching in with their enormous army. There were 6,000 regular troops, 14,000 foot soldiers, a sizeable cavalry and the small mercenary army of Indian soldiers accompanying Shah Shuja. To feed and support this army, there were 38,000 camp followers, among them there were also men to cut the grass and look after the sheep.

More than an army on a purposeful mission, this vast group seemed more like one on a picnic outing.

They needed 30,000 camels just to carry their baggage. One of the generals needed 260 camels to carry his uniforms, while a brigadier had to make do with only 50 camels. Another group of 30 camels was reserved for carrying claret, six camels carried only cigars and cheroots and one camel carried only eau de cologne. One regiment employed two camels to carry Manila cigars, while other camels carried jams, pickles, cheroots, potted fish, smoked salmon, hermetically sealed meats, plates, glass, crockery, wax candle and table linen. Seeing all this extravagance, one of the more conscientious generals remarked that many young officers would have left behind their swords or double barrel pistols rather than travel without their dressing cases, perfumes and Windsor soap.

This well-provisioned army broke off in three different directions. One main branch took off in the vague direction of Kandahar via Balochistan. The Khan of Kalat, upon seeing their splendour, is said to have remarked, 'You are taking an army in, but how do you propose to take it out again?'

As a matter of fact, even before reaching its destination, a quarter of the army died of thirst and dehydration because they had not cared to find in advance the sources of water along the route.

This was not the only blunder in this foolhardy plunge of the British. They were venturing into the battlefield without a clear battle plan, or a definite idea of their objectives. What did they plan to do after conquering Kabul? Did they plan to stay in Kabul forever? Or was their objective limited to replacing one Amir by the other? If that was the case, then was this massive exercise worth the effort? As a commercial enterprise, the East India Company should have made at least a rough cost-benefit analysis of the effort. But none of this was done, not even a military plan of the tactics and tricks that the Afghan rival might employ. But there was one man who predicted the result even as this huge assemblage was passing under his eyes.

'You will see,' remarked a British colonel who watched the army go, 'not a soul will reach here from Kabul except one man, who will come to tell us the rest are destroyed.'

Three years later, he had the gloomy satisfaction of seeing Dr William Brydon, sagging in the saddle, come down from the hills alone. 'Did I not say so? Here comes the messenger.' The colonel said acidly.

At first, the army's march went off without any major resistance. There was one difficult battle at Ghazni when they had to blast their way into its formidable fort. Dost Mohammad had hoped that the British forces would find it hard to breach its walls. That would have been the case, but for the resources of Mohan Lal Kashmiri. One of his informers in Ghazni gave him the information that one section of the fort had a weak wall which could be dynamited and blown apart relatively easily. Acting on this cue, Major General Henry Durand, laid the dynamite charge which provided the breach and the British force its entry into the fort.

Durand laid the dynamite at considerable personal risk. Actually, he had to light the cord thrice because in the first two attempts it failed to catch fire. Meanwhile, the noise of enemy footsteps, going back and forth, alerted the guards posted on top of that portion of the wall. They started firing at the shadows, but Durand and his men managed to escape the bullets.

For this act of bravery, the British army was later to institute a medal in his honour. There is no doubt that this was a well-deserved recognition. However, credit should have been given to Mohan Lal as well. After all, it was on the basis of the information he had obtained about the weak portion of the wall, which ensured easy and early British victory. Mohan Lal, too, had procured the information at some personal risk.

The Legend of Mohan Lal

There were many other extraordinary acts that this man had performed in the British employment. The British Secret Service had selected ambitious Pandit Mohan Lal Kashmiri in 1831 to accompany Alexander Burnes. He was only 19 years old at that time and his salary of ₹1,000 per annum was not insignificant. But he was a deserving candidate and his selection had been recommended by his mentor, Charles Trevelyan, who had seen him graduate first in his class from Delhi English College.

It is said that Mohan Lal was the first Kashmiri to become proficient in English. As a quick learner in the art of espionage, he assumed the name of Mirza Quli Kashmiri when he reached Kabul. He did not stop just with the change of name, but had carried his act to perfection. One sure way he found of getting access to the secrets of the high and mighty of the land was to marry into a family of some status. Over the years his marriages were spread all over the field of his operations, from Central Asia to Persia, Kabul and finally Delhi, where he met his seventeenth and favourite wife, Haidri Begum, near whom he lies buried in Lal Bagh close to Azadpur in Delhi.

Mohan Lal had led a colourful life like his boss Burnes and, like him, was proficient professionally. There was definitely a strong bond between the two, otherwise, he wouldn't have gone all the way to England, at his own expense, to hand over Burnes's diary to his family.

But he left England a sad man because he was not reimbursed for the loan of ₹79,496 that he had taken from his Afghan friends on behalf of the British soldiers during the difficult days of the First Anglo–Afghan War.

Somewhere in his heart he may have also felt let down that Alexander Burnes had referred to him dismissively in his book, *Travels into Bokhara*, as the 'Hindu lad who helped me with my correspondence.'

As Pandit Nehru wrote, 'In a free India, a man like Mohan Lal would have risen to the top most rungs of the political ladder. Under early British rule, whatever he might be or whatever he might do, he could not rise higher than the position of a "Mir Munshi" or at most a "Deputy Collector".'

Though Mohan Lal was short-changed by British, the fall of Ghazni fort came as a big disappointment for Dost Mohammad. He had expected fierce resistance and considerable British losses. But as the news of the Afghan defeat reached Kabul, Dost Mohammad's commanders began to desert him one after the other. When he found himself with just a small band of faithful, he fled Kabul towards Bamiyan.

With that, the stage was set for the transfer of power from the Amir that the British did not like to one who was their puppet. Shah Shuja entered Kabul on 6 August 1839 after an exile of thirty years.

5

A Kabul Wife

For the first time in its history, a British army was in control of Afghanistan, and a large force was stationed in Kabul. Since they were expecting to stay there for some time, they should have occupied the Bala Hisar fort because it was situated at a height overlooking Kabul. Besides, the fort was surrounded by high walls. All this should have made it just the ideal place to house an army. But the Amir wanted to keep the large number of his wives, concubines and children there.

As staying in the fort was ruled out, British officers should have looked for some other place located at an elevation. Instead, they laid out their tents in the valley outside Kabul. And rather than build a wall around it, they opted to dig a ditch and put up a palisade. The net result was that they were in an indefensible position and exposed on all sides. It is ironic that a century-and-a-half later, Americans should have picked precisely this site to build their embassy.

Henry Durand was uncomfortable about many of the decisions that the political head of the mission, Sir William Macnaghten, was making. In a number of cases relating to that expedition, Henry Durand was to prove prophetic. He had advocated that as the mission of the British forces in August 1840 regarding installation of Shah Shuja as the Amir had been achieved, they should withdraw for a triumphant return to their frontier.

But Macnaghten wanted to govern from Kabul.

Even there, Henry had suggested that the British Indian troops should make the Bala Hisar fort overlooking Kabul their base, as it would give them military advantage. Once again, he was overruled. But as luck would have it, he was passed over for a military mission to Kunduz. In protest, he resigned and left Kabul to return to India. At that time, Sir John Keane had told him,

'I cannot but congratulate you on quitting the country, for mark my words it will not be long before there is some signal catastrophe.'

Once the British army had settled in Kabul for the long haul, it went about the business of making itself comfortable. Alexander Burnes, who was an experienced Kabul hand, was the man to follow. Like him, many other officers began to stay in the city in hired accommodations rather than in the army encampment. And emulating him, they too started keeping mistresses. Seeing their officers do so, the British soldiers first and then their Indian counterparts began to seek women regularly. A rhyme popular among the British soldiers summed up this state of affairs well,

A Kabul wife under burkha cover
Was never known without a lover

But the nobles of Kabul were not amused. As the resentment spread they began to complain about British philandering. Mirza Ata reflected this sentiment when he wrote in *Naway Maarek*, 'The English drank the wine of shameless immodesty forgetting that any act has its consequences and rewards.'

This was an ominous warning. The British commanders should have taken note of it and disciplined their men. But they were led by an ineffective Macnaghten. Finally, the Amir took up the issue with him.

'You should stop this traffic by punishment,' the Amir urged. 'Otherwise this tree of wickedness is going to bear unwholesome fruit.'

However, Macnaghten was not the one for subtleties or a quick reaction. In this case, he should have said something reassuring to the Amir and followed it up with firm steps. Some disciplinary action was needed urgently and it should have seemed so to the locals. Instead, Macnaghten took the line of least resistance and allowed the situation to drift. This fuelled the Afghan anger further. Even the Amir was shocked because instead of appreciating the gravity of the situation, Macnaghten had replied to him flippantly, 'If we stop the soldiers having sex the boys will fall quite ill.'—(*Waqiat-i-Shah Shuja*)

Turning Kabul into a vast prostitution arena was not the only grudge that the men of Kabul had against the British. There were other missteps as well.

The expense of maintaining a vast army in Kabul had led to financial losses for the East India Company. Consequently, Macnaghten was asked to reduce the number of soldiers and staff under his command and send them back to India. Here, he was quick in taking action and sent back a good number of soldiers. He followed it up with some initiatives of his own which would weaken his position further.

As a first step, he interfered with the Afghan system of recruitment. Thus far, it had been a source of patronage for the Afghan tribal chiefs who were allocated a quota of men to be recruited. Macnaghten wanted to change it to a professional system of recruitment, thereby cutting out the chiefs.

As if this wasn't bad enough, Macnaghten also reduced the payments that the chiefs received from East India Company from ₹1.3 million in 1839 to ₹1 million in 1841. Most of these cuts were going to apply to the Ghilzai tribes, who controlled the vital passes between Kabul and the Khyber. The British were soon going to find to their peril what a disastrous decision that was.

Towards Catastrophe

With their complaints against the British presence multiplying, the tribal chiefs were looking for a spark. That did not take long in coming. On the evening of 1 November 1841, a female servant of Abdullah Khan Achakzai went over to the house of Alexander Burnes. On hearing this Abdullah Khan sent his men to fetch the girl back, but instead of realizing that the situation could get out of hand, Burnes did what he had done earlier on so many similar occasions. Rather than have his pleasure interrupted, he asked his men to thrash those who had come to take the girl.

This was too much for Abdullah Khan to bear. He and his relatives went to Aminullah Khan Logari and with the Koran in hand sought his help. Logari, in turn, summoned a Jirga of the local chiefs where Abdullah beseeched, 'We are justified in throwing off this English yoke; they stretch the hand of tyranny to dishonour private citizens, great and small…' (Mirza Ata, *Naway Maarek*)

After picking up rumours from his sources, Mohan Lal Kashmiri went later that evening to Alexander Burnes's house to warn him that the situation could get dangerously out of hand. But being a veteran of many such escapades, Burnes thought otherwise. He patted Mohan Lal on the shoulder and told him to get a good night's sleep, while he returned to the servant girl.

By the following morning, the crowd around Burnes's house had swelled to such an enormous level that even he was alarmed. But there was still a swagger in his walk, and sufficient confidence that he would be able to pacify the crowd either by his words or by offers of money. With this in mind, he went up to his roof to harangue them and talk his way out of a very hostile situation. When he found that the crowd could not be pacified, he changed into Afghan clothes and tried to escape through a back door. But he was soon discovered and though he tried to shoot his way out he could not escape. In a matter of minutes, he, along with his brother Charles, and Captain Broadfoot were slaughtered.

The crowd then marched to the houses hired by other British officers and systematically hounded them out. Their next target was the army camp.

General William Elphinstone, the commander of the British army in Kabul, was a veteran of Waterloo. He had fought well there, but that was twenty-seven years ago and he had been young then. Now, he was old of body and weak in spirit. At a time like this, when a quick decision could have made the difference between life and death, he temporized. On the evening of 2 November, we find him writing this note to his colleague Macnaghten who was probably sitting in the adjoining camp, 'We must see what the morning brings and then think what can be done...'

Many mornings came after that but none brought any cheer to the British. Each new day brought fresh demands of money and hostages from the Afghans led by Akbar Khan. Two days short of Christmas, Macnaghten was slaughtered by a mob instigated by Akbar Khan. One version maintains that he was shot by the gun he had presented to Akbar Khan before his body was cut to pieces. Another version suggests that he was beheaded first and then the rest of his body was cut in tiny bits. Whatever it was, the end was grisly and the message to the British could not have been grimmer.

Despite this, they were fatalistically drawn to Akbar Khan's promises.

When the British army decided in December 1841 to retreat from Kabul, Mohan Lal warned them repeatedly of the dangers. He sent them a series of notes warning that they were being set up for a trap, and that they would all be targeted in an ambush. But, as before, his warnings were ignored. Like Mohan Lal, Shah Shuja was also deeply sceptical of the British move. He wrote to a young officer, Lt Henry Pottinger, 'To leave the cantonment...is the height of folly. Beware, do not even think of going to Jalalabad.' (*Waqiat-i-Shah Shuja*)

In the end, Mohan Lal made one desperate attempt by appealing to the treaty obligation. But even that was disregarded. Writing in *The Life of Dost Mohammad,* he mentions, 'No regard was shown (by the British) to the Articles of the Tripartite Treaty. Shah Shuja was left at the mercy of his enemies… Had it not been for us; he…would have destroyed the Barakzais, and thus have freed us and himself from these fatal consequences.'

Lt Pottinger too wrote ruefully, 'I was hauled out of my sick room and obliged to negotiate for the safety of a parcel of fools who were doing all they could to ensure their destruction.'

Pottinger was right because even at that time the British had a chance. They still had the numbers and the guns. In contrast, Akbar Khan's party was disorganized and its unity suspect. But Elphinstone was not up to the task—he was infirm and indecisive. So the British opted for the easy way out, or so they thought.

The retreat of Elphinstone's Army of the Indus began on 1 January 1842. If they had thought the New Year would bring them better tidings, they were in for a series of shocks.

At every pass, the Afghans had arranged for an ambush and a new set of demands for more money and hostages. In every ambush, the British army lost officers and men. Sixteen thousand men, women and children had set out of Kabul. Around mid-January, a solitary horseman, clinging somehow to his horse's neck, was seen approaching the British fort at Jalalabad.

This solitary horseman was Dr William Brydon, the one about whom the colonel had predicted, 'You will see, not a soul will reach here from Kabul except one man, who will come to tell us the rest are destroyed.'

Butcher and Bolt

G.R. Gleig, who was attached to the defeated army as a chaplain, wrote, '… it was a war begun for no wise purpose, carried on with a strange mixture of rashness and timidity, brought to a close after suffering and disaster, without much glory attached either to the government which directed, or the great body of troops which waged it. Not one benefit, political or military, was acquired with this war.'

Very few people recall today the devastating effect this war had on British morale. However, a sombre reminder of it exists in Mumbai. The

Church of St John the Evangelist located in Navy Nagar, commonly known as the Afghan Church, was dedicated in 1852 as a memorial to the dead of this war.

The rout and slaughter of the British at the hands of their 'uncivilized' Afghan neighbours marks a dividing line of sorts. Up until then, the British travellers had described the Afghans they met as tolerant, friendly and respectful.

After the First Anglo–Afghan War, the same Afghans began to be described by the British as marred with a reputation for barbarity, treachery and fanaticism. It was also the beginning of a long period of hatred between the two.

Since the British had the monopoly on the written English word, their prejudice became global conviction. From the mid-nineteenth century onwards that British labelling of Afghans as wild beasts has stuck.

The British also suffered. Their loss was both the economic consequences of defeat and the humiliation of losing the 'respect' of their Indian subjects. In order to salvage their reputation, they wanted revenge—just like the Afghans want their *badal* when they have been hurt. But there is an important difference in the two attitudes. Afghans seek *badal* when they are hurt by someone. But the British wanted revenge despite the fact that it was they who went into Afghanistan with the declared intent of defeating the Afghans and changing their Amir by force.

However, the powerful do not like to be corrected. It soon became clear that they would not let bygones be bygones. They were seeking revenge and it was going to be very bloody. It will be reasonable to suggest that from then on cruel retribution became a feature of their colonial policy. The British army was later to term this policy as 'butcher and bolt', meaning 'slaughter and run'.

By October, another British army reached Kabul where they exacted their revenge. It was in Kabul's covered bazaar that Macnaghten's corpse had been found. This famed bazaar was razed to ground by British dynamite, but it took them two days to complete the task. Meanwhile, there was mass scale looting. There is no count of the number of people killed or the number of houses destroyed, but the stench from the bazaar persisted long after the British had left Kabul a second time.

Mortimer Durand describes Lord Auckland's policy pungently in his book, *Life of Sir Henry Durand*:

> In order to repel the shadow of Russian aggression, we had resolved to force Shah Shuja, a weak and worthless exile, upon the Afghan people, till then well disposed towards us; and this great and unprovoked injustice, the cause of all our subsequent troubles in Afghanistan, was to be effected by military measures of which the rashness and folly seem at the present day almost inconceivable.

Durand was right in his assessment about this sorry chapter. But there were also whispers among the British that his father, Henry Durand, had deserted his post in Kabul.

London Misinformed

The leadership in London had been uneasy about the developments in Kabul from 1840 itself. Alarming reports from Afghanistan were pouring in regularly from India. But the public at large was still unaware of the magnitude of this disaster. At last, a member of Parliament asked the question on 8 February 1842 whether the newspaper reports about the insurrection in Kabul were correct. Prime Minister Sir Robert Peel stalled, and did so again a month later. In May, when parliamentarians persisted in having a response, Peel pleaded public interest in withholding the information.

Finally, in June 1843, H.J. Baillie demanded that the whole correspondence leading up to the massacre in Kabul be produced in the Parliament. He went on to say, 'The resources of our Indian Empire are being wasted in the vain attempt to subdue a race of men no less fierce…a country…so remote by its position as to render war on a large scale almost a hopeless undertaking… The boundary of our Indian possessions should lie on the Indus.'

This sentiment was shared by other politicians. A prominent British statesman and novelist, Benjamin Disraeli, speaking in support of Baillie, said, 'If ever we lost India it would be from financial convulsion. It would be lost by the pressure of circumstances which events like the war in Afghanistan would bring about…'

Regarding Auckland's argument about establishing a barrier in Afghanistan, Disraeli remarked, 'If the British left Afghanistan alone it would constitute the finest barrier. The soil is barren and unproductive. The country is intersected by stupendous mountains...where an army must be exposed to absolute annihilation... The people are proverbially faithless...Here then are all the elements combined that can render the country absolutely impassable as a barrier if we abstain from interference.'

Disraeli's assessment about the country was right on the mark. Yet, the same parliamentarian changed his views when he became the prime minister. In fact he was then going to be the main driver of the 'Forward Policy.'

As is sometimes the case, the debate in Parliament led nowhere; the papers that were demanded about the debacle were not produced because Foreign Secretary Henry Palmerston cited improved relations with Russia. No one questioned him on the non-existent role of Russia in this purely Anglo–Afghan affair. Rather, the parliamentarians accepted Palmerston's plea when he said the papers would serve no purpose except to open old wounds.

Later, however, it was found that the correspondence forwarded by Auckland had been deliberately cut and edited to misinform London. But the blame for this should not rest with Auckland alone. There were others who had a share of responsibility for this deceit. These two men, Macnaghten and Wade, used to either tamper with or, through their overriding comments, change the import of the reports sent by Burnes from Kabul.

This was one reason why the disaster of the First Anglo–Afghan War had been agitating the British people, its politicians and press. They were convinced that the humiliation was avoidable and that the expedition was launched on a false premise. In 1860, the report of the Newcastle Foreign Affairs Association confirmed this feeling. The first paragraph of the report was damning of the entire episode. Quoting from an official compilation called the 'Correspondence relating to Afghanistan', it maintained that the 'report that was said to have been sent by the mission of Sir Alexander Burnes to Cabul in 1837, was declared by Burnes himself, as soon as he saw it, to be "a fraud".'

It then went on to apportion the blame:

> We find that the charge of forgery against the members of the (India Board) of 1839, is fully substantiated. We find that the purpose with which this was done was twofold: to mislead Parliament as to the necessity of the invasion of Afghanistan and the deposition of Dost Mohammed, in order to counteract Russia; and further to oblige Russia

> by suppression of evidence, the publication of which would have been inconvenient to Russia. And we find that, to effect these purposes, not only were whole documents suppressed and others mutilated, but… certain words were erased from despatches and other words substituted.

The case of forgery and deceit was strong, but Lord Palmerston counselled restraint.

Ripples Beyond the Indus

The defeat of the Army of Indus in 1842 had effect beyond Afghanistan as well. Indian soldiers and camp followers had provided the cannon fodder for the British folly. For their compatriots back in India, the Afghan victory in the war became a symbol of possibility. It showed that the British army was not invincible. The British defeat gave them hope that freedom from foreign rule was feasible. It may have been a passing phase, but it certainly was the germ of an idea.

When in 1857, Indians launched their uprising, the 'Indian Mutiny' (as this piratical term is known in Britain), the 'Revolt in India' (as Karl Marx called it in a dispatch for *The New York Tribune*), or the 'First War of Independence' (as it is known in India); it was partly inspired by the war that the Afghans had won.

There were other consequences as well before and after the uprising of 1857. In a minute of 8 February 1854 on the subject of Defence of India, British General Sir James Outram had written, 'the natural and impregnable boundary of our Empire is the Indus.' Soon there were more endorsements of this view. The shock of 1857 had its effect on the earlier British policy of continuous expansion. John Lawrence suggested that the trans-Indus territories be restored to Afghans.

This invited a terse telegraphic rebuke from Governor General Lord Charles Canning, 'Hold on to Peshawar to the last.'

Lawrence was to later become the viceroy of India and in that position he held on to his views and seconded General Harry Lumsden's prescription in 1858 that 'the best way to deal with Afghans was not to deal with them.' But just then both Lawrence and Lumsden were relatively junior in the hierarchy and not powerful enough to affect a fundamental policy change.

Both events were interconnected and both dates, 1842 and 1857, were to keep pricking the British pride. An Indian, otherwise loyal to the British, traced the mutiny of 1857 in a great measure to the Afghan campaign of 1841–42:

> It was a direct breach of faith to take the Sepoys out of India. Practically they were compelled to go for fear of being treated as mutineers, but the double pay they received by no means compensated them for losing caste. The Sepoys mistrusted the Government from that time forward, and were always fearful that their caste would be destroyed; besides, the Kabul disaster taught them that Europeans were not invincible.

The British atrocities in India after the First War of Independence were far greater than those they had inflicted in Afghanistan. Victor Kiernan writes in *The Lords of Human Kind*: 'India was never forgiven for what it did in 1857, still less perhaps for what it exasperated the English into doing, or allowing to be done.'

Much British brutality followed the mutiny; the benevolent gloss over the British presence melted away by the open hostility and massacres that came with insurrection. Karl Marx, writing in 1857, quotes a young Englishman saying: 'Every nigger (Indian) we meet with we either string up or shoot.'

If the atrocities of Indian states under princely rule had been widely publicized as a pretext for British annexation, now the insurrection of the Indians became the justification of dominion and enforced subordination.

But the consequences of the British blunder in Kabul were not just limited to the massacre there or later in India. Parallel to it another drama was unfolding in Central Asia. It demonstrates how Britain and Russia, despite their differences and rivalries, were often interconnected and supportive of each other even as they continued to play the Great Game.

6

Side Effect

IT IS REMARKABLE THAT THE methods of the colonial powers were almost similar and so, too, was their opinion of the people they were colonizing. Reading their views now, it would appear as if they were doing a favour to inferior races by agreeing to colonize them.

The entire caricature was of 'dynamic, progressive, orderly, and civilized' Europeans acting upon 'static, backward, apathetic, anarchic and chaotic' Asians.

A member of the Viceregal Legal Council, Sir James Stephen, put it rather bluntly. In his discussion of the Afghan question, he laid down principles which would seem to override the rights of every Asiatic state, and place them entirely at the mercy and discretion of the British government. 'Our relations with these states,' he wrote, 'must be determined by the fact that we are exceedingly powerful and highly civilized and they are comparatively weak and half barbarous.'

The British attitude towards Indians generally held that they were 'grossly ignorant, steeped in idolatrous superstition, unenergetic, fatalistic' and, thus, in need of 'the essential parts of European civilization'.

Russia was equally contemptuous in its attitude towards its colonies. If the British were busy 'stringing up or shooting niggers in India', a Russian General, after committing carnage in 1868 in Khiva, had this to say, 'In Asia, the harder you hit them, the longer they remain quiet.'

Russia's imperial tradition depicted the neighbouring nomadic (Central Asian) people as 'wild, untamed horses,' 'unruly, and disloyal peoples', whose Khans practised 'savage customs', while the Russian Empire was 'the world's respected and glorious state'.

A Kazakh scholar, Abdizhapar Abdakimuhli, describes the Russian colonial attitude towards Kazakhs in this manner,

> ...nomads...cannot even be placed on a level with human beings. They are...ascribed the position of being the offspring of demons and devils who suddenly came forth from hell...

The British opinion of Afghans and Indians may not have been as ghastly, but their contempt of them was no less.

Who were more civilized—the colonial powers or the colonized? The ultimate verdict on this issue will be given by history. But this example should be illustrative of how humane the two sides were—the so-called civilized of the West, or the allegedly barbarians of the East,

> A curious thing was the water supply for the (British) Block Houses. This came by a pipeline laid over the hills from the pumping station below. The pipe could have been easily cut by the Pathans, but this was never done. They considered rules as necessary in warfare as we did. Cutting the water pipes of the Raj would be as immoral as the use by us of poison gas.*

Yet, the British army used poison gas on Afghans.

Barbarism at Bukhara

Occasionally, however, a Central Asian potentate acted with sufficient savagery to have the entire region tarred unfavourably. One such ruler was Nasrullah Khan of Bukhara.

Unfortunately for Colonel Charles Stoddart, he offended Nasrullah Khan from the moment he arrived in Bukhara in 1838. It was customary for dignitaries visiting Bukhara to dismount, lead their horses into the square

---

*M.C.A. Henniker. 1951. *Memoirs of a Junior Officer*. HMSO, p. 235. M.C.A. Henniker's company was engaged in building a blockhouse on a hilltop overlooking the Khyber Pass. Pathans could have, but they did not stop the life-giving water supply to the British, yet the British army used poison gas on the Frontier Pathans in the early twentieth century. This was only to be expected because the British Manual of Military Law stated that the rules of war applied only to conflict 'between civilized nations'. In fact, the Manual of 1914 clarified that 'they do not apply in wars with uncivilized States and tribes'.

or leave them with servants outside and bow before the Amir. Stoddart was told this but he decided to follow British military protocol, which meant that he could remain seated on his horse and salute the Amir from the saddle. Nasrullah Khan stared at Stoddart for some time, and then stalked off without a word.

Colonel Stoddart continued to commit similar mistakes during his audiences with the Amir. Finally, Nasrullah Khan could not bear the insults any longer, and had Stoddart thrown into the 'Bug Pit'—a vermin-infested dungeon under the Ark fortress.

Despite many notes from Stoddart to his colleagues in India and his family in England, no attempt was made by the British to rescue him. The British were engaged then in a desperate situation in Kabul. They had neither the troops nor the will to launch a military force into Bukhara and rescue Colonel Stoddart. Finally, in November 1841, Captain Arthur Conolly arrived on a rescue mission all by himself. But he was the wrong man for this mission because he was an evangelical Protestant from Dublin, whose goals were to unite Central Asia under British rule, Christianize the region and abolish the slave trade.

The Amir of Bukhara treated Conolly well initially, but when he realized that Conolly had not brought a reply from Queen Victoria to his letter, he sent him to the same dungeon as Stoddart. When the news of British massacre in Afghanistan reached him, Nasrullah lost all interest in aligning Bukhara with the British.

A few weeks later, on 17 June 1842, Nasrullah Khan ordered Stoddart and Conolly to be brought to the square in front of the Ark fortress. The crowd stood quietly while the two men dug their own graves. Then their hands were tied behind them, and the executioner forced them to kneel. Colonel Stoddart did not miss this last opportunity to offend the Amir. He shouted that the Amir was a tyrant. As if on cue, the executioner sliced off his head.

The executioner offered Conolly the chance to convert to Islam in order to save his life, but the evangelical Conolly refused. He, too, was beheaded.

A Flawed Strategy

It was not all gloom and doom for the British during this period. There were occasional bits of positive news too. One such silver lining was provided by General Sir Charles Napier. One autumn day in September 1842, he was pulled out of an obscure post in Poona. He knew instinctively that late in his life he had finally been given a chance for glory, and he was determined not to let the opportunity slip away.

The task that he had been given was to capture the upper and lower Sind. It was a gateway to Balochistan and the frontier, but neither that land nor its people had committed any act of aggression against the British power; their offence was geographical in nature. It was the access to the frontier that the British craved and Sind just happened to lie in their path. Napier admitted as much while he was packing his bags for the journey to Karachi.

'We have no right to seize Sind,' Charles Napier wrote in his diary, 'yet we shall do so and a very advantageous, humane and useful piece of rascality it shall be.'

By March 1843, he had defeated the Amirs of Sind. And in that exuberance, he sent the single-word telegram, 'Pecavi' (I have sinned). With that single word, he had achieved the fame that he had long lusted for.

During this decade, the month of March seemed to be propitious for the British. As in 1843, March 1849 was also to prove momentous for them. The British Empire already had Sind in its firm control for several years now. After the death of Maharaja Ranjit Singh in 1839, his successors somehow carried on with the facade of being in control, but Punjab was, for all practical purposes, easing into British grip bit by bit.

This was bound to happen because while Sikhs were good soldiers, their administrative capacities were not such as to ensure effective control over a conquered but restive population. As a result, their writ seldom ran beyond the military cantonments in the territory they had conquered. After Ranjit Singh's death, the Sikh rule did not survive long over the trans-Indus territory. Watching that slow decay, Amir Dost Mohammad was waiting in the wings for his chance to strike. Had the British not taken over Peshawar, he would have retaken possession of Peshawar for Afghanistan.

But the British made their move first. On 30 March, Lord Dalhousie read out the proclamation, 'The East India Company would take over the Punjab and all the Sikh properties in part payment of the debt due by the State of Lahore to the British Government, and of the expenses of war.'

They should have stopped there, because their Raj now extended to the furthest corners of Punjab and Sind. But this only whetted their appetite for more. If they could get so much so easily, why not go a bit further. The British, especially the younger military lot, wanted to secure the borders from raids by Pathan tribesmen. And when in doubt about getting the go ahead from the authorities in London, there was always the convenient bogey of the Russian bear lurking in Central Asia.

It was in this frame that Dalhousie wrote to Sir John Hobhouse (a British writer and statesman) on 24 March 1849, 'I have never felt, more especially since the Afghans came on stage, the tremor of a doubt or seen reason to question for a moment the necessity of the policy of annexation which I submitted to you.'

Between 1843 and 1849, Britain had extended its territory right up to the Indus as its 'manifest destiny'. The result was 100,000 square miles of 'India's most fertile soil, destined to become the breadbasket of the British Empire.'

That should have been enough territory, because beyond lay lands that were inhospitable and different. There inhabited people who were formidable fighters. Alexander had described this land and its people in this manner to his mother; '...where every foot of the ground is like a wall of steel, confronting my soldiers. You have brought only one Alexander into the world, but every mother in this land has brought an Alexander in the world.'

The British encounter with them was no different. An extract from the diary of Herbert Edwardes, a British agent in the tribal areas who was one of the first officials to meet a Waziri chief in 1853, should have been warning enough about the people living in the frontier. He described the dramatic effect the meeting had on him in these words:

> Mullick Swahan Khan, chief...of the Vizeerees [waziris], came into camp by invitation to see me. He is a powerful chief, and his country boasts that it has never paid tribute to any sovereign, but exacted it in the shape of plunder from all tribes alike. Swahan Khan is just what one might picture the leader of such a people: an enormous man, with a head like a lion, and a hand like a polar bear. He had on thick boots laced with thongs and rings, and trod my carpets like a lord. The Hindostanee servants were struck dumb and expected the earth to open. With his dirty cotton clothes, half redeemed by a pink longee over his broad breast, and a rich dark shawl intertwined into locks that

> had never known a comb, a more splendid specimen of human nature in the rough I never saw. He made no bow, but with a simple 'Salaam aleikoom' took his seat.

Going by this, the British should not have ventured further into the wilds. But they wanted to unseat the tribals and to that end they kept advancing. Like a petulant child who wants a toy he has taken fancy to, the British wanted to govern the frontier that they little understood.

In fact, the British approach on the frontier was shaped by geopolitical goals. They were not concerned with a border but with access. Their interest was limited to controlling the passes to check the tribal communities who used these passes to raid Punjab and loot the caravans going through them. The British control of these passes also gave them a veto over access to Afghanistan. That was their limited objective—they were not interested in developing the region or promoting the welfare of people living there.

This approach may have suited the British military mind, but it was a flawed strategy. It was also the crux of British contradictions in the second half of the nineteenth century. As a result, the British policy about Afghanistan vacillated. They wanted secure borders ending at the frontier which could be defended against an attack by Russia. But they also needed to defend Punjab against raids by Pashtuns from the frontier. Yet, and this was their dilemma, the British were fearful of including under their control areas and people who they could not effectively govern.

That's why their aphorism for policy in these parts was, 'rule the Punjabis, intimidate the Sindhis, honour the Baluch and buy the Pashtun.'

An About-turn

But the British had their weaknesses too. One among many of these was the fact that like a weathercock they were fickle in their affections. Take for example the way they treated Dost Mohammad. This was the Amir they had sworn once to get rid of. In the late 1830s, they had waged a war against him. That costly enterprise had set the East India Company down by £11 million. They had lost an entire army and the war had dented their prestige, all of it because the Governor General wanted to dethrone Dost Mohammad. Yet, they were reversing all that and wiping the slate clean as if nothing had happened. Now, in a remarkable about-turn in 1843, the British decided to set him free.

Dost Mohammad was received in triumph at Kabul, and from the beginning set himself to re-establish his authority on a firm basis. At first, in 1846, he allowed his emotions to guide his foreign policy—the bitterness of the rough treatment by the British still rankled. Accordingly, he allied himself with the Sikhs, but that was an ill-fated move. After Maharaja Ranjit Singh's death, the Sikhs were a dispirited lot. Therefore, after the defeat of his Sikh allies at Gujarat on 21 February 1849, he abandoned them and led his troops back into Afghanistan.

Dost Mohammad was more successful on his own. In 1850, he conquered Balkh, and in 1854, he acquired control over the southern Afghan tribes by capturing Kandahar.

In March 1855, Dost Mohammad decided to forget the bitterness of the past and turned to the British again. He held discussions with Lawrence and Edwardes and concluded an offensive and defensive alliance with the British government. These negotiations of Dost Mohammad were to have another result of great advantage to the British. As a direct result of this understanding, Dost Mohammad chose not to assist the insurgents during the 1857 Indian War of Independence. Had he decided otherwise and sent in his men, the British would have faced a much bigger problem during that uprising.

But, in this second reign, Dost Mohammad was always stretched financially. He described his reduced condition thus to Edwardes and Lawrence:

'See these coarse garments,' said Dost Mohammad, opening his vest, 'how old and patched they are. Are these the proper robes for a ruling Prince? This shawl around my head is the sole piece of finery I possess. I have no money whatever. My sons and my Chiefs take everything I have. They leave me nothing, and they tear me into pieces with their dissensions. I live from hand to mouth among them, a life of expedience. I wish to Heaven that I could turn a Faqueer, and escape from this heavy lot.'

Dost Mohammad was not the only one to suffer privations. The Great Game affected many in a most fundamental way. Industrialization in Russia and Britain along with the Russian imposition of a state banking infrastructure in Central Asia effectively removed Indians from their central role in the region's rural credit system. In just a few short decades, the centuries-old financial monopoly of Indian traders in Central Asia came to an end. But Indians must have been an important part of the trading society then, because memories of their presence continue to linger. Even today, if you go to the main bazaar in Bokhara, the traders there will proudly point to a lane and say, 'this is where the Indian money changers used to sit.'

Their presence in Central Asia wasn't just limited to trade and finance. It must have been a secular and benign influence on the society as well. Their departure, however, must have affected the leverage India had in its political and, possibly, religious relations with the Central Asian states. Unfortunately, the Great Game had put a halt to a link that had prospered for centuries on the Silk Road.

7

Pleasure Hill Sanatorium

BRITAIN WAS NEVER SERIOUSLY KEEN on extending its reach into Central Asia. It had posted spies there, but their brief was to keep a watch on Russian moves and alert Calcutta about any Russian designs towards Afghanistan. This was a self-imposed limit. If the Indus was 'Hud-e-Sikandar', then the frontier in Afghanistan was 'Hud-e-British'.

It was Afghanistan that preoccupied the British mind throughout the nineteenth century for its Tibet-like exoticness and its untamed tribes. Afghans irritated them for their defiance and for repeatedly rubbing the British nose in the ground. Unlike Indians, they were neither malleable nor compliant. The British had got the measure of Indians; they could assimilate their culture and understand their traditions. But the Afghans remained inscrutable to them.

Moreover, British officers were hidebound by the administrative structures they worked in and constrained by the policy goals they were instructed to achieve. If at all some among them stayed on long enough to be curious about the country, the modus operandi of these early accumulators of Afghan knowledge was just as tribal as the communities they were trying to understand.

Rudyard Kipling was an exception to this rule, but he was not an officer. He was a writer and a journalist; it was his business to be curious. That's the reason his writing about the region was insightful and incisive. Weighing a Pathan against an Englishman for their valour in *The Ballad of East and West*, Kipling exclaims:

Oh, East is East and West is West, and never the twain shall meet,
Till Earth and Sky stand presently at God's great Judgment Seat;

But there is neither East nor West, Border nor Breed, nor Birth,
When two strong men stand face to face,
Though they come from the ends of the earth!

But Kipling's was a rare literary voice about the region and its people. Otherwise, Afghanistan remained largely unloved and little understood. There weren't as many books written on Afghanistan, as, for example on India. On the rare occasion if someone had the time and inspiration to write a book, the manuscript was unlikely to survive long. The wars were a great destroyer of paper.

If the written word about Afghanistan was difficult to find, so was the country itself. Afghanistan did not open up for tourists till well into the twentieth century, even then the window between the 1960s and 1970s was agonizingly brief. For the rest, only military expeditions ventured into this forbidding land.

Still, Afghanistan has made the occasional dramatic entry into books. Arthur Conan Doyle introduces his fictional Sherlock Holmes through this greeting by Dr John H. Watson in *A Study in Scarlet*, 'You have been in Afghanistan, I perceive.'

These stray references in fiction have continued to intrigue the world about Afghanistan. In recent times, Harry Potter* too got interested in the country,

> 'Sir, does the Thaumentors coming back have anything to do with the Curse of Durand?' Harry asked.
> Dumbledore smiled behind his beard. 'I see that as usual, Mr Potter, you seem to have found the answers to all your own questions before you even pose them.'

That curse, as Harry Potter chose to describe it, visited the world in 1893. A lot was to happen before that. Most of it was driven by the conviction of the narcissistic colonial powers that they were the civilized ones who had a mission to tame the uncivilized Asians.

---

*Harry Potter fan fiction by nomadicwriter. 2005. 'Harry Potter and the Curse of Durand'. Chapter 17. http://archiveofourown.org/works/50074/chapters/65917

A Prudent Course

It wasn't that the empires were aggressive all the time. A lot depended on the temperament of the people in power. Secretary of State Lord Cranborne accepted Viceroy Lawrence's arguments and wrote to him in October 1866, 'I quite concur in your views as to the impolicy of meddling in Afghan or Russian quarrels.'

On the specific question of the proposal to occupy Quetta with British forces, Cranborne echoed the views of the viceroy, though with a little more humour: 'I would as soon sit down upon a beehive.'*

But this benign phase was an aberration. It did not last long. After Cranborne, the new secretary of state, Stafford Northcote, had little time to find his feet on Afghan affairs when Lawrence's letter conveyed news of the almost certain defeat of Sher Ali Khan (the Amir of Afghanistan and son of Dost Mohammad). Lawrence's letter explained that Sher Ali would probably now ask for aid, 'with an intimation that if we decline he will be compelled to seek for assistance from the Persians or even the Russians.'

It was a replay of the same old game and the same old fear. Someone just had to whisper the word 'Russia' into British ears and they would jump out of their seats. It was to keep such a reaction in check that Northcote wrote to Lawrence, 'We are very reluctant to intermeddle in any way with these complicated civil wars—and hope you will adhere to your policy of entire neutrality.' ** This was also largely the feeling in the Russian camp, but the spoiler was the trust deficit.

In 1869, Alexander Gorchakov, Russia's foreign minister, held discussions in London with Lord Clarendon, the British secretary of state. It was at this meeting that he gave the assurance on behalf of the Russian government that 'Afghanistan lay completely outside the sphere within which Russia might be called upon to exercise influence.'

These were not empty words. Russia's actions, thereafter, did not violate this assurance. In fact, she was to concede territory three years later as per the communication recorded by the then British secretary of state, Lord Granville, on 17 October 1872, by which Afghanistan was to have control of 'Badakhshan with the dependent district of Wakhan; Afghan Turkistan

---

*Cranborne to Lawrence, 10 December 1866, Lawrence Mss/27, no. 46.

**Northcote to Lawrence, 10 April 1867, Lawrence Mss/28, no. 17.

comprising the districts of Kunduz, Khulm and Balkh the northern boundary of which will be Oxus...'

In a letter of 19/21 January 1873, addressed to the Russian ambassador in London, Prince Gorchakov conveyed Russia's acceptance of terms proposed by Britain. By this formal communication, Russia had ipso facto agreed to exercise restraint. And with this it had also accepted the northern boundary of Afghanistan, principally along the Oxus River. This became the Rubicon that Russia promised not to cross. It is a matter of recorded fact that Russia did not violate that understanding either then or later.

This suited the British policy which, at that time, was one of 'masterly inactivity'. This interesting term was first used by J.W.S. Wyllie in an article in the *Edinburgh Review* of January 1867. But some historians go back to ancient times and ascribe the phrase to that period. The idea seems to be found in a sentence about one of the Hebrew prophets: 'His strength is to sit still.'

However, the term masterly inactivity did not imply a state of somnolence; its essence was watchfulness. But its opponents found it convenient to align masterly inactivity with inefficiency and what is worse, cowardice. To be fair, masterly inactivity was a policy of peace at home and non-interference in the internal affairs of neighbours. Unfortunately, this usage began to take on a negative meaning. And it encouraged the misunderstanding that Lawrence favoured non-interference in Afghanistan under all circumstances.

In fact, it would be more accurate to describe his policy as one of 'reluctant interference' or 'limited interference', though these terms lack the elegance of Wyllie's words.

It is no doubt true that Lawrence was reluctant to intervene beyond India's northwest frontier. To some extent, this was a reaction to the disasters of the First Afghan War. But masterly inactivity was also a consequence of Lawrence's administrative priorities. According to his assessment, the greatest threat to the security of British India came from within its existing borders. Therefore, consolidation within India, after the turmoil of 1857, took priority over everything else.

Lawrence had made the right choice, but critics called it a soft option. This prudent course was set to change soon.

Pax Britannica

The history of Afghanistan, almost throughout the nineteenth century, reads stranger than fiction. It was a story full of greed, intrigue and violence. It need not have been this way. And it may not have been so but for the misjudgements of small men.

But why blame the small men; those considered great are fallible too. Recently declassified documents of the Soviet politburo show that at a meeting in Moscow on 23 September 1989, the British Prime Minister Margaret Thatcher told Soviet Union President Mikhail Gorbachev, 'Britain and Western Europe are not interested in the unification of Germany. It would lead to changes in the post-War borders and we cannot allow that.'

'We cannot allow that!' Isn't that an incredulous statement to make in this day and age? Yet, it was said. And it was not some tiny dictatorship or a minor banana republic that Thatcher was talking about. She was trying to determine the destiny of a fellow European state, and a powerful one at that. The colonies had long gone, but colonial habits die hard and Thatcher was obviously suffering from that hangover. The attitude was still the same; just as it had been in the nineteenth century. The empire's will, right or wrong, must prevail. However, in this case, neither Gorbachev nor the German people cared much for her will, and the two Germanys were soon united.

It was definitely an error of judgement by Thatcher. But why censure her. As Colonel Arnold Wilson, the territorial architect of today's Iraq, wrote, '...we were the acolytes of a cult—Pax Britannica—for which we worked happily and if need be died gladly.'

This is what the players in the Great Game of the nineteenth century were busy doing. Some of them were certainly heroic, achieving the unthinkable for their country. But, by and large, they were men of action, not of reflection. They were the type who leaped first, leaving the thinking part to others. In this unending tournament of empires, the young were the heroes, the old pondered. Look, for example, at the age of some of these heroes.

If we start with the interpreters of action, there is a very impressive roll call of young writers. Rudyard Kipling had barely turned 20 when he wrote authoritatively about Amir Abdur Rahman and his confabulations at the durbar in Rawalpindi in 1885. Young Kipling's writings were to have considerable influence on British decision makers. Winston Churchill was not much older at 23 years when he became the interpreter of the frontier's rage, and the British outrage at it, to his nation.

On the action side, the field was packed with youth. Some of them were still in their teens when they went into battle for the glory of the empire. Some others were a little older, but just about. Alexander Burnes was only 25 years old when he ventured up the Indus and supped with Maharaja Ranjit Singh, before proceeding further to open up Afghanistan for the British. Eldred Pottinger was barely 26 years old when he led the defence of Herat against the invading Persians.

There is no doubt that some of them were gifted young men, but many more were tempestuous. Some of them were mere adventurers who had come to the wilds looking for fun. They were the ones who saw conspiring Russians behind every Afghan rock. It was largely these people who misread the signals. As men of action, their understanding of the Russian motives was way off the mark and the reason for many of the fruitless wars. Sadly, many of these young men became victims of their own misjudgement—they died for negligible British gains in Afghanistan.

Yet Afghanistan was not an end in itself; the jewel was India which had to be protected from the lusting Russian eyes. As J.R. Seeley noted,

> ...we have the possession of India, and a leading interest in the affairs of all those countries which lie upon the route to India. This and this only involves us in that permanent rivalry with Russia.

Two of the world's greatest powers then, Victorian Britain and Czarist Russia, were engaged in this tournament of shadows; the so-called permanent rivalry which profited neither country. When they started in the beginning of nineteenth century they were 2,000 miles apart. Within a hundred years they were within sniffing distance of each other; some Russian positions were just about 20 miles away from India.

Sandwiched between the new Russian possessions in Central Asia and the advancing British Empire in Punjab was Afghanistan.

This was the dangerous Afghanistan which Kipling was to describe later as, 'When you are wounded and left on Afghanistan's plains, and the women come out to cut up what remains, jest roll to your rifle and blow out your brains and go to your gawd like a soldier.'

To checkmate Russia, Afghanistan had to be secured. Ironically, it was in pursuit of this goal that Britain would repeatedly go to war with Afghanistan. One such war was summed up by 23-year-old soldier–reporter Winston Churchill as, 'Financially it is ruinous. Morally it is wicked. Militarily it is an open question and politically it is a blunder.'

Long before Churchill's warning, the East India Company had convinced itself that its survival in India was at stake. And to protect itself the Russian bear had to be kept away. At least this was the theory that East India Company's generals promoted.

As early as the 1830s the imagined Russian advance towards India became an obsession with British officers. By then, the Russians had advanced up to the Oxus. The next step, the British feared, would bring them to India via Afghanistan.

During this period, the combination of players was such that friction between Britain and Russia was a natural consequence. Any voice for understanding the other viewpoint was scoffed at.

Let's start with the unlikely location of Tehran. Under normal circumstances, this post should not have had a say in Afghan affairs. But Sir John MacNeill, the British ambassador in Tehran, had a phobia of Russia and its expansionist plans. His advice to the foreign office in London was, 'The only nation in Europe which attempts to aggrandize itself at the expense of its neighbours is Russia… Russia alone threatens to overturn thrones, subvert Empires and subdue nations…'

He could have said the same thing about his own country, but no one in Britain was in a mood for such introspection. The temper in London was bellicose; welcoming of every dark prognosis about Russia. Therefore, recommendations like that of John MacNeill reinforced that conviction.

In London, Foreign Secretary Lord Palmerston, who was given to patriotic extremes, was convinced that a weak and corrupt Persia was already almost in the Czar's pocket and when the Persian forces tried to conquer Herat, the city known as the gateway to India, his fears were magnified.

It is true that Prime Minister Melbourne was sceptical of Palmerston's concerns, but he chose not to interfere because the foreign secretary had recently married his widowed sister.

Meanwhile, in India, Governor General Lord Auckland began to refer Herat as the 'western frontier of India', though Herat was a thousand miles away from the Indus!

It must be bizarre conjectures like this that made the military historian Sir John Kaye write about Simla as, '...that pleasure hill sanatorium where Governor Generals surrounded by irresponsible advisers settle the destinies of Empires.' He added, 'Simla had been the cradle of more political insanity than any place within the limits of Hindustan.'

He could have also said that the decisions these grand men sitting in Simla made were to cost thousands of men their lives.

But they were not aberrant all the time. Sometimes, there was sufficient cause for their apprehension. One such case was when Prince Gorchakov, the foreign minister of Russia, explained his country's Forward Policy in Central Asia in this manner, 'The position of Russia in Central Asia is that of all civilized states which are brought into contact with half savage, nomad populations.' As if that was not enough he went on to add, 'Border security and trade relations impel the civilized state to exert a certain authority over Asiatics who only respect visible and palpable force.'

This statement was read two ways by the British overlords in India. The alarmist view was that Gorchakov had just confirmed what they had suspected all along—that the Russian march forward in Central Asia was going to be relentless. At another level, the statement was proof that both the colonial powers shared a similar view of the Asian people.

To that extent, Gorchakov's comment about the Asiatics must have been music to British ears. It seemed as if the two powers had coordinated their thoughts, because the British pronouncements about the natives were almost along similar lines. While this may have been a mere coincidence, the two did consult from time to time about their areas of influence in the region. Yet, misunderstandings also developed, and the territorial advance of one led to counter moves on ground by the other.

Therefore, Gorchakov's Forward Policy was soon matched by one of their own by the British. In Britain, Sir Henry Rawlinson was the catalyst for the Forward Policy. He considered the uprising of 1857 as a warning that the Raj was fallible. Combining that fear with the threat from Russia he wrote in a memorandum in 1868,

> If the Russians were to get a foothold in Afghanistan, the disquieting effect will be prodigious. Every Indian ruler who has, or imagines he

> has, a grievance, or is even cramped or incommoded by our orderly government will begin intriguing with the Russians.

Then, he gave his fancy a free run. 'It was therefore essential,' Rawlinson asserted, 'for Government of India to maintain a mission in Kabul, annex Kandahar, hold Herat, garrison troops at Quetta and lay rail and telegraph lines to NWFP.'

But John Lawrence, the viceroy in India in 1867, thought otherwise. To him, the Russian bogey was overhyped. Sounding a note of caution, he said, 'Afghanistan was too poor to support a large occupying army and too fractious to be controlled by a smaller force.'

About the possibility that Russia might occupy Afghanistan to advance into India, he said, 'Let them undergo the long and tiresome marches which lie between the Oxus and Indus: let them wend their way through poor and difficult countries among a fanatic and courageous population, where in many places every mile can be converted into a defensible position; then they will come to the conflict on which the fate of India will depend, toil worn with an exhausted infantry, a broken down cavalry and a defective artillery.'

This was a sensible and sound diagnosis. There was little chance that an already extended Russian army would take on Afghans and then the British. But this was no season for prudence. Times had changed and so had the cast of men. In this new, rash climate, those counselling caution were slotted dismissively as from the school of masterly inactivity. The new Prime Minister Benjamin Disraeli wanted action and the man he chose to advance that policy was Edward Robert Bulwer-Lytton, the viceroy of India between 1876 and 1880.

8

Russia Draws Closer

SOMETIMES DESTINY PLAYS A ROLE in the lives of people in the most unexpected way. Edward Robert Lytton had recently inherited an estate on the death of his father. He had planned to finish his tenure as minister at the embassy in Lisbon, and retire to his estate to a leisurely life of tending to his lands and writing poetry. Though the governorship of Madras had been offered to him in 1875, he had refused it on the advice of his doctor. Lytton was suffering from piles and his doctor's view was that the hot climate of Madras and its spices could aggravate his condition.

But on 28 November 1875, he received this letter,

> My dear Lytton,
>
> Lord Northbrook has resigned the Viceroyalty of India, for purely domestic reasons, and will return to England in the spring. If you be willing, I will submit your name to the Queen as his successor. The critical state of affairs in Central Asia demands a statesman, and I believe if you will accept this high post you will have an opportunity, not only of serving your country, but of obtaining an enduring fame.
>
> Yours sincerely,
> B. DISRAELI

At first, Lytton had demurred fearing for his medical condition but when Prime Minister Disraeli pressed him again, he agreed.

At this, Disraeli boasted to his secretary of state for India, Lord Salisbury, 'We wanted a man of ambition, imagination, some vanity and much will—and we have got him.'

Salisbury was not enthused. As Lytton's neighbour in Hertfordshire, he knew the man well and was wary of his imagination.

This is where destiny played its hand. Had Northbrook stayed on as the viceroy in India, British policy on Afghanistan may have maintained its placid sameness. But that was not to be.

The policies of former Prime Minister William Ewart Gladstone had already been replaced by the more aggressive Disraeli in London. In India, Northbrook and his policy of masterly inactivity in Afghanistan was now going to be replaced by the aggression of Lytton. He wasn't just aggressive in his policies; he was also abrasive in his personal conduct. He smoked like a chimney, flirted outrageously and caustic critics ascribed his Forward Policy to the pressure of piles.

Mortimer Durand writes in his book, *Life of Sir Alfred Comyn Lyall*, that 'Lord Lytton came to India as the Viceroy in 1876 with the instructions to take decisive measures for counteracting the dangers of Russian advance in Central Asia, and in particular for re-establishing our influence in Afghanistan.'

This was an abrupt change in policy. But it was not due to any transformation of the situation on the ground. There was no new threat and the Russians were not making ominous moves. In fact, it was only three years earlier, in 1873, that at British urging Russia had agreed to the Oxus as the northern extremity of Afghanistan's borders. Some of the territory that had been conceded by Russia was more than what the Afghan Amir had wanted or hoped for. What then had changed in 1876 for Britain to sound the alarm?

Historical record shows that nothing had changed either in 1876 or in the first quarter of 1877. To be more precise, nothing in and around Afghanistan was different. Yet, suddenly everything seemed to fall apart.

Detestable Russians

In April 1877, Russia declared war on Turkey and began their advance on Constantinople through the Balkans. When the news reached London, Queen Victoria took it as a personal slight. She wrote in her hand to Disraeli, 'If the Russians reach Constantinople, the Queen would be so humiliated that she thinks she would abdicate at once.'

She also told the Prince of Wales, 'I don't believe that without fighting… those detestable Russians…any arrangement will be lasting…'

Meanwhile, without any real idea of what was at stake, peoples' passion had reached hysterical levels. War seemed almost certain and the music halls in Britain were setting up a jingoistic beat,

We don't want to fight,
But, by jingo, if we do,
We've got the men; we've got the ships,
We've got the money too,
We've fought the Bear before,
And while we're Britons true,
The Russians shall not have Constantinople

Britain had responded to the Russian advance in the Balkans by sending 5,000 Indian troops to Malta. This was by way of conveying a military message to Russia. In its turn, Russia responded by conducting fresh military activity in Central Asia. General Kaufmann had assembled a large force of 30,000 men in Turkestan waiting for orders to launch them into Afghanistan.

The Russian army's progress in the Balkans had been slow but by February 1878, its forces were standing at the gates of Constantinople. However at the last moment Czar Alexander backed down.

In the end, as Queen Victoria wanted, the Russians did not have Constantinople.

None of these developments were of any serious concern to Afghanistan. Yet, it was this separate and seemingly unrelated chain of events that was to raise Russian–British tensions and alarm the Afghan Amir.

Meanwhile in India, Viceroy Lytton's aggression was boundless. And he was not the one for subtleties while expressing his views regarding the British right to press on towards Afghanistan.

Writing to the secretary of state for India in April 1877, Lord Lytton mentions:

> I believe that our North-Western Frontier presents at this moment a spectacle unique in the world; at least I know of no other spot where, after twenty five years of peaceful occupation, a great civilized Power has obtained so little influence over its semi-savage neighbours, and acquired so little knowledge of them that the country within a day's ride of its most important garrison (Peshawar) is an absolute terra incognita

and that there is absolutely no security for British life a mile or two beyond our border.

If Peshawar was terra incognita, whose fault was it? Were the Pashtuns to be blamed? Or was it that the thrusting young men who the British had sent to lord over the area had absolutely no interest in getting to know the 'semi-savages' (as Lytton described them).

If the viceroy's missives were so vitriolic, was there any chance that his officials might cast a kindly eye at the frontier?

Sadly, those in Simla had miscalculated on the strategic front too. Much more than the Afghan side, it is the developments in the northern reaches of India that should have worried the British more.

In 1875, Russia had taken Kokand. With that in their grip they had taken in Central Asia, in a space of ten years, a territory half the size of USA. It was now within 200 kilometres of Kashgar and within the sight of control of passes which could lead them to Ladakh and Kashmir. But the British wizards were fixated on the Great Game.

When prejudice shapes policy, every move by the other side appears ominous. And Russia was indeed moving at a rapid pace in Central Asia. The Russian army led by General Konstantin Kaufmann had conquered Khiva in 1873. After this, all that separated Afghanistan from Russians was the oasis of Merv. But around this time, Russia had given the assurance that they did not intend to advance any further. However, this failed to satisfy Sher Ali, so he sent his representative to Simla to lobby his case with the British.

Viceroy Northbrook was sympathetic and he recommended to the secretary of state in London that Britain should take advantage of the situation and press the Amir that 'he should unreservedly accept the British advice on all external relations. In turn Britain would help him with arms, troops and money.'

Sher Ali was sounded along these lines and he had not found the proposal objectionable, but Gladstone turned it down as too interventionist.

This put the Amir in an awkward position. Thus far, Britain had been promoting the Russian bogey to gain more and even more traction in Afghan affairs. Yet, now that Russia was knocking at Afghan doors, Britain had declined to step forward to be by the Afghan side. At least this is how Sher Ali saw it.

It was only after he was rebuffed by the British that Sher Ali turned to Russia. But the Russian General Kaufmann played straight and passed on copies of letters he had received from the Amir to the British. This act by itself should have assuaged British fears. But, as it often happens in such situations, circumstances change and with them policies change too. Both Gladstone in London and Northbrook in Calcutta had been replaced. The new duo of Disraeli as the prime minister and Lytton as the viceroy viewed things entirely differently.

Even though Kauffmann had played straight earlier, Russians soon decided to send General Nikolai Stoletov on a diplomatic mission to Kabul. The provocation for this move was the British dispatch of its troops to Malta. And, as previously mentioned, this Russian move was made before the understanding they had reached with Britain at the Congress of Berlin. In so far as the Afghan Amir was concerned the fact is that he was not consulted by the Russians; he was presented with a fait accompli.

However, the British interpreted this as a joint Afghan–Russian conspiracy against their interests. So they decided to respond to Stoletov's arrival in Kabul by dispatching their own mission.

Had they been considerate, if there was a steadier hand in India, the matters would not have blown into a crisis. In fact, all indications were pointing to a thaw.

The Congress of Berlin in July 1878 had done much to clear up the misunderstandings that had cropped up between the two powers. Prior to the meeting in Berlin, British forces had been flexing their muscle in the Straits and Malta. Russia had reacted by dispatching a mission to Kabul. After the Congress, an understanding was reached by which Russians had agreed to withdraw their mission from Kabul.

But, as is sometimes the case, there was a gap between that decision and its implementation, and the poor state of communications was to blame for it. Major General Nikolai Stoletov had already reached Kabul with a small military detachment. He left Kabul when he received instructions from Moscow, but he kept behind a small force, alarming both the Amir and the British.

This Russian misstep was just the opening that Lytton was seeking. He primed up London against the Amir Sher Ali by describing him as, '...not only a savage, but a savage with a touch of insanity.'

While he was at it, he also took a swipe at the procrastinators in London, 'We were told that our warnings were witless, our anxieties nightmares; our calculation the crude excursions of an untutored fancy, our conclusions airy fabrics.'

What Lytton was trying to burnish was a view at odds with verifiable facts. The Russians had not posted a large army in Kabul. Even the small detachment left there was at the mistaken initiative of an officer and not by the grand plan of the Russian state. A simple cross-check of the facts with the Amir or with the Russians themselves would have calmed things down.

But Lytton was looking for an excuse and he had the support of Prime Minister Disraeli. No one in London wanted to challenge him just yet, so Lytton was going to have his way. Sadly, it was on the basis of outbursts such as this that the British armies were repeatedly launched into Afghanistan.

On a chessboard, such moves may have seemed logical. But with the benefit of hindsight, it is now equally logical to condemn them as hasty. After all, Disraeli, as a parliamentarian, had opposed any intervention in Afghanistan. In 1843, while speaking in support of Baillie he had said, 'If ever we lost India…it would be lost by the pressure of circumstances which events like the war in Afghanistan would bring about…'

Disraeli should have remembered these words when he became the prime minister of Britain. But he was no longer just an MP, now imperial ambitions guided him. Disraeli gave the new viceroy the go ahead to pursue the Forward Policy.

Lord Lytton did not need any further encouragement; and from that point onwards his behaviour towards the Afghan Amir was that of a school bully.

The Amir's Predicament

This put Sher Ali in a difficult position. He drew a large British 'pension' with two main provisos: keep peace along the northwest frontier of India and reject any diplomatic advances from Russia. It was a part of their unwritten understanding that accepting the Czar's men would invite Britain's retaliation. It would reflexively mean withdrawal of British funding and it might even lead to a British invasion.

On the other hand, if he rejected the Russian mission, then Russians had the excuse to march through Afghanistan and overthrow him. It was a fraught situation for Sher Ali. He thought he was opting for the least troublesome solution when he accepted the small Russian mission, but kept it confined in Kabul. There, he began to engage the delegation in protracted negotiations and noncommittal promises, hoping thereby that the British Viceroy would understand that he was only playing for time.

But his hope that Britain would appreciate his predicament was soon dashed. Lord Lytton was furious and demanded that the Amir should welcome a British embassy, along with conditions that were likely to reduce his powers and that of his country.

In making this demand, Lytton was not taking off by himself. He had received instructions from London that he should tackle the task Northbrook was so reluctant to fulfil. His mandate was to convince the Amir to let Britain establish a permanent envoy in Kabul. Thus far, there had been a Muslim 'vakil', who carried out some of the envoy's duties. But the secretary of state for India, Lord Salisbury, did not trust this model; he wanted to replace the vakil with a permanent British representation in Afghanistan.

For this, the Conservative government in Britain was ready to offer Afghanistan much more than the previous Whig government. But this generosity came at a price. It demanded bigger concessions from Afghanistan for these services; a significant influence on its foreign policy and a good overview of its domestic policy.

The first cracks in the Conservative plan appeared almost immediately. Amir Sher Ali refused permission for a British envoy to travel to Kabul on the plea that he could not guarantee his safety. But the real reason was his worry that in case he did not meet the envoy's demands, it would worsen relations between Britain and Afghanistan.

Lord Lytton was displeased with the Amir's response. He said that if the Amir refuses a 'hand of friendship' it will compel him to 'regard Afghanistan as a State which has voluntarily isolated itself from the alliance and support of British Government'. The sting in the threat was obvious.

Alas, the issue was not that simple. The situation was complicated by the fact that the Amir's son and heir to the throne had died recently, and the Amir was still in mourning. His response to the British requests was therefore hostile, 'It is as if they will come by force…as if they wish to disgrace me; it is not proper to use pressure in this way; it will mean a complete rupture and breach of friendship...'

Lytton Has His War

That breach was the way to which their fragile bond seemed to be heading. Whether by circumstance or deliberate design, the British military preparations picked up steam in September 1878 when the British Parliament was in recess and ministers were at their country homes away from interference in the affairs of colonies.

Still, Lytton was instructed to suspend action till the Russians had responded to the British query about Stoletov. In fact, when the Russian response was received, Disraeli felt that Russians had responded fairly and he wrote, 'As far as I can judge the explanations of the Russian Government are satisfactory.'

That should have settled matters but Lytton was not convinced. He asked General Neville Chamberlain to move to the border at the head of a military delegation. However, the Afghans stood firm and denied the British team entry.

Finally, on 30 October, the Amir received an ultimatum demanding admittance for the mission by 20 November, or face an invasion. The Amir did not respond. Chamberlain reported this colourfully to Lytton saying that, 'Sher Ali had no more intention of apologizing than of turning Christian and applying for a Bishopric.'

It was a difficult situation and London was hesitant to plunge into another war. But in India, Viceroy Lytton was not worried about the consequences. His goal was straightforward, he wanted to replace Sher Ali with a pliant ruler. In contrast, in London, the Cabinet was unsure about risking another military disaster in Afghanistan, and a consequent collapse of public confidence. While both Salisbury and Lytton pushed for a war, the British Cabinet was opposed to it. The doubters in the Cabinet were worried that another setback in Kabul might lead to a repeat of the Indian War of Independence of 1857.

However, Lytton had raised the stakes so high that backing off was no longer possible. It would have undermined British authority in the subcontinent, which depended to a great extent on the perception of

British might. In the end, Lord Salisbury prevailed and the Cabinet decided reluctantly to let Lytton have his war.

On 21 November 1878, at the end of the ultimatum period, Britain declared war on Afghanistan. It was the start of a conflict which, like the First Anglo–Afghan War, is regarded as a great failure.

9

Second Anglo–Afghan War

IN 1878, THE BRITISH GENERALS, unlike their bumbling predecessors, worked to a well-thought-out plan. They were to invade from three sides. One column of 13,000 men, under Major General Sir Donald Stewart, marched from Quetta to Kandahar. A second 16,000-man column, commanded by General Sir Samuel Browne (designer of the famous Sam Browne belt), was to move in from Peshawar through the Khyber Pass to Jalalabad. The third, led by 46-year-old General Frederick Roberts, numbering only 6,600 men, was to secure the Kurram Valley and then proceed to Kabul.

All three military columns advanced without much resistance towards Kandahar via Quetta and through Kurram Valley towards Kabul. Yet another force ejected Afghan troops from Khyber valley. Ironically, this invasion of Afghanistan was accompanied by a British manifesto proclaiming friendly disposition of Britain towards Afghanistan!

This military expedition though had been launched much to the displeasure of an otherwise indulgent Prime Minister Disraeli, who complained to Cranbrook, 'Nothing would have made me consent to such a step ... When Viceroys and Commander-in-Chiefs disobey orders they ought to be sure of success in their mutiny.'

Lytton was aiming way beyond a simple military expedition; he wanted to carve Afghanistan into three. But on this point, at least, those sitting in London stood firm. They opposed the scheme because they were convinced that it would do more harm than good.

The military expedition had some political officers accompanying it. Mortimer Durand was one such. He was a young political officer, but his superiors thought it would be good exposure for him to accompany

General Roberts in this military campaign. As an impressionable young civilian officer, his reaction to bloodshed was naturally different from a hardened army man. In a letter that he was to send to his biographer's sister on 12 December 1879, he recalled,

> Two Squadrons of the 9th Lancers were ordered to charge a large force of Afghans in the hope of saving our guns. The charge failed, and some of our dead were afterwards found dreadfully mutilated by Afghan knives… I saw it all.

Still, it was not a particularly gruesome war by colonial standards. The military contingent's march through Afghanistan had been largely unremarkable except for one ambush after they had crossed a particularly steep pass. There they came under fire from the Mangal tribesmen. The 3rd Sikhs lost five men in that skirmish. Mortimer Durand records this incident with some pride, '…a Sikh soldier, who had been shot, handed over his rifle and belt to a colleague. Then he urged him, "Run my brother run. It is the Government property."'

'A moment later this Sikh soldier was cut to pieces by the Afghans,' noted Durand in his diary.

Overall, however, it was not difficult for this army to have its way, nor was it difficult for Sher Ali to know that his time was up. Even before the British troops entered Kabul, Sher Ali fled to Turkmenistan. There he asked for assistance from the Russians. But Kaufmann advised him to make friends with the British government. A heartbroken Sher Ali died within a matter of weeks; his predicament was described thus in Alfred Lyall's *The Amir's Soliloquy*:

> *And yet when I think of Sher Ali, as he lies in his sepulchre low,*
> *How he died betrayed, heartbroken, 'twixt infidel friend and foe,*
> *Driven from his throne by the English and scorned by the Russian…*

That last line by Lyall captures the essence of Afghan predicament. Its Russian connection was a false reed that pierced those who leant on it for support. This, in turn, was a boon for the British who found the field vacant for their machinations. It was not the imaginary Russian advance, but the desire for military glory by some ambitious British policymakers which was the cause of Afghan misery.

The Condemned Treaty

By the time the British army reached the outskirts of Kabul, Sher Ali's son Yakub Khan had been installed as the Amir. But he was not the best person for the job. In fact, Sher Ali had once described him as 'undutiful son, that ill-starred wretch.'

Obviously, an uninspiring leader like Yakub Khan could not rally his men to put up a fight. So he sued for peace. In the background of brute British force, is it any surprise that this weak Amir was forced to sign the Treaty of Gandamak, more often called the 'Condemned Treaty'. This humiliating document was signed on 29 May 1879. Under this treaty, Yakub Khan gave up Kurram Valley, Khyber Pass and a few other frontier districts. Britain also got the control of Afghanistan's foreign policy and a permanent British embassy was to be established in Kabul. In return for those concessions, the British agreed to withdraw their troops from Kandahar and Jalalabad and pay Yakub Khan an annual pension of £60,000.

For the British, it was all very agreeable so far. The war was over, the new Amir had been installed and the humiliating Treaty of Gandamak had been signed to Britain's satisfaction. Now, a mission had to be established in Kabul.

The man chosen to head this mission was Louis Cavagnari. He was the principal negotiator of the Treaty of Gandamak, and for that reason he was hated by the Afghans. There were misgivings among the British, too, because of his arrogant ways. In fact, General Neville Chamberlain had remarked that Cavagnari was '…more the man for facing an emergency than one to entrust with a position requiring delicacy and very calm judgement… If he were left at Cabul as our agent I should fear his not keeping us out of difficulties.'

Yet Lytton had insisted on sending just this man for a delicate mission to Kabul.

The British troops had withdrawn from Kabul by the time Cavagnari reached there on 24 July 1879 with his assistant, a surgeon and an escort of seventy-five soldiers. They occupied a compound inside the Bala Hisar fortress, close to the Amir's quarters.

For the first few days all seemed well. Kabul was calm and the British mission went about the task of settling in for the long haul. But this calm did not last long. Six Afghan army regiments arrived in August from Herat. They demanded two months' of pay arrears from the Amir. When they were beaten back by the Amir's guards, the resentment among them began to peak. Some of this was directed against the British.

A retired Rissaldar-Major of the British Guides warned Cavagnari, but he replied nonchalantly, 'Never fear. Keep up your heart, dogs that bark don't bite!'

'But these dogs do bite. Sahib, the residency is in great danger!' the Rissaldar persisted.

'They can only kill the three or four of us here and our deaths will be avenged,' Cavagnari said dismissively.

His confidence was boundless. On 2 September, just the day before he was to be killed, he sent this last message to Lord Lytton: 'All is well in the Kabul Embassy.'

On 3 September, the Herati regiments gathered again in the Bala Hisar fort demanding their pay, but the Amir's staff offered only one month's pay. At this point, someone suggested that the British had gold in their Residency. The mutinous soldiers then went to ask Cavagnari to pay their salaries. He refused to pay, claiming that the matter was of no concern to the British government.

A scuffle broke out, and, inevitably, shots were fired by the British troops. At this, the Afghan soldiers withdrew to their cantonment to collect their weapons, while Cavagnari prepared the compound as best as he could, and sent a plea for help to the Amir.

Soon, 2,000 Afghan soldiers returned and invaded the Residency. Cavagnari was the first casualty. He was hit in the head. By noon, the Residency was on fire, and only three British officers and some soldiers were alive to keep fighting. In desperation, a messenger was sent again to the Amir. It is inconceivable that he had not seen the massacre from his neighbouring quarters. But he sent back the message that he was powerless to help.

The First Anglo–Afghan War had ended in British retreat and the slaughter of its entire army on its way out of Afghanistan. That had been followed within months by brutal British revenge. This time the revenge was quicker. General Roberts left India and collecting a hurriedly assembled force marched up to Kabul. He reached there in early October.

One of the first to visit Roberts was the Amir Yakub Khan. He said straight away that he wished to abdicate.

'His life,' he said, 'had been miserable and he could not bear it any longer. Better be a grass cutter in the English camp than ruler of Afghanistan. You see,' he added, 'what the people are. Who would rule over them? I have fought battles for Amirship like my father and grandfather, but it is over now. I have nothing to do with them now. Let me go to India or London… They rebelled against my father and abandoned him in his need. Now they have rebelled against me. I have not one friend in this country, not one friend.'

Yakub Khan and his family were eventually given asylum in India. But the immediate priority for General Roberts was revenge.

Lytton and Roberts imposed a reign of terror upon the people who had dared to oppose the British occupation of Afghanistan. As a result, this weak, poor and divided state was ravaged by hangings and rounds of savage cruelty. Sitting in Calcutta, Lytton relished this vindictive hostility greatly. He had even considered burning down Kabul completely, though he later abandoned the idea.

When the scale of British savagery became known in London, Lytton tried to distance himself from any association with it. But it is a fact that as the viceroy of India, Lytton gave this direction to General Roberts,

> Every Afghan brought to death I shall regard as one scoundrel less in a nest of scoundrelism… It is our present task to shed such a glare upon the last bloodstained page of Indian annals as shall sear the sinister date of it deep into the shamed memory of a smitten and subjugated people.

After the Second Anglo–Afghan War, and the subsequent occupation of his territory by the British, Abdur Rahman, the soon-to-be crowned Amir, became aware of the deadly nature of the Great Game where people were mere pawns. He was also beginning to understand the new geopolitical realities. Shocked by the sheer scale of British retribution, he asks this rhetorical question in a book that is promoted as his alleged memoir,

> How can a small power like Afghanistan, which is like a goat between two lions or a grain of wheat between these two strong millstones of the grinding mill, stand in the midway of the stones without being crushed to death?

Then, he provides his response and the possible way out of this quandary. According to him Afghanistan had to adopt a policy of equidistance from both powers, verging on isolation, and reject commercial ties with his neighbours:

> The greatest safety of Afghanistan lies in its natural impregnable position… Allah has given us every peak of the mountains for a fortress of nature, and foreigners know that the Afghans, being born warriors, can go on fighting forever and ever, as long as they can hide themselves behind the stones and do not have to face the enemy in the open field.

Even if the authenticity of the memoir is in doubt, it is hard to quarrel with his assertion that, 'Afghans, being born warriors, can go on fighting forever and ever…'

10

A King Arrives

THE STAGE WAS NOW SET for the entry of the future Amir of Afghanistan, Abdur Rahman. From a young age, Abdur Rahman had led a life that alternated between royal comforts and the misery of exile. In between, he had to contend with scheming courtiers.

Once, a relative told his father Afzal Khan (the Amir of Afghanistan from 1865 to 1867) that young Abdur Rahman drank wine and smoked Indian hemp. Thereafter, Afzal Khan's treatment of his son became punitive, so much so that Abdur Rahman decided to run away to Herat. But before he could bolt, the plot was discovered and his father put the young rebel in prison.

The future absolute ruler of Afghanistan remained in the lock-up, bound in chains, for the next one year. Luckily for him, the army chief of his father passed away and Afzal Khan needed a man of his confidence to replace him. It was this fortunate circumstance that saw Abdur Rahman come out of the jail.

But Abdur Rahman's struggles were far from over and bad luck continued to dog him. When Dost Mohammad died in 1863, Sher Ali took over the crown of Afghanistan. A few years later in 1869, in the differences that arose in the family Abdur Rahman was forced to flee. He was accompanied only by his uncle and a few followers.

Of Abdur Rahman's exile in Central Asia, Sir Alfred Lyall writes in *The Amir's Soliloquy*,

> *They hunted me over the passes and up to the Oxus stream,*
> *We had just touched land on the far side, as we saw their*
> *spearheads gleam*

At one stage, when they entered the Wazir country, Abdur Rahman told his followers that he had not eaten for several days. The collective financial condition of his followers must have been really desperate because all they could produce was a single coin. What happened thereafter is best described by the future Amir, '...with this little money they brought some mutton, butter and onions... My men managed to procure an iron saucepan and in this I cooked some of the meat, making also some gravy.'

Just imagine the condition of a man who had not eaten for several days. The smells from the meat being cooked must have been tantalizing, and every passing minute would have seemed like an eternity. When the meat was ready and they were preparing to take the saucepan off the fire, a tragedy struck this hungry party. Abdur Rahman describes this further,

> I had been obliged to tie the saucepan to some sticks to hang it over fire, and as I was going to take the cooked meat out of the saucepan, a dog thinking the hanging string was the intestine of some animal seized it in his mouth and ran off with the whole thing... Three days before I had 1000 camels to carry my cooking utensils, and now one dog could run off with my cooking pan, together with the food.

Abdur Rahman spent the rest of 1869 travelling through Helmand, Persia and finally arriving in Samarkand where he was given a house and some allowance by Russia. For the next eleven years, he waited patiently for his chance, and in the meanwhile cultivated the travellers and traders from Afghanistan. His misfortunes came to an end only in 1880.

At last, destiny seemed to have arranged all the cards in his favour. Sher Ali had died, and as the grandson of Dost Mohammad, it was Abdur Rahman's right to make a claim to the throne. General Kauffmann saw this as a good opportunity to place his man in Kabul before the British could do so. Therefore, he encouraged Abdur Rahman to rush home.

When he crossed the Oxus and began to march towards Kabul, the tribes on the way began flocking to him. The news of this popular advance set those in Delhi and London thinking. The consensus in London was that General Roberts and his army should be withdrawn from Kabul at the earliest. In part, this was because of the fear that the local resentment against the atrocities committed by them might erupt into violence. Second, over the longer term it would be financially ruinous to sustain a large army in Kabul.

Abdur Rahman's march towards Kabul had been without prior British concurrence, but they decided to back him because he seemed to be the only one capable of providing a steady hand at the throne. As for the possibility that he might be a Kauffmann protégé, British experience was that in the past Afghan Amirs had been unhappy with Russia because it had not lived up to its promises.

Therefore, it was decided to engage Abdur Rahman before he reached Kabul. In the negotiations that followed, it was agreed that the British would withdraw from Kabul leaving behind a Muslim as their agent (incidentally replacing the Muslim with a British agent was a principal reason for waging the costly Second Afghan War). In return, Abdur Rahman agreed that he would not have foreign relations with any country other than Britain. On its part, Britain agreed not to interfere in the territories ruled by him. All of this was set in a series of letters exchanged between the British representative Griffin and Abdur Rahman. Griffin's salutation in his letters changed from a dry 'My friend' to respectful 'Your Highness' after Abdur Rahman was installed as the Amir on 22 July. But beyond this cosmetic change, the British policy remained as before.

However, there was some favourable news from London for the Amir. Disraeli had been defeated in the elections and the details of British atrocities in Kabul had shocked the country. As a consequence, Lytton resigned from his post. The new Prime Minister Gladstone was opposed to the 'colonial lobby' generally. His term saw not only the end of the Second Anglo–Afghan War, but also that of the First Boer War and the war against the Mahdi in Sudan. Gladstone appointed Lord Rippon as the viceroy, and his liberal Cabinet decided to abandon the Forward Policy.

Reign of an Absolute Ruler

It was under such a favourable constellation of stars that Abdur Rahman returned to Kabul. But once there, he must have found a desolate city half burnt by General Roberts's soldiers. The few citizens who could dare to venture out into streets must have looked shell-shocked. Even the view that the new Amir may have had from the Bala Hisar fort must have been grim. It is described by Lyall as,

I look from a fort half-ruined, on Kabul spreading below,
On the near hills crowned with cannon, and the far hills piled with snow,
Fair are the vales well-watered, and the vines on the upland swell,
You might think you are reigning in heaven—I know I am ruling hell

Strangely, at this dark moment the cause of which was British atrocities, he was anxious to obtain the nod of British approval. This recognition, that he was indeed the Afghan Amir, was grudgingly extended to him on behalf of Queen Victoria as a favour.

However, he did not seek a similar endorsement from the Russian government even though it was Russia which had provided him with refuge and sustenance for close to eleven years. Moreover, it was they who had encouraged him to seize the moment and march towards Kabul when the Afghan regime was in a state of flux.

That apart all was not well with him. The throne had come to him after many trials. It was only natural that eleven years of exile and trauma should have left their mark on him. That, plus a year in his father's jail, had turned him bitter, and made him suspicious and cruel.

When he became the Amir, the least infraction of law by his people was punished by horrible cruelty; blinding, flaying, starving, beating and mutilations were common punishments. The Amir was adept at making the penalty fit the crime.

This is best illustrated in Rudyard Kipling's poem *Ballad of the King's Jest*, which is a tale of cruelty like the *Ballad of the King's Mercy.* A young man, keen to win the favour of the King, brings him vague rumours of foreign invasion. He is ordered to stay up in the branches of a peach tree until he sees the enemy coming. Below are bayonets, and after a few days, he falls to his death.

Rudyard Kipling was not employing artistic licence when he told of this incident thus,

Hotfoot, southward, forgotten of God,
Back to the city ran Wali Dad,
Those who would laugh restrained their breath,
When the face of the King showed dark as death

Some of the lesser punishments were those where a nose was cut off, someone's beard was plucked out one hair after the other, or men were made to stand for several days and nights without moving. In some other cases, snuff was rubbed into the eyes. In more severe cases, men were hanged or beaten to death or rolled off a hill. The Amir confessed once to Frank Martin (the author of *Under an Absolute Ruler*) that during his reign, he had put 100,000 people to death. A vast number of them were men, but there were women and children too.

Among the methods that he used for giving the death sentence was this: the executioner would bend the tops of two young trees towards each other and fasten them to the ground. The person to be executed was tied, one leg and arm to one tree, and the other leg and arm to the other tree. When all was ready, the ropes binding the trees were cut simultaneously. As the two trees rose again from the ground, the body of the person tied to them was gradually torn apart in the middle. The other methods used for execution were blowing of the body by an artillery gun, hanging and bayoneting.

But the more gory methods were reserved for the cases of adultery. Once, while ordering the punishment of such a couple, the Amir said that since the man was so excessively fond of the woman, he should have her as completely as possible. So the woman was thrown alive into a huge cauldron of boiling water, and boiled down to a soup. This soup was given to the man, who was forced to drink it, and hanged soon after. The Amir gave particularly savage punishment in rape cases. The accused would be buried in the ground up to the chin, and left there until dead, after which the dogs were allowed to come and eat as much as they could get of the body.

With cruel games such as these, it was little wonder that Abdur Rahman was hated as much as he was feared, and that a plot was set in motion after his death to seize his body and cut it into pieces to feed them to the dogs.

Yet, he had his virtues too. He had graduated from the hard school of adversity and eaten the bread of exile, and many a times he had been hunted like a partridge on a hill. All in all, he was a king of exceptional ability. It was his practice to sit working till late into the night, often as late as four in the morning. This habit of keeping awake most of the night may have been due to the fear of a coup attempt or some other type of treachery that is usually attempted at night rather than during the day when people are up and about.

He spent comparatively little time in the company of the women of his harem. His amusements were few. Sometimes, he would indulge himself and play a game of chess, a skill that he had picked up when he was a refugee with the Russians.

Occasionally, he also went out for duck shooting, but his great passion was flowers. Above all, he was committed to bettering the lot of his people; he wanted to teach them the technical skills of other countries in order that they might raise themselves to a level with the people of other nations. But his efforts were not wholly successful. He used to complain that in spite of all he had done for them, his people were still the same. It was ironical of him to complain that though he had killed thousands, it had still not made the others disciplined and willing workers.

His single biggest handicap was the lack of deputies who were able and who he could trust. Moreover, corruption was endemic in his kingdom. A majority of officials took bribes and many of them were sloppy in their habits and at work.

11

A Case of Mervouneness

THERE IS NO DOUBT THAT within a year of taking over as the Amir, Abdur Rahman had enforced some order in Afghanistan. But it was a fragile order at best; the entire edifice was held together by the fear of punishment. Therefore, the lawlessness was bound to return the moment security forces were diverted elsewhere.

Moreover, the external factors which had turned benign towards Afghans may not have always stayed so. British India's views were notoriously fickle and they could harden any moment. A small misunderstanding or the sighting of a Russian in Afghanistan was enough to change the mood.

The manner of British decision-making was also abrupt to the point where Afghanistan, its best interests or the views of its people were not a factor. Every British official of some consequence had a view of his own regarding Afghanistan, and how to keep it in check.

For instance, General Roberts had recommended the division of the country into provinces ruled by governors who were to be subservient to Britain.

Alfred Lyall was of the view, 'We shall now, beyond doubt, disintegrate the country; there is no other course left.'

But Mortimer Durand differed. He felt that attempting the disintegration of Afghanistan would mean playing into Russian hands by making it easier for her to annex provinces situated to the north of the Hindu Kush. Therefore, he was in favour of outright annexation.

In 1880, after Kandahar was handed over to Afghanistan by the British forces, Durand wrote, 'So ends this vexed question. Convinced as I am that Afghanistan must someday be ours...'

Imagine then the situation of a person who has gone through the misery of an exile for the last eleven years, and who, upon return to his kingdom, finds it under grave threat. This was so despite the fact that Britain now had a liberal government in place. It was under these ominous conditions that Abdur Rahman found himself at the beginning of his rule. There were multiple problems within the country and many irritants outside with the two great powers of the day. The reality of his kingdom was that his writ ran till about the circumference of Kabul. The rest of the country was ruled by independent Sirdars.

It is to the credit of Abdur Rahman that he went about methodically changing this state of affairs by expanding and consolidating his empire. Kandahar was the first city to fall and merge with his kingdom. Herat followed soon thereafter and so did other minor chiefdoms.

The situation at the border was even more tentative. The financial condition of Afghanistan being precarious at best, there was hardly any money to post soldiers at the borders. It was this reality that led Abdur Rahman to the conclusion that he needed to settle his borders for peace and stability. This pragmatic touch led him to write to the viceroy in October 1882,

> I think it is high time to have the question of my boundaries settled with such a powerful enemy as Russia, through the good offices of the British Government… The troops that I have collected serve only like the officials of a police force in their respective cities… Should I augment the army where is the money to come from? And if I do not augment it how will frontiers be guarded? My affairs are hanging by a fine gossamer thread which cannot support a heavy weight.

Though it was the British who had been grabbing Afghan territory steadily, the Amir's fear was about Russian intentions. He was also frank enough to admit that he just did not have sufficient money in his treasury for the country's defences. All this was going to be put to a test shortly.

Mortimer Durand summed up the situation in a note in January 1884, 'The only statesmanlike course is to come to an understanding with the power which we have hitherto tried to thwart and impede in a half-hearted way. I would, if possible, embody that understanding in a formal treaty precisely defining the limits of Afghanistan…and recognising the extension of Russian influence up to those limits.'

But sometimes events overtake the best-laid plans. In this case, the plans had not even taken a concrete shape before they began to be overwhelmed.

Russia Draws Nearer

On 13 February 1884, the Merv oasis was captured by Russians. For them, it was of considerable military and strategic importance. With its capture, their control of Central Asia was complete. Durand's diary entry of 23 July said it pithily, '...in the meantime the Russians have occupied Merv...'

This news was received with great alarm in Kabul, Calcutta and London. The intensity of feeling in England was summed up by the Duke of Argyll as, 'Mervouness'.

In London, the news of the Russian annexation of Merv had worked the media up to frenzy. One of the more prominent contributors on the subject, Charles Marvin had already a number of anti-Russian publications to his credit. Now he thundered, 'Mr Gladstone's Cabinet is notoriously given to making concessions, and Russia, well aware of this, is resorting to every artifice to squeeze it.'

Ironically though, after making 1885 annus horribilis for Gladstone with writings such as this, Marvin went back to his native Hungary.

The Afghan Amir did not help matters by sending his troops to the trans-Oxus districts of Shignan and Roshan. This was a clear provocation to the Russians. In contrast, Russia's occupation of Merv was not a violation of any treaty; it just brought Russia that much closer to Afghanistan. But the Afghan occupation of Shignan and Roshan was a direct violation of its Agreement of 1873 with the Russians. These two territories were clearly outside Afghanistan.

A related problem was the fact that at that time British officials did not have full knowledge of the boundaries in northern Afghanistan.

Still, the British were alarmed by the Russian move. The hero of the Second Anglo–Afghan War, General Frederick Roberts, described the capture of Merv in 1884 as, 'by far the most important step ever made by Russia on her march toward India.'

The British worry was that the next step would take the Russians to Herat and from there they would come knocking on Indian doors. This spectre began to haunt the British grandees assembled in Simla. The fall of Merv brought home to Lord Ripon and the British public the possibility that the jewel of the British crown might be at risk. If Afghanistan fell, how could a common border with Russia be defended?

The British journalists based in India did not wait long to jump in with their analysis.

A *Civil and Military Gazette* commentary on 7 January 1885 by Kipling boldly sketched the implications of the Russian advance for India: 'We may safely assume that Russia will annex, more or less formally and completely, every inch of ground in Central Asia.'

What was left unsaid in this assertion was the fear that after Merv, the takeover of Herat was only one blow away for Russia. Once Herat was taken, the path would be open in the direction of India.

An insight into the diplomatic manipulations of this time is provided by the secret diary kept by Arthur F. Barrow, the private secretary of General Lumsden,

> The Viceroy of India telegraphed the India Office on Feb. 24, 1884, emphasizing… The problem facing the British government had to be stated in the plainest terms. The Russian outposts have been pushed up to the very frontiers of Afghanistan; and it is a moot point whether that frontier had not already been violated. Russia's agents are in Cabul, emissaries are working in Shignan and Wakkan; and if she is not yet prepared to advance on Herat, she has reached positions from which such an advance, if unopposed, can be made with ease. (Precis respecting Afghan Frontier from January 1884 to April 9th, 1885)

London stirred itself finally and approached Moscow to appoint a trilateral commission to resolve the boundary issue. As the contingent representing British India wound its way towards Herat, a report appeared in the *Civil and Military Gazette* on 8 October: '…an interview with Sir Peter Lumsden informs that the work of the Commission has been practically settled at home.' Sir Peter Lumsden said that he 'would concede nothing that has not or may not be conceded by the British Government.'

Bluntly speaking, this meant that Peter Lumsden had gone out with very little negotiating flexibility in his pocket. It was also clear that he had not been given the full powers that are generally granted to the head of an important commission.

According to this news report, Lumsden also said, 'in the preliminary negotiations the British Government had expressed their willingness to allow the Russians to extend their frontier from Sarakhs to Pul-i-Khatun, some fifty miles further south, and consequently fifty miles nearer Herat...'

Media Frenzy

It is true that the journalist was only doing his job. But by and large, the times were such that people were ready to believe the worst about Russia. The media in England and their British counterparts based in India were generally not unbiased reporters. Their dispatches and columns were coloured with the pride that Britain was the greatest power the world had seen after the Roman Empire. This glory was now under threat from the Russian bear. At least this is how they laced their reports. They, in turn, were influenced by the young and ambitious Indian Civil Service and British Indian army officers.

Among the India-based journalists, Rudyard Kipling was the most remarkable. His reportage was notable for its passion, descriptive colour and literary flow. Many of the books that he wrote later also drew heavily from what he had experienced and witnessed in these formative years.

That Kipling's reports should be coloured by British interests was natural because he was writing for a largely military readership of *Civil and Military Gazette*. But he was not alone. His colleagues in London, too, were of the same view. Witness, for example, this extract from *The Observer* in 1879, 'On our status in Afghanistan, that land of rocks and ruffians depends in great measure our influence in Central Asia, and indirectly the strength of our position in India.'

This was one of the milder sentences to appear in the British press. Otherwise, the media was baying for Afghan blood. And Russia was being uniformly projected as the ogre waiting to pounce on Afghanistan.

At a political level though, the assessment in London was far less jingoistic. For instance, Lord Salisbury was a proponent of the Forward School, but he was practical enough to tell a peer, 'A great deal of misapprehension arises from a popular use of maps on small scale. If the noble lord would use a larger map, he would find that the distance between Russia and British India was not to be measured by finger and thumb, but by a rule.'

That indeed was the case on ground. Russians were nowhere near a menacing position and, as they had repeatedly said to the British representatives, the Oxus River was the limit of their territorial ambition in Central Asia. True to their word, Russians did not cross that limit, but suspicion is hard to cure.

Rout at Punjdeh

Separately, in a case typical of the games being played then, Abdur Rahman's forces began to make a pre-emptive move on ground. The Afghan commander pushed some of his troops into Punjdeh in 1884 and the Amir in a follow-up move threatened to send an even bigger force. This angered the Russian commander, General Komarov, who decided to meet the challenge with countermoves by his forces. By November, the situation became grave.

The Russian forces pushed forward steadily towards Badghiz giving the British representative the unenviable task of somehow keeping the two armies apart. When the Russian forces pushed a little further to a post called Pul-e-Khatun, which was just 12 kilometres short of Punjdeh, the Afghan commander General Ghas-ud-din was infuriated enough to shoot off a letter to the Russian colonel calling him a liar and a thief. The Russian colonel wasted no time in sending an equally poisonous response.

By March 1885, London and Moscow had also got into the act working themselves up into a real spat. The British ambassador in Moscow, Sir Edward Thornton, warned Russian Foreign Minister Nicholas de Giers that an attack on Punjdeh would have disastrous consequences and that an approach towards Herat would be interpreted by Britain as a declaration of war by Russia.

Had the communications been better and speedier in that age, this outburst may have been entirely unnecessary. The field commanders of the two sides would not have taken the sort of aggressive actions that they took. But matters were brought to a head and the Russian and the Afghan armies were straining at the leash. A single misdirected shot could have started the conflict at any moment. It was now up to the two capitals in London and Moscow to somehow untangle the mess.

In India, two army corps under the command of General Roberts were being mobilized just in case they had to be sent to defend Herat. Queen Victoria considered the situation grave enough to send a telegram to Czar Alexander appealing that he should prevent the calamity of a war.

Russian Foreign Minister de Giers was quick to get a grip on the situation, treating it as misplaced enthusiasm on the part of local commanders. For good measure, he assured the British ambassador that Russia had no intention of attacking Punjdeh or moving towards Herat.

The foreign minister's soothing words may have mollified the diplomat, but his Russian commander in the field was reacting to the situation on ground as he saw it. And what he saw was not reassuring for the military man.

An Afghan force of 900 cavalry with infantry men and eight guns had crossed the Kushk River. When the Russians asked them to withdraw, the Afghan commander refused. To add to the provocation, someone from the Afghan side fired at Russians. This was enough for Komarov to order 4,000 men armed with modern equipment to charge across the plain into the Afghan ranks. It was a one-sided battle in which the Afghans were massacred and the only survivors were those who could run away from the battle.

By 1885, the Punjdeh oasis was in Russian hands.

12

The Amir's Journey

MEANWHILE, IN MARCH 1885, AN advance of a different sort was taking place in India. Anticipating the need for a settlement of Afghan borders to the north with Russia, Viceroy Lord Dufferin had invited Amir Abdur Rahman to a durbar in Rawalpindi. This suited the Amir because he had been anxious to remove the ambiguity and settle his borders. So he was happy to set forth from Kabul for Rawalpindi.

Rudyard Kipling was reporting this visit for the *Civil and Military Gazette*. Since the Amir was to take a train from Peshawar to Rawalpindi, Kipling sent a series of dispatches from there to his paper. Anything that Kipling wrote had to be interesting; after all, he was blessed with a golden pen. But, for a 20-year-old to write so fluently, excites wonder even now. Kipling's dispatches of the events in Peshawar and Rawalpindi continue to rank among the finest in descriptive and satirical journalism. His first report was about Peshawar, a city which he called the 'City of Evil Countenances':

> ...the City of Evil Countenances has become shrouded from sight by the incessant rain, and a journey to the Edwardes Gate means a mile-long struggle through soft oozy slime... Under the shop lights in front of the sweet-meat and ghee seller's booths, the press and din of words is thickest... Pathans, Afreedees, Logas, Kohistanis, Turkomans, and a hundred other varieties of the turbulent Afghan race, are gathered in the vast human menagerie between the Gate and the Ghor Khutri... The main road teems with magnificent scoundrels and handsome ruffians; all giving...the impression of wild beasts held back from murder and violence, and chafing against the restraint. The impression may be wrong; and the Peshawari, the most innocent creature on earth, in spite of History's verdict against him; but not unless thin lips, scowling

> brows, deep set vulpine eyes and lineaments stamped with every brute passion known to man, go for nothing. Women of course are invisible in the streets, but here and there instead, some name-less and shameless boy in girl's clothes with long braided hair and jewellery—the centre of a crowd of admirers. —*Civil and Military Gazette,* 1 April 1885

Since this was one of Kipling's first journalistic assignments, his reports were frequent and his language unrestrained. He followed up this dispatch with another report when the Amir and his entourage of attendants and horses were getting ready to board the train at the Peshawar station. Kipling was particularly amused by the coincidence that this was going to be the first train journey for both man and beast:

> ...pitch dark and the platform of the Peshawar station, covered with the Ameer's horses, which are at the present moment entraining for Pindi. Unless you are actually on the platform, in serious danger of your life from flying heels and panic stricken horses, you will not appreciate the beauty of the situation... Neither Cabulies nor horses have seen a train before; but the former are adapting themselves wonderfully to circumstances. In the first place they are absolutely fearless; plunging head first, into the squealing, kicking truck-loads of yaboos (Afghan horses), without a moment's hesitation. Hyder Ali, Commander-in-Chief of the Ameer's army, has recognized the gravity of the situation... Three horses are down in a wagon of eight, and from the appalling noise inside, seem to be kicking each other to pieces. Hyder Ali, guided by a single lantern, dives into the tumult, directs, superintends, harangues... If one restive grey stallion could speak, he might even tell us how the Commander-in-Chief backed him, protesting and snorting, up the slippery gangway and into his fellows once more.

Then, Kipling describes the scene at the platform,

> Ammunition cases, in red wood, home-made Martini-Henri rifles; tent poles, furs, food, samovers, hookahs, saddles two feet high, and every other sort of odds and ends, lie about in wild confusion. Everything is wet and clammy to the touch, and in the black darkness one stumbles across men and horses at every step... Usbeg lancers and locomotives cheek by jowl; tartars and telegraphs, jostling each other; western civilization

> and eastern savagery, blended in the maddest fashion... After an hour and a half of hard work, the Commander-in-Chief retires; the Assistant Commissioner, soaked from head to foot, follows his example, in order to snatch a little rest before the Ameer's 'special' is taken in hand, and the wagons of horses and men steam off into the darkness...

Kipling had nothing but sympathy for the Amir, who was honked out of his comfortable divan, and torn from his 'pipe of contemplation, and worst of all, just after the evening meal, about nine o'clock.' Then he was compelled to discourse affably until the special train was ready. Kipling added in parenthesis, 'Fancy turning out into the wet, with twinges of gout in your left knee and an amiable smile on your countenance, at such an unearthly hour of night.'

While the train was getting ready to steam out of the Peshawar station on a pitch dark night, the Punjdeh incident was casting dark shadows politically.

An American military historian, Theophilus F. Rodenbough, was worried enough to say, 'England is just now not without serious perplexities, but none are so fraught with possibilities of mischief as the storm which is now gathering on the Afghan frontier.'

The response in Moscow to the victory in Punjdeh was ecstatic but in London they began to fume.

Nervous English

When news of the Russian attack on Punjdeh reached Rawalpindi, Lord Dufferin was playing host to the Amir. The reaction in the British camp was one of great panic.

Durand rushed to the Amir's accommodation to inform him of the development. As Durand records it, '...I drove at once to tell him of the slaughter of his people and the death of his General. The Amir took it coolly. He said the loss of two hundred or two thousand men was a mere nothing...' He added, '...and as for Generals, we have many more in Afghanistan.'

This was not just off-the-cuff bravado on the part of Amir. The real reason for this show was his disinterest in the people of Sarik Turcoman because according to him, they were ruffians and as difficult to control as the Afridis.

Dufferin was greatly relieved that the Amir happened to be with him at the right place at the right time. Had it been otherwise, if, for instance, he was touring in some remote valley in Afghanistan, the course of events may have been different. Therefore, it was a relieved Dufferin, who noted this in a report,

> But for the accidental circumstances of the Amir being in my camp in Rawalpindi, and the fortunate fact of his being a prince of great capacity, experience and calm judgment, the incident at Punjdeh...might have been the occasion of a long and miserable war (between Britain and Russia).

It was only natural for an overwhelmed Lord Dufferin to add that the Amir was 'a prince of frank and even bluff, yet courteous manners, quite at ease... with a look of Louis XI or Henry VIII—that is now never seen in civilized life.'

Dufferin and Durand were most impressed by the Amir's balance and his mature reaction. The viceroy, in particular, was happy that a clash with Russia had been averted.

But historians have not paid careful attention to the Amir's reaction. Unlike his hosts who derived comfort from his calm response, he was disappointed that Britain had not lived up to its commitments. Later, he was to record his impression with some contempt for the British behaviour in Punjdeh, 'The English army and officials were so frightened and nervous that they fled in wild confusion not knowing friends from foes...'

Despite this, Abdur Rahman continued to place more faith in Britain rather than in Russia. He was of the view that Afghanistan faced a greater threat from Russia, which was expanding menacingly southwards. He was often heard saying that Russia was like an elephant which crushes everything in its way, 'The Russian policy of aggression is slow and steady, but firm and unchangeable.'

War Clouds Loom Large

If the political landscape was fraught, the weather in Rawalpindi was merciless. Lord Dufferin must have tried to make the arrangements most agreeable to the Amir, but his Viceregal powers did not extend to the weather gods. Rawalpindi remained unusually wet for almost the entire period of the Amir's stay. Because of the wet and soggy grounds, much of Amir's time was spent inside the tent.

Meanwhile, British officers spent hours speculating on the chances of a war with Russia and in finding fault with the Gladstone government for not having anticipated the crisis in Punjdeh. So the Sunday of 5 April, which should otherwise have been spent outdoors in team sports, was wasted on fretting and fuming.

The final day of the Amir's stay in Rawalpindi was 8 April 1885. A grand open air durbar was organized in his honour with a military parade, the band and the mandatory gun salute. An interesting aspect of the durbar on the final day was that Durand acted as the interpreter for the Amir's speech in Persian. The viceroy was in his finery with a row of medals on his chest. The Amir too had his medals dangling from his chest, but his dress was a plain grey suit and a black fur cap. The only concession to extravagance in his attire was a large diamond star in his cap. But that was necessary—after all he was the King.

The burly thickset bulk of Abdur Rahman limped ponderously towards the dais. From a distance it might have looked as if a bear had just strayed into the regal arena.

Kipling termed this studied simplicity in the midst of so gorgeous an assembly as, 'the last protest of the savage against the civilization that could not let him rest where he was...'

He goes on to describe the durbar in this manner for his column,

> From that point of vantage, he (Amir) proceeded to take stock of the assembly and then turned to begin the conversation...with Lord Dufferin. What was said, what was translated and what was the reply, was utterly inaudible at two paces distance; and for twenty minutes the Durbar watched in silence a most edifying piece of dumb-show.

It might be true, as Kipling insists that what was said between the two was not audible. But it is equally true that what might have transpired then and subsequently was to the Amir's advantage.

All through the celebrations, the mood in Rawalpindi was grim. Reports trickling in from the Russian press had the effect of humiliating the British further. The media there was in a jingoistic mode wanting the Russian forces to carry on further south. Had it been their decision they would have liked to have control of Herat. It was an achievable objective because the Afghan forces were weak; they could not have defended Herat against a Russian offensive. The British army could not have come to Afghan aid readily because it needed time to travel up to Herat and mount an effective defence.

But the British were working themselves up without reason. It was not the Russian objective to carry the issue beyond a point. They wanted to convey a message to the Afghan Amir that they too were a formidable force, and this message had been conveyed effectively through the capture of Punjdeh. It was not their intention to raise antagonism to a point where it risked becoming a war with Britain.

However, the incident was a severe blow to the prestige of the British lion.

A few weeks later, the British public began to get the first reports of the humiliation at Punjdeh. An anonymous letter was published in *The Times* on 25 May 1885, which summed up the issue. This letter also described the British predicament at Punjdeh:

> Long before this reaches London it will be known that the Russians and the Afghans have fought at Punjdeh and that we escaped from the latter place by the skin of our teeth. The action commenced on the morning of the 30th of March, and was over in about 45 minutes. The Afghans were driven back and lost heavily. They formed up outside our camp, and we were for some time anxious as to whether they (Russians) would attack us or not. Luckily for us they never attempted it.

Prime Minister Gladstone was under considerable pressure for action by the public and in the Parliament. Finally, succumbing to it, Gladstone asked the House of Commons for a special budget grant of £11 million for a war against Russia. And instructions were telegraphed to India to muscle up two army corps quickly.

However, the semi-official *Journal de St. Petersburg* continued to maintain the line that 'the Czar has no present intention of even laying hands on Herat.'

Just as quickly, better sense began to prevail all round. Russians were the first to make a peace overture; in any case they had no intention of keeping a desolate piece of land. London was quick to clutch at this peace offering.

In response, Russians acted reasonably and agreed to exchange Punjdeh for Zulfiqar Pass. Amir Abdur Rahman was satisfied with this arrangement and he viewed it as a fair settlement.

While the immediate crisis was averted at the intervention of the two capitals, the feelings at the ground level remained fraught. Even after the exchange of territory, there were still some portions of the Afghan boundary with Russia that remained to be settled. They were small in number and area but they were there. Therefore, the next crisis was only a misunderstanding away.

Throughout this period, the Amir proved himself to be a shrewd man. He did not let a minor battle on the furthest corner of his realm to develop into a war. Yet, he had achieved his objective of drawing British attention to the fact that the northern part of his boundary needed to be settled with Russia.

Admittedly, the Amir had indulged in some brinkmanship. It was risky, but it was a calculated move. This, to him, was necessary to draw attention to a perilous border. The Amir succeeded in his gamble and the agreement that was eventually reached between Russia and Britain meant that the Amir did not lose a penny of revenue, a single subject or an acre of land.

The Great Game Peaks

The negotiations went on in short spurts over a period of two years. At the end, a document dealing with the Russo–Afghan boundary was signed in 1887. This agreement was accompanied by an unwritten British warning that a Russian movement towards Herat would constitute a provocation. The Russian foreign minister gave the assurance that had been given earlier too that for Russia it was clear that Afghanistan lay within the sphere of British influence and added, *'C'est la parole de l'Empereur que vousavez, non seulement la mienne.'* (It is not just my word alone; you also have the promise of the Emperor.)

This statement was significant. It conveyed clearly a fundamental shift; a turn away from a policy of feudal expansionism to expansionism driven by economic imperatives and new geopolitical realities. The Russian expansion was no longer just military driven.

There was another interesting side to it. In that era, the tension between Russia's westward-looking metropolises and its vast Asian hinterland provided novelists and playwrights with rich material to cogitate on. Ivan Turgenev and Fyodor Dostoevsky could debate which direction Russia should take, but no one doubted the existence of the West–East dilemma. Nor was it a purely geographical phenomenon. The institution of serfdom meant that until the 1860s at least, a Russian grandee merely had to take a ride through his estates to leave Europe far behind. In essence, Russia still remained a feudal power.

The thaw in British–Russian relations was due to a variety of other factors too. Some were integral to each other; many others were a syndrome of action-reaction. In that sense, the period from 1874 to 1885 marked the climax of the Great Game. But it was not its end. The result of all this was a strategic stalemate.

Russia realized that it would have to abandon whatever plans it might have had in the past to attack British India, though there is doubt if it had thought of such an Indian venture seriously after that first attempt by Paul I. On its part, Britain's actions made it clear that its menace to Turkestan had lost its urgency. With this, the focus of the Great Game shifted to other parts of Asia—the Pamirs, Tibet and Manchuria.

There were other considerations as well which pointed to the fact that change was in the air; that new alliances were taking shape, not just in this part of Asia, but in Europe as well. Therefore, it was a good time for Britain to make a decisive move in Afghanistan.

The British also noted with some concern that after over a decade in power, Abdur Rahman was getting more sure-footed in acquiring territory for Afghanistan. Some of his moves were in areas which the British thought were of their interest. As Mortimer Durand noted in his diary in June 1891, 'We are getting very bad news all along the border, from the Black Mountain to the Waziri territory. The Amir is threatening Kurram; the Afridis are in very shaky condition…'

13

A Troublesome Ally

AMIR ABDUR RAHMAN WAS AS unstable as water, but he kept all others in a constant state of tension. He was restless, vigilant and always anxious about foreign designs on Afghan borders. In 1892, Mir Yusuf Ali, the Beg of Shignan province, had welcomed a Russian explorer named Dr Albert Regel to his territory. When this news reached the Amir, he decided to depose him, and not long afterwards, St Petersburg's *Novoye Vremya* would report that the Shignan province had been occupied by the Afghans.

A month later, the Amir's men brought Yusuf Ali to Kabul and imprisoned him there. In his place, Gulzar Khan, a native of Kandahar, was appointed as the governor of the occupied Shignan. At around the same time, the Amir deposed Ali Mardan Shah, the native chieftain of Wakhan, and replaced him with his own official, Ghafar Khan, extending his influence northward.

This was not welcome news for the Russians. They had been concerned about the Amir's motives ever since 1885. This latest expansion into the Beg territory bordering Russia was certainly a big source of their anxiety. But they were also convinced that the *real* threat was not from the Amir of a small country, who also happened to be their former pensioner and asylee, but from the British government. The monetary and political support that the Afghan Amir received from Britain made his occupation of the Begdom look like British expansion into the areas bordering Russia.

Not surprisingly, a few months later, the Russian Imperial Cabinet gave a memorandum of remonstrance to the British ambassador at St Petersburg. The document noted that the Amir in Afghanistan had encroached into an independent territory bordering Russia. It added that based on the 1873 Anglo–Russian Agreement, the provinces of Roshan and Shignan were now under the unlawful occupation of the Afghans. Russia wanted the British government to put pressure on the Amir to withdraw from these provinces.

The British ambassador was quick to respond. But his response contained the surprising confession that British India had limited knowledge of the region. The ambassador's reply also conveyed that the Amir of Afghanistan had claimed that the province of Roshan and Shignan belonged to Badakhshan, which was clearly stated as Afghan territory by the 1873 agreement.

Given the fact that by the 1870s the British were already completing almost a century-long period of involvement in Afghan politics, it was highly unlikely that the British had only a limited knowledge of the region.

Instead, there could be two possible reasons behind the British response. First, the Anglo–Russian treaty was only clear on the boundary demarcated by the Oxus River, while Roshan and Shignan lay beyond the length of the river. Second, and perhaps a more likely interpretation, the more territory rested between British India and Russia, the bigger would have been the 'buffer zone' between the two empires. By this line of reasoning, it was a British charade for more territory.

Whatever may have been the British plan, the subsequent response from Russia was blunt. The Russian message made it clear that they were not in the mood for negotiations. Seeing their attempt fail, the British quickly turned towards Afghans; after all, the whole point of establishing a buffer zone was to avoid a conflict with a strong Russia.

The viceroy in India asked the Amir to retreat from Roshan and Shignan. But the Amir avoided the British call and his officials continued to resist the small expeditions in the area by Russian explorers. At that time, the British did not read too much into it; they thought it was merely the Amir's usual habit of procrastination. But the Amir had begun to realize that both the British and the Russians were keen to delimit their boundaries with Afghanistan, so his plan was to lay hands on as much land as possible and earn himself some leverage for any future negotiations.

Expansionist Ambitions

In the north, he had occupied Shignan and Roshan, and to the southwest, he was slowly encroaching into the Pashtun tribal areas. But here the Amir's encroachment was relatively diplomatic. For this purpose, he would often invite chiefs from the tribes bordering British India to pledge allegiance to Afghanistan. The Turis, Orazkaiz, Wazirs, Sheranis and the inhabitants of Zhob were all invited, at different times, to accept the Amir as their sovereign. But gaining overlordship in these parts was not always easy for the Amir; his expansion there could be categorized under three fronts.

The first front was the Kafir (infidel) areas; the area between, roughly speaking, Kashmir to Badakhshan and down to Kafiristan (now known as Nuristan). These areas seemed to be the least problematic for him in the southeast, because the residents there were non-Muslims, and as a Muslim ruler, he knew that he was able to rally support easily against the non-believers of the area. In fact, he had successfully done so in the past. When some Hazara chiefs supported Sher Ali Khan's rebellion against the Amir, he labelled the Shiites as infidels and his men massacred a large number of Shiite rebels. Sayed Askar Mousavi, the author of *Hazaras of Afghanistan*, has provided detailed accounts of such atrocities committed against Hazaras by the Amir. Some of these involved the Amir's men making small mounds with severed human heads.

Beyond the Kafir areas, in the second front, was the portion to the south. There, his chance of winning over the fiercely independent tribals seemed thin. His expansion in this area faced several challenges. At first, the Amir had extended some authority over the territories west and north of Peshawar, and the border tribes in Swat, Kunar and Bajaur. But he could not make any serious moves further, as in doing so he would have had to confront the heavily armed tribes. Moreover, the Amir was preoccupied internally because of constant rebellions against his rule.

Due to these reasons, the Amir had been able to force his way only up to Asmar in Kunar. Beyond Asmar his progress was checked by Umra Khan of Jandol, the 'Napoleon of the Frontier'. This leader of the tribals could not be subdued by either the British or the Amir.

The Amir did not have sufficient military power to defeat him and the British never seriously made the attempt to do so because Umra Khan was a useful foil against the Amir's encroachment into the tribal areas. This state of stalemate was fine with the British because by their philosophy of governance a divided subject were easily ruled.

Still, Amir's advance was worrying enough for Durand to write in a letter to Captain W. Evans about the Amir's intentions and the British response to it,

> He is holding on to Asmar and other places where he has no right to be. If he goes on we shall have to turn him out of there as we turned him out of the Waziri Country, but I think he will go without giving serious trouble. He is merely a swaggering Afghan with his head full of wind.*

Finally, on the third front, further down towards Balochistan was the strategically important district of Zhob, a caravan route by the Gomal Pass which was located at an important point between Punjab and Ghazni.

In January 1892, the Amir sent two of his officials, the governors of Katawaz and Mukur, to the area with an escort of over a hundred horsemen. They marched down the Gomal River and arrived at Gahkuch to establish an outpost there. In the following July, another detachment of the Amir's troops, under the leadership of Sardar Gul Mohammad Khan, advanced to Zhob. From there, he wrote to the British political officer, saying that the people of Gustoi were subjects of the Amir and the British must not interfere with them. The same men would later travel to Wana and Waziristan and repeat this procedure there.

Due to these moves, the Amir caused the British some distress, and in response, the viceroy in India decided to contain the Amir's forces into a certain boundary.

By 1893, their relations were fast deteriorating and some sort of boundary settlement was in the minds of British authorities. In a blunt letter to the Amir, the new viceroy of India, Lord Lansdowne, wrote that regardless of whether the Amir would accept the offer or not, it was imperative for the British to decide which territory should and should not be part of Afghanistan.

The Amir must have been disappointed to receive this viceregal missive. But it was too strong a nudge for him to ignore. The border settlement was now only a question of time.

Mortimer Durand—The Man

Empires have mainly depended on violence. Killing, torture and the destruction of property are essential to the tasks of destroying resistance,

---

*Durand to Captain W. Evans. 'Durand papers' MSS, S. No. 384, 16 November 1892 EUR. D. 727/11. India Office Record, British Library, London.

extracting information and collaboration and demonstrating dominance that underlay all conquest. The moment a challenge to its authority succeeds, the empire stands reduced.

In 1879, when Mortimer Durand was in Kabul attached to General Roberts, he happened to read the General's proclamation to the people of Kabul, declaring the murder of the British mission diplomats 'a treacherous and cowardly crime, which has brought indelible disgrace upon the Afghan people.'

Young Durand was alarmed by what he had read and by its implication. How could an entire civilian population be held accountable for the excesses of its army?

This was not all. There were extremely harsh punishments that the General had planned already. The followers of Yakub Khan, General Roberts declared, would not escape and their 'punishment should be such as will be felt and remembered…all persons convicted of bearing a part in [the murders] will be dealt with according to their deserts.'

Durand confronted Roberts over his proclamation. 'It seemed to me so utterly wrong in tone and in matter that I determined to do my utmost to overthrow it…the stilted language, and the absurd affectation of preaching historical morality to the Afghans, all our troubles with whom began by our own abominable injustice, made the paper to my mind most dangerous for the General's reputation.'

After this protest by Durand, General Roberts softened the text somewhat, though still not entirely to Durand's satisfaction. He thought it was merely 'a little less objectionable'.

The planned action against the population was indefensible, but the crimes during the battle were gruesome too. Durand, however, was well aware that the Afghans were not the 'fiends in human form' of popular fiction. In 1893, he describes the Afghan army commander, Ghulam Hyder, as an inquisitive and generous man,

> Today we talked about the size of London, and how it was supplied with food…about religious prejudices, the hatred of Sunnis and Shias, the Reformation and the Inquisition, the Musselman and Christian stories of Christ's life and death, the Spanish Armada, Napoleon and his wars, about which Ghulam Hyder knew a good deal, the manners of the Somalis, tiger shooting…

However, let's pause here a bit and see who Durand was. Mortimer Durand was born near Bhopal in central India in 1850, and his background fitted him perfectly for a career as a high imperial official.

His father, Major General Sir Henry Marion Durand, was the illegitimate son of a brother of the Duke of Northumberland, and, in the course of his own career, helped crush the 1857 Indian Mutiny with efficient brutality. When he felt it necessary, the senior Durand did not shrink from burning the Indian villages that had harboured insurgents, or ordering prisoners to be shot in cold blood.

However, Henry's son was not of a military mind. Actually, Mortimer Durand was intensely shy all his life, and to hide that shortcoming, he assumed a somewhat rigid and officious manner even at social occasions. This gave him an ill-deserved reputation of being aloof. He was not a gourmet; in fact he took little interest in food. But he liked a good bottle of claret.

Mortimer was only seven when he was sent away to school in Switzerland. It was there that he learnt that his pregnant mother, Annie, had died of a fever, having been forced to make a series of marches to escape the rebels who had captured the family's home at Indore.

This early loss must have made him yearn for a woman of mature years. It was probably due to this longing that later, in his early twenties, when Durand read for the Bar at Lincoln's Inn, he began a passionate affair with an older widow, Mrs Neville.

Once he had even promised Mrs Neville that he would take her with him when he took up his first Indian Civil Service posting in 1873. But his family was scandalized. They were fearful that his career would be ruined. Durand was adamant at first, but in the end he caved in to the family pressure. He announced his surrender in a letter to his sister Madge, his closest confidante for more than fifty years,

'There is one argument in your letter which seems to me unanswerable—that of letting Mrs Neville be subject to "Talk"... No one knowing her would think evil of her making her home with me, but I suppose you are right. The world is hatefully malicious.'*

She did not accompany Durand to India, but a sense of guilt did. And from then on, he would refer to his jilted lover as 'poor Mrs Neville'. He

*David Rose, 'The Man who Drew the Fatal Durand Line', *Standpoint*, March 2011.

also wrote a long poem of uncertain quality called 'Love':

Why did she love him? A deathless love
For a coward who could never feel its worth
Ask of the terrible gods above,
*Who mould and fashion the loves of earth**

It was partly the effect of this first calf love that Mrs Neville continued to stay with him as a memory. That may have been so, but it is equally likely that it was symbolic of his sensitive nature. There was also the fear of losing one more anchor of his life after having lost both his parents; his mother in 1857 and father in 1871 when he fell from an elephant.

When he reached India as a new arrival in the civil service, Durand used to worry that he was not, as most senior civil service officers from pre-Mutiny days were, a 'Haileybury' man. Haileybury was the training college in Hertfordshire which was once run by the since disbanded East India Company, a place where Britain's old aristocracy was trained and tutored to govern India.

Having sat for the civil service exams a little more than a decade after the 1857 war, Durand saw himself as a 'competition-wallah' and, therefore, different from the former who were of a higher social class and, according to the conventional wisdom of those times, more suited to the job of governance.

But this complex, of not belonging to the superior class, did not stand in the way of his personal life. He fell in love almost immediately after arrival in India. One fine day, he saw Miss Ella Sandys whom he described as, 'a graceful sunny haired girl in a grey habit who rode her bay stallion on the race course as no girl had ever ridden a horse before.'**

They got married in the spring of 1875 and moved to Simla. One immediate effect of marriage was a change in his fortunes. He was selected for the Foreign Service; and, as a committed professional, he lost no time in mastering Persian, a proficiency that remained unrivalled in Foreign Service for long.

But the difference in the young couple's temperament soon began to tell on the relationship. Ella was vivacious and a splendid dancer. Mortimer

---

*Percy Sykes. 1926. *The Right Honourable Sir Mortimer Durand-A Biography*. London: Cassell & Co Ltd.

**Ibid.

felt miserable on the dance floor. And he expressed his anguish bluntly, with a touch of jealousy, 'We went to a dance together and I spent a rather unpleasant night… I wish that damned waltz had never been invented. That and the low dresses of the period madden me sometimes. I wish… I had between me and a brick wall the man who invented waltzing, with free leave to work my vengeance.'*

Young Mortimer seemed to have been driven by contradictory impulses in his family life. He was intensely possessive of her, but he was too career-minded to give her all the attention that she craved. He wanted children, but he was afraid that it might lead to division of affection by Ella between them and him. 'If Ella ever showed one moment's hesitation between me and her children I believe it would break my heart… I would never see her face again, nor the hated faces of the children who had robbed me of her love…'

Yet, as they grew older, Durand became exceedingly protective towards their children.

Ella longed for the company of her husband, but Durand kept long hours in his office. Bizarrely, his relationship with Mrs Neville resurfaced just as he started his negotiations in Afghanistan in 1893. Its damaging effect on his marriage suddenly became a major distraction.

On 13 October 1893, as he settled in his Kabul quarters, he began his journal entry by discussing his diplomatic prospects. However, he couldn't help but mention what was really on his mind: 'Ella unhappy about Mrs Neville.'

'No letter from Ella, which makes one's day a blank,' he wrote the next day. 'I fear she is vexed about poor Mrs Neville.' With Durand unable to reassure his wife in person, her anxieties continued to dog him until he returned to India two months later.

It seems that his insecurities on the personal front may have had some effect on his work life. For example, was Mortimer Durand a good judge of people? Well, the verdict on that is a bit iffy.

He was certainly not astute in judging Abdur Rahman. For instance, he wrote in his diary on 26 January 1881, 'The Liberals have the right policy; to keep Afghanistan united, failing annexation, but they have been saddled

---

*Percy Sykes. 1926. *The Right Honourable Sir Mortimer Durand-A Biography*. London: Cassell & Co Ltd.

by the Lytton regime with the wrong man. If we could throw him over, we should have a united Afghanistan tomorrow.'

This is a remarkably revealing minute. Let us try and understand it bit by bit.

As long as Lytton was in position as the viceroy, Durand had endorsed his Afghan policy completely. But soon after Lytton's departure, he began to find fault with the choice of the Amir that he had helped install!

Incidentally, Abdur Rahman, the Amir installed by Lytton and the one that Durand was complaining about, turned out to be the most successful Amir of Afghanistan in the nineteenth century. It was Abdur Rahman who united Afghanistan in the shape that we see today. And it was this united Afghanistan that Durand was writing about in his minute of 26 January. Yet, this was the man Durand wanted overthrown!

Finally, if Durand had such a low opinion of Abdur Rahman, why did he lobby in 1893 to go to Kabul and negotiate with him for the Durand Line?

Tryst with Fame

Sometimes circumstances dictate your career. Then, there are some people who anticipate opportunities, grab them and mould their careers. Yet others pursue an issue because they are convinced that it is the right course for their country, and as professionals, they are obliged to get the best out of it for their nation. Durand had been following developments in Afghanistan from the very beginning because of a combination of these factors. In that respect, his choice of learning Persian was no accident.

It followed, therefore, that he should take keen interest in the settlement of Afghan borders. As he wrote in his journal in January 1884, he was concerned about the favourable position Russia enjoyed, '...a big nation absorbing a number of small weak tribes...'

This was a realistic assessment of Russia's position. But it did not prevent him from noting with a touch of pride that Britain was lucky to get away with a huge prize like India, 'We, on the other hand, are a small body of foreigners holding two hundred and fifty millions of Asiatics in leash...'

It was because of this objective reality that he advocated an early settlement of Afghanistan's boundary with Russia. With that in view, Durand recommended that the British Raj should, 'precisely [define] the limits of

Afghanistan…and [recognize] the extension of Russian influence up to those limits.'

He was of the opinion that the sooner this understanding was reached the better it was for everyone. Durand's initial view of Amir Abdur Rahman Khan, however, was not very favourable. He considered the Amir as 'a troublesome and unsatisfactory ally…thoroughly detested throughout the country. His cruelties are horrible…especially as he shows the utmost jealousy of ourselves… I should not be sorry to see him driven out of the country.'

These were strong words. But was he justified in handing down this harsh an indictment? Were some of the British any less cruel? Had Durand been truly objective, he would have compared Amir Abdur Rahman's actions with those of Lord Lytton, General Roberts or even his own father, Henry Durand. Each one of them had been responsible for ordering mass killings.

This is not to deny the fact that the Amir was cruel. Any ruler who takes pride in saying that he had ordered the execution of a hundred thousand people during his reign had to be extremely cruel. But that was one part of his rule. The other was the role he played as the leader of his country in pulling it out of the morass that it was in. There is no doubt that he was successful as a consolidator of his country, and was a pragmatist in his relations with Britain and Russia.

According to Durand's notes, Abdur Rahman once told him that, 'The Russians want to attack India. You do not want to attack Russian Turkmenistan. Therefore the Russians want to come through my country and you do not. People say I would join with them to attack you. If I did and they won, would they leave my country? Never. I should be their slave and I hate them.'

Despite that optimistic view of Britain, it was she and not Russia, which had repeatedly attacked Afghanistan. This diary entry by Durand raises the doubt whether he had always faithfully recorded his conversations with the Amir. Or had he written them down as he might have wanted the Amir to say them?

Whatever be the truth in that, at least Durand was not leading a military mission to Kabul. In fact, he was not meant to lead any mission to Kabul. The viceroy had initially wanted to send General Roberts to negotiate with the Amir. But this was opposed by the Amir because of Roberts's oppressive role during the Second Afghan War. So Durand was opted in as a substitute.

However, some in the British government were filled with foreboding about Durand's mission to Kabul in 1893. They wondered if it was the proper time for a British team to visit Kabul. They feared that this group might share the fate of Sir Louise Cavagnari, the leader of a similar British mission, who, after negotiating the Treaty of Gandamak, was killed by mutinous Afghan troops in Kabul. For that matter, they also recalled with horror the betrayal and wiping out of an entire British army by the Afghans in 1842.

In this present case, the risk of a perilous end was far greater because Durand was going without an army; not even a nominal escort was accompanying him.

But the decision to send the mission had been made, and the Afghan ruler's consent had been received with considerable difficulty. If there were risks, it was too late to think of them.

At the Indian end, they had taken a deliberate decision to keep the team small. There was no point in sending a large military contingent with the team because it would have made the Afghans suspect the motives of this visit. On the other hand, sending a small escort was pointless as it would have been ineffective against an Afghan attack. So it was decided to take a calculated risk and leave the security of the mission to the Afghan hosts.

Durand's novel, *Helen Trevelyan, or The Ruling Race*, published just a few months before he went to Kabul, was his manifesto, 'There are few things on earth, if any, to come up to the joy of starting on a campaign when head and heart are young,' Durand wrote. 'Behind lies civilization and its trammels; before is freedom and excitement, and the hope of seeing great deeds, with the chance of distinction.'

Like his fictional character, he was going to Kabul with the hope of 'seeing great deeds, with the chance of distinction'. Durand was reasonably certain that he would not be disappointed; that this was going to be his tryst with everlasting fame.

14

Durand Reaches Kabul

MORTIMER DURAND WAS MET BY Afghan army Chief Ghulam Haidar at Landi Khana, in the Landi Kotal Mountains. After exchanging greetings with Haider, Durand looked around to see the escorting party. At first, their appearance disappointed him.

Durand noted that, 'the cavalry in short red coats and yellow trousers, with rough low boots; the infantry in loose blue trousers, black coats with red collars and cuffs, and country shoes with upturned points appeared as awful ragamuffins.' Durand was not sure if his delegation was going to be secure with this lot.

Anyway, they were stuck with this escort for lack of a choice. But there were more surprises in store during their journey. As the small party of British officers led by Durand was approaching Kabul, this was the sight they saw at Latabund,

> It was a ghastly illustration of Amir's methods. On a post by the roadside was an iron cage with some bones in it. These were the remains of a noted highway man, who was caught and left in the cage to die. There he lingered without food and water for sixteen days.

However, the escort accompanying them proved to be a lot more kind. Durand observed to his great relief that the proficiency of the Afghan soldiers had more than made up for their looks. Soon, his team was on the best terms with the soldiers of the escort. They considered them a willing and good-tempered body of men. They would accompany their British guests almost everywhere, even if they had to climb a mountain.

It can happen only in an insecure and disorganized society that they make a hero out of an ordinary foreigner belonging to some economically advanced country. Either that or in a colony that suffers from a deep-rooted inferiority complex. Unfortunately, Afghanistan, being what it was at that stage, was a sorry mixture of both these tendencies. So a Caucasian man had a reasonably good chance of being made much of by Afghan society. Mortimer Durand was soon going to meet just such a fellow white man.

Amir's Confidant

Sir Thomas Salter Pyne's was an amazing success story in Afghanistan. He had left England when he had just touched 16. He was largely uneducated but armed with two essential skills of survival; he was street-smart with a gift of the gab and had learnt the basic skills of a technician.

His first, and only, employment in India was as a clerk-cum-junior engineer in a Bombay firm. In an account that he was to relate to an Australian newspaper after his retirement, he revealed the dramatic story of how he got to Afghanistan. In fact it was a Frenchman, not him, who should have been there.

If that had happened, if the Frenchman had stayed on in the Amir's employment, the Durand Line may never have come about, nor indeed all the troubles that have followed since.

This is the report based on what Pyne related after his retirement to the Australian newspaper *Kalgoorlie Miner* of 19 January 1901, 'He was still in Calcutta when the Ameer of Afghanistan paid a visit to Lord Dufferin at Rawalpindi. A portable engine, with a dynamo and flashlight, caught the Ameer's eye, and gave him the idea of introducing machinery into Afghanistan.'

A Frenchman who was in charge of the machinery accepted the Amir's invitation to go to Kabul, but he made his way there disguised as a dumb Afghan. He could not, however, summon up enough courage to last him long. Shortly after his arrival at Kabul, he looked out of his window one morning and saw two men hanging on the gallows and two women having their throats cut. This spectacle proved too much for the Frenchman. Since he could not just pack up and leave, he waited for his chance. Fortunately, this was not long in coming. When the Amir sent him to England to buy machinery, he decided not to risk his life again.

While the machinery was dispatched to Kabul, the Frenchman never returned.

This is where the British played a clever hand. The Afghan Amir needed someone urgently to install the machines that were coming all the way from England. So he sent a request to the Indian government asking for an engineer to replace the Frenchman. But the government played coy; it declined to appoint one officially on the pretext that it could not force its nationals. There was also the hint that a stay in Kabul was considered equivalent to suicide.

However, young Salter Pyne, by then 25 years old, volunteered for the position. Isn't it interesting that he should have become conveniently available precisely then? One moment the British government says sorry it could not suggest a man for the position, yet the very next moment, one of its own volunteers for the post. The fact that emerged later was that Salter Pyne was working for British intelligence. And they had played this little game to establish Pyne's credentials as an independent man, with no connection to the government.

He set out for Kabul in 1885 escorted by a squadron of Afghan cavalry. His first night on Afghan soil was spent in a small chamber in the wall of a town, while fighting went on all round him. He would have liked to turn back right then, but it was too late.

When he began work in Kabul, the Amir found qualities in him as a sound manager and a good engineer. So the Amir gave him a contract to construct a godown for ammunition and thereafter to manage it. That was the beginning of Pyne's rise in the Amir's esteem, and he managed to make himself so indispensable that over time he became the second most powerful person in Afghanistan, next in importance only to the Amir and outranking even the army chief of Afghanistan.

Pyne had won the Amir's trust to such an extent that when he had to send a personal confidant to convey a message to the viceroy, he chose Pyne over an Afghan.

On paper at least, Pyne is said to have faithfully conveyed that the Amir considered Mortimer Durand to be his personal enemy. He also passed on the Amir's impression that it was because of Durand's misguidance that the viceroy had become inimical in his attitude towards Afghanistan. In addition, Pyne took care to convey the Afghan concern about the British occupation of various tribal territories belonging to Afghanistan.

At the same time, it is claimed that Pyne's stay in India was opportune from the British point of view. When he went back to Kabul, his principal agenda was to assure the Amir that the British had nothing but his good in their heart and that Durand was genuinely nice. He is said to have been eminently successful in achieving both these objectives.

This wasn't all. Pyne was going to play a critical role in Durand's mission as well.

Talks, Tasks and Tales

As Dan Brown wrote in *The Da Vinci Code*, '...everyone loves a conspiracy.' Since the truth may be frightening, let us also turn to conspiracy. Moreover, new documents are emerging from the vaults where so far they had been kept in great secrecy. And new interpretations about the nature of Durand's mission are coming up regularly. While much of it remains an enigma, there are enough straws in the wind to support the suspicion that it was a fixed match. Did Mortimer Durand know the outcome even before he had set foot in Afghanistan?

We will come to all that later. Let us for the moment look at the challenges that the mission had to overcome. They had travelled to Afghanistan because the Amir had begun defying the British and Russian rules in the region. He had been gradually reoccupying territories in the northeast and southeast Afghanistan. While the former moves angered the Russians, the latter incursions needled the British.

As a prelude to the talks, the British forces, too, had been harassing Afghan officials in the frontier region. Over the previous few months, the viceroy had choked off arms and ammunition supplies to Afghanistan. Both sides were, therefore, busy putting pressure on the other before the talks started.

To be historically fair, it must be said that these territories were once ruled by the Amir's ancestors when Afghanistan was at its prime. Now, these places were either claimed by the Russians or the British. Although it may seem that the mission was sent to deal with British claims, in reality, it was the opposite.

Durand's primary task was to advise the Amir that Russia wanted a literal fulfilment of the Agreement of 1873, which Russia claimed the Amir had breached.

The reason for such prioritization was clear. The British saw Russia as a threat, not Afghanistan. They were no longer worried about checking the Afghan invasions of Punjab, because there was almost a zero chance of that happening now. The internal wars in Afghanistan had weakened its government to such an extent that the country was regarded by foreign powers as a 'corridor' or a 'buffer zone' rather than a powerful sovereign land. Accordingly, Mortimer Durand had outlined certain objectives for his mission.

When he was nominated to go to Kabul to negotiate with the Amir on issues concerning Afghanistan's northern borders, Durand had made this entry in his diary in June 1893:

> I cannot say it is a duty I look forward to with unmixed pleasure, for the Amir is not fond of giving up territory and he is likely to be extremely unpleasant on the subject… However the thing must be done… I think I shall be able to persuade him not only to come back behind the Oxus, but to be reasonable about our frontier.

It is remarkable, in view of the major concession that the Amir was soon to make, that Durand records in this diary entry his professional opinion that the 'Amir is not fond of giving up territory.'

We should add to this the fact that the issue of the southeastern Afghan border did not figure high on the ledger drawn for the delegation. Durand was told that he 'might probably take the opportunity of his presence in Kabul' to discuss the 'differences of opinion' that the Amir had with the Government of India.

Therefore, the frontier areas were nowhere in the list of 'must do' things for Mortimer Durand in Kabul. That, at least, was the story spun by the British prior to the talks.

And talking of tales, were the British right in portraying the Amir as hostile to their interests? The facts point otherwise. Though he had spent over a decade in Russia, Abdur Rahman was more comfortable with the English ideas and the English people. He had a British governess for his children, an English tailor, an Irish dentist and a cockney engineer Salter Pyne whom he confided in.

The first three days of their stay in Kabul were given to rest and recuperation. It was not out of their choice, but a schedule imposed upon them under the Amir's instructions.

Actually, both sides were wary. Each had a low opinion of the other. Further, their reputations did not inspire confidence that these two rigidly opinionated men would be able to find common ground. Durand was stiff, almost a rude man. He was officious in his behaviour with his juniors and others of an inferior status. When on his arrival in Kabul, Salter Pyne helpfully suggested that he should make an offer of guns to the Amir as a way of softening him on the boundary negotiations, Durand's immediate retort was, 'I don't carry guns about in my waistcoat pocket…'

In his opinion, Abdur Rahman was a brutal savage, 'The Amir is not the Emperor of Germany, and to treat Afghan filibusters with diplomatic tenderness is pure folly. What they understand and expect is action, not talk.'

This was the less than favourable setting for their meeting. But when they first met on 5 October, the Amir was cordial in the Afghan manner as Durand writes: 'He held my hand so long, and was very affectionate, that I began to feel quite uncomfortable.'

In the beginning, when serious discussions first started, some ground rules were set as Durand termed them,

> …I began by informing His Highness that, in deference to his strongly expressed desire, the Government of India had decided that for the future the Persian text of all communications between them and the Amir would be regarded as binding. His Highness seemed much pleased at this concession… His Highness was somewhat troublesome, declining with real or simulated indignation to be bound by any agreement made by his predecessor, Sher Ali, and denying the accuracy of our maps, and questioning the genuineness of our documents, and raising a variety of objections.

It is important to note here that Mortimer Durand tells the Amir right at the start of their negotiations that 'for the future, the Persian text of all communications between the Government of India and the Amir would be regarded as binding.' Despite this British undertaking, the Amir was made to sign only the English text of the Agreement on 12 November. But moral issues and broken promises did not unduly trouble Durand.

A second important observation was the Amir's refusal to be bound by any agreement made by his predecessor Sher Ali. More importantly, the Amir makes it clear at the outset that he did not believe in the accuracy of British maps. Interestingly, he also questioned the genuineness of British documents.

These points are important indicators of the red lines, which in Durand's words, were drawn by the Amir at the beginning of their negotiations. It is also worth noting that Durand had not recorded any opposition to Amir's objections. If the main objective of Durand's mission was to secure the Amir's assurance that the Agreement of 1873 with Russia should be respected, then there were some issues on the Afghan side too. A primary one was the Amir's suspicion regarding the extension of the British Indian railway to Chaman; so much so that he had forbidden his citizens to use the railway. He had also shown deep hostility to the British having direct contacts with the tribes, especially with the Waziris, Afridis and the people of Bajaur and Swat.

Durand's instructions were to change that attitude of hostility because only Russia would gain from that state.

At their first meeting, the Amir made it clear that it was not his intention to violate the terms of the 1873 agreement with Russia. The impression that he sought to give was that the Afghan transgression into the Russian side was the inadvertent result of enthusiasm at the local level. This, of course, was an act on the Amir's part because not even a leaf could flutter in the Afghan kingdom without his permission.

After their meeting, this is what Durand recorded,

> He seemed much more interested in the British frontier than in the Russian, which was perhaps mere acting. But on the whole I was extremely pleased with the interview. At the end of it he said to me, "My people will not care or know whether I go backwards or forwards in Roshan or Shignan (in north), but they will care very much to know exactly how they stand on your side."

This last bit was important, especially when you consider what happened eventually. If Abdur Rahman was so conscious of his people's sensitivity on the borders to the south, why did he then give in without first consulting them? In his notes of that meeting, Durand also wrote, 'My impression is that he will give way about the Agreement of 1873, and push us harder on our side, but I am by no means confident. His line was that Sher Ali was a fool and did not know what he was doing…'

A few days later, Durand records, 'I cannot help a sort of feeling of pity for the Amir; standing there fighting his game out against Russia and England, absolutely alone...'

In writing this, he was more or less echoing the words that Lyall wrote in *The Amir's Soliloquy*,

> *Shall I stretch my right hand to the Indus that England may fill it with gold?*
> *Shall my left beckon aid from the Oxus? The Russian blows hot and blows cold*
> *The Afghan is but grist in their mill, and the waters are moving it fast,*
> *Let the stone be the upper or nether, it grinds him to powder at last*

Abdur Rahman was truly in an unenviable position because he was caught between two powers, both of which were in an expansionary mode. As Lyall wrote, he could annoy neither.

But there was no shortage of the macabre in Kabul. Once, in late October, as Durand set out to ride towards the Amir's palace, he saw bodies of four men who had been executed earlier that morning. They were lying by the roadside as a warning to others. Further on, they saw a General half-buried in the ground. His head and torso were sticking out of the ground, awaiting slow death.

15

The Line That Divided Pashtuns

As far as the negotiations were concerned, there was hardly any progress. At one point, Durand was so frustrated with the Amir's antics that he wrote in his diary, 'The Kabul mission has broken down; the Amir is going to Balkh to arrange matters. I believe he was afraid of having us, lest we should ask too much.'

Mortimer was not in any great hurry to return to India, but his frustration with the Amir's stalling tactics was growing steadily. As the negotiations about the frontier with India dragged on, Pyne counselled patience. He told Durand, 'Amir never gives any real decision on any other day except Sunday.'

Accordingly, one lucky morning the wheel turned. There is no explanation as to why the Amir changed tack suddenly, and became amenable. The British texts of the period give copious details about the settlement of the boundary on the Russian side. But they fall strangely silent when it comes to the Agreement on the Indian side. Why did the Iron Amir buckle under in the manner that he did?

One can guess what actually happened on that fateful day of 12 November 1893. We can also try and piece together stray bits of evidence to form a picture. There were no Afghan nationals in the room with the Amir, just an Indian named Sultan Mohammad Khan (father of the poet, Faiz Ahmed Faiz) and the British delegation. To be absolutely correct, even Sultan Mohammad was not in the room. He was hiding in purdah behind the Amir so that he could keep notes of the meeting. These notes could have provided a clue to what actually transpired, but there is no trace of them.

As far as the Agreement itself is concerned, the only thing remarkable about it is its shortness. There are just seven small paragraphs to it.

When this British group emerged from the royal chamber, they came out with two signed documents. The agreement about the northern part fixes the 'boundary' between Afghanistan and Russia (see Annexure I). The agreement with the British is about the 'spheres of influence' in Afghanistan's eastern and southern frontier. This latter piece of paper was to become known as the Durand Agreement (see Annexure II). It was signed in a language that Amir Abdur Rahman had no knowledge of.

A Deed of Deception

Was the Iron Amir goaded into signing a one-sided Agreement? There was only one man in the entire kingdom who could have made him do this—Salter Pyne, the joker in the British delegation's pack. Seeing how successfully Pyne was able to manipulate the Amir in the direction he wanted, Durand noted, 'He is a very useful man. It is amusing to feel that the mission is being personally conducted by a little cockney trader.'

That was not the only deception. The Durand Line passes through present-day Pakistani provinces of Khyber Pakhtunkhwa (NWFP), Federally Administered Tribal Areas (FATA) and Balochistan. It also includes ten provinces in Afghanistan. According to some accounts, the British, under a false pretence, assured the Afghan ruler that Balochistan was a part of British India. Therefore, they were not required to have the consent of anyone from Balochistan while finalizing the Agreement, or later for the demarcation of the boundary on ground. This was incorrect because by a treaty signed with the Khan of Kalat in 1876, the British had recognized the independence of this state. By internationally accepted norms, Balochistan too should have been a party to the Agreement because a part of its territory was also involved. But, the British kept the Baloch rulers in the dark about the Durand Line Agreement to avoid any complications. Therefore the Agreement was drawn as a bilateral document between Afghanistan and British India only. It intentionally excluded Balochistan. Hence, from a legal standpoint, the Agreement became null and void as soon as it was signed.

By this act of exclusion the British were being economical with the truth. As Bernard Shaw once said, this typified the British character, '...he (Britisher) does everything on principle. He fights you on patriotic principles; he robs you on business principles; he enslaves you on imperial principles.'

In the case of the Durand Agreement, the Amir was being robbed of territory, and his people were being enslaved.

The way the British writers treat this issue reeks of self-censorship on a vast scale. They skip over the subject and make it out as if the entire Durand trip, and the negotiations with the Amir, was a lark, not a case of strenuous and serious negotiations.

Let's try and view the negotiations through a sarcastic lens. It might then spin out in this manner:

> Durand, it would seem, had gone to Kabul with his small band to get away for a few weeks from the worries of office. They were entertained there by an Iron Amir who seemed most anxious to please the visitors. When they had had enough of this idyllic stay in the Amir's palace, they decided to head back to work in Simla. As a going away present, the Amir produced two sheets of paper; one was blank, the other had a map of Afghanistan on it. Durand was reluctantly dragged away from the piano that his host had thoughtfully placed in his room, and scrawled a few short some-things in English, which would have ordinarily made no sense to the Amir. But since it was Durand who had written them down, the Amir jumped with joy and grabbed the nearest pen to put his Royal signature on it.
>
> But Durand wasn't done yet. He was still in a state of ecstasy which comes from playing an exceptionally fine aria on the piano. So he waved his magic pen again, quite like an accomplished conductor, and drew a line across the map. And pronto, he had given Afghanistan a new border. The Amir felt blessed that the visiting Englishman had given him a scientific border. All seemed to have been decided except a slice of the Waziri territory which the Amir wished to retain. Now, if we were to continue in that same supercilious manner, then British historians will also make us believe that the Amir wanted this small piece of Waziri territory for sentimental reasons because his old nanny used to live there.

However, here the British accounts make a slight concession to truth and quote a real conversation, 'When Durand asked him why this insistence on a piece of land where population is small and revenue meagre, the Amir turned towards him slowly and held him in a steady gaze before responding with a firm voice, "Nam-name-honour"'.

This last bit of conversation is what actually happened. All the rest that

I have described in the satirical piece above about the way the Agreement was signed is imaginary. In part, this is atonement, a regret that Afghans should have been denied a factual and historically correct peek into what really happened on 12 November 1893.

A Compliant Marionette

It is established practice during negotiations that you do not reveal all your cards in one go. Moreover, if you are making a concession, it is done after hard bargaining. Even then, you do not concede everything all at once. You make concessions in driblets and in return for something from the other side or upon instructions from your superiors.

In this case, there was no concession from the British side. The only sweetener that Durand had offered was to increase the annual money grant given by Britain from ₹12 lakh to ₹18 lakh. But this additional ₹6 lakh could hardly be called a significant addition to the Amir's revenues. In any case, that increased fund was largely for the maintenance of his administration in the Wakhan corridor, which he had very reluctantly agreed to absorb at British insistence.

The British were keen to staple Wakhan on to Afghanistan because this additional territory added to the buffer between their Indian possessions and Russia. But adding that distant piece of territory to his kingdom did not give any strategic or revenue benefit to Abdur Rahman or his country.

Moreover, even the enhanced British purse of ₹18 lakh given to him in 1893 was a modest offering especially when you keep in view the fact that as far back as 1841, the British were paying ₹13 lakh to Afghan tribal chiefs. One reason for the massacre of the British army in that year was the British decision to reduce that purse by ₹2 lakh annually.

If the tribal chiefs were being given ₹13 lakh in 1841, surely an additional grant fifty-two years later of only ₹6 lakh to a king was not a great bonanza.

Is it likely that the king of a country could have agreed to partition his country for this extra ₹6 lakh? It appears even more improbable when that king happens to be a very proud Abdur Rahman. It is also a fact that despite its economic problems, Afghanistan was not a poor country. In fact, when Shah Shuja abdicated in 1842, he had left behind £2 million in the treasury. So to say that either of these two—a message from top or need for greater money—was the reason for Abdur Rahman to change tack and capitulate, will be stretching credulity.

The Amir could not have given in to blackmail or temptation of the sexual kind; his visits to the harem were generally limited to once a week. Therefore, there was hardly any scope there for the British to blackmail him. What then could have made him take so dramatic an about-turn? This is a mystery.

It is also worth recalling that once, not too far back in time, Mortimer Durand was himself against the division of Afghanistan. His logic was that the division would be an invitation to Russia to grab the northern part. He had then said, '...attempting the disintegration of Afghanistan would mean playing into Russian hands by making it easier for her to annex provinces situated to the north of the Hindu Kush.' Yet, and against his own logic, Mortimer Durand had now divided Afghanistan.

Unfortunately, there are no Afghan records on the issue and even if there was a scrap of paper somewhere in the official or a private collection in Kabul, it would have been bombed out in one of the many wars that have been inflicted upon this unfortunate land.

To consider the issue from another angle, let us look at the Amir's record. Did he give up territory? Or did he add to it? The fact is that after a long period of strife and instability, he was successful in bringing sound administration and a reasonable amount of stability to Afghanistan. He had not removed discord entirely, because there were still the rebellious Afridis and Mehsuds, but, by and large, Afghanistan was free from great convulsions.

Besides consolidating, the Amir had successfully added territory to Afghanistan. These were the parts which were under independent Sirdars earlier, but Abdur Rahman had subdued them one after the other absorbing Kandahar, Herat and all the smaller ones in his orbit. By the time Durand came in with his mission, Abdur Rahman had expanded Afghanistan by three times in size from the truncated state he had inherited. It is, therefore, difficult to believe that an Amir whose track record was one of expansion should, in a fit of generosity, have given away a large chunk of his land to a visiting Briton.

The only area that was given to the Amir was Kafiristan. And that too, as Durand would write later in a secret letter to the viceroy, was granted to the Amir because Kafiristan was 'miserably poor'. It was severed from

Chitral by the Shawal Mountains, and the area was not easy to supply during winters. Moreover, its remote location had made it a difficult place for the British to govern. But the Amir was happy to keep the area because as far as his wishes went, it would greatly please his subjects. The real reason, as the Amir told Durand, was to send in his army and convert the Hindus living there to Islam. This was the only concession made by Durand; otherwise, the entire Agreement was a losing proposition for the Amir.

The Agreement did not make sense for a very practical reason too. Abdur Rahman was a Pashtun. He derived his basic strength from the majority Pashtun population rather than from minorities like Tajiks, Uzbeks or Hazaras; the last being Shias were not trusted by him for anything other than menial jobs. For such an Amir to cut off over 50 per cent of Pashtun lands, and to part with more than 50 per cent of the Pashtun population, did not seem logical at all. It defied reason then, and it continues to defy logic even now. Could it have been something personal; was it due to a medical condition that turned him temporarily into a compliant marionette for the British?

It will be unwise to rule out this possibility. The Amir had his local hakeem, but he relied more on a British doctor to cure him of serious ailments. Some of these were of a grave nature, requiring heavy doses of tranquilizers.

As a rule, British accounts tend to be copious especially where they have won a great diplomatic victory. They go into considerable detail describing every aspect of the negotiation, because they write with an eye on history and as a guide for their future generation of negotiators. This was the case with the three Afghan wars. Durand's journey to Kabul and the negotiation over the northern part of the Afghan border with Russia have also been amply written about. The question that intrigues is this: how is it that we have a complete picture of the whys and why nots of the northern border part of the negotiations, but there is next to nothing about the far more important Durand Agreement? Why and how was the Amir brought about?

It is strange that even Percy Sykes, who wrote a rather authoritative biography of Mortimer Durand, simply skips over the crucial issue as to how the Amir turned around. He does not give us a clue as to when and by whom the Durand Line was drawn on the map. Further, the biography does not touch on the fact that if Durand was so adept at Persian why did the two sides not sign the text in Persian? After all, the Durand Agreement was the most important agreement that was ever signed by the two sides. And both the Government of India and the Amir had recently agreed that only the Persian text would be considered as binding. Yet just the English text of the Agreement was signed by the two sides.

After the signature of the document, the Amir held a great durbar where he spoke and lauded both the Agreement and Mortimer Durand to the assembled Sirdars. Interestingly, he made Durand speak in Persian to this assembly.

In fact, many in Afghanistan assert that the Amir did not sign the document. They suspect his signatures were forged on the document. That may be an emotional assertion rather than a statement of fact. But the doubt about it persists to this day, indicating the strength of resentment against an unfair agreement and a line drawn unfairly. In the latter case, even the signatures are missing.

If you look at the map and see that line, you cannot help but remark as to why the line was drawn on such a small-sized map. The line travels in a zigzag fashion across the map, which makes you wonder as to how this casual romp of a pen could become the dividing line of people's destiny?

Such lines should be the result of careful work done by cartographers over several weeks. To give an example, Radcliffe Line between India and Pakistan is roughly of the same length as the Durand Line. But Cyril Radcliffe did not casually draw a line across a small map. He spent a full forty-nine days in India poring over documents and large-scale maps. He was assisted by a team of professionals, consulted a variety of people including politicians, bureaucrats, cartographers and many others. He had a team of trained draftsmen who had carefully and meticulously drawn the borders between India and Pakistan. Yet, he was criticized by both sides for spending only seven weeks in deciding the destinies of people. In fact, the level of rage against him was so high that he left India immediately upon completion of the border plan. And he vowed never to return again because he was afraid of being killed by one side or the other. W.H. Auden mentions it in his poem 'Partition' (1966) thus:

The next day he sailed for England, where he quickly forgot
The case, as a good lawyer must. Return he would not,
Afraid, as he told his Club, that he might get shot

In contrast, Durand, if he is the one who is suspected to have drawn that zigzag line across the map, got away with it all. It is true that like Radcliffe, Mortimer Durand too had spent seven weeks in Afghanistan, but most of that time was spent lying in wait for the right opportunity to bait the Amir. Once the Amir was brought around, the map-making was a casual affair. Durand's was an instant line, drawn on a small copybook-type map and covered nearly 1,600 miles. Mortimer did not have the time to consult anyone, nor did he have the professional help of the kind that is necessary in such a major undertaking. And he considered neither the historical evidence nor consulted any representative of the affected regions. People who were to live on the two sides of this line were given no say in the matter. Nor was their approval sought. Durand did not spend time worrying over the future of those divided by his line.

Unfortunately for the people, the Durand Line was a diktat to which the dictatorial Iron Amir submitted meekly! There was not a squeak against the line by the Sirdars either. Wasn't this strange, eerily strange? And unlike Radcliffe, Mortimer Durand did return to Afghanistan.

16

A Very Ill Amir

A MYSTERY RETAINS ITS ALLURE until the last fig leaf is in place. Till then, the imagination has a free run, making you wonder and taking you to fanciful turns. It is like a visit to 221, Baker Street in London. The house is still maintained just as it was when Sherlock Holmes may have lived in it. You walk across from the bedroom into the drawing room thinking that Dr Watson might be sitting in one of the chairs smoking a pipe with a newspaper in hand. When you don't find him there, the guide tells you helpfully to try the next room with a view of the street. Maybe he is there keeping an eye on the people walking by. You step in softly, expecting Sherlock himself to leap across the room to consult Dr Watson on some urgent case. Once again you see just a well lived-in room. The denouement comes at the end of the tour when the guide tells you that neither of the two had ever lived there, or on the face of this earth.

Like many others, I too have puzzled over the mystery of the Durand Line. Why did the Iron Amir sign on the dotted line? Why were there no Afghans in the room when he signed it? Why, in his so-called autobiography, there is considerable detail about how he agreed to settle the northern boundary during his talks with Durand, but almost next to nothing about the frontier where he gifted away 40,000 square miles of Afghan lands to the British? If Mortimer Durand was such a formidable diplomat, why did he need Salter Pyne to pull a trick on the Amir?

As for his being a wizard at diplomacy, the fact is that the American President Theodore Roosevelt took a rather dim view of Durand's abilities and had him sent back prematurely from Washington. Demanding the recall of an ambassador is a grave affair. Such a drastic step is rarely taken in international diplomacy, and it is rarer still in a relationship as close as the one between the United States and the United Kingdom. So was Mortimer Durand really such a great diplomat?

If he wasn't a wizard at diplomacy, and this is our little puzzle here, then how could he mesmerize Amir Abdur Rahman into blindly signing the English text of the document? And what is more, how did this hugely suspicious Amir agree happily that a small unsigned map with a hastily drawn line was to be his country's 'scientific' border henceforth?

These issues continue to preoccupy the Afghans. Alas, unlike in a tour of Baker Street, the puzzle here concerns the real-life tragedy of the Pashtun people; a tragedy that continues to draw blood a century after that line was forged through an unwilling land.

Periodically, questions have also been asked about the Amir's medical condition. Was he disabled naturally or purposely when he signed the document?

The sketch that Salter Pyne's successor Frank Martin draws in his book, *Under an Absolute Ruler*, is of an Amir who was meticulous to a fault and cautious in every detail:

> Possessed of very exceptional ability, he was as conscientious in all matters of routine as Philip II of Spain. His whole time and attention was given to the task before him, working from the hour he quitted his bed until he lay down again. He put off no work until a later date that was possible of completion, but tried to get each day's work finished the same day. It was his custom to sit up working most of the night and not to retire to rest until about four in the morning… This habit of keeping awake most of the night was probably due to fear of a rising, or treachery, which would be attempted at night rather than during the day when all the people were about.

If that is an accurate portrait of the man, then how could he commit a blunder like signing blindly on a piece of paper? Is it possible that he may have been persuaded into doing so under a medical condition?

It will be unwise to rule out that possibility. After all, there are many examples in history where states have employed dubious means to achieve their ends. Murders have been sanctioned and honeytraps have been used. Poison and drugs were given in the name of higher national interest. The British put an entire people on opium because it was profitable business. As

Bernard Shaw said, they were capable of employing every trick in the trade to achieve their goals.

Moreover, they were accomplished at covering their tracks well, and equally good at broadcasting as evil the same fault in their adversaries. For instance, they were quick to inform the world about the cruel practices and the spy network of the Afghan Amir. But the British themselves had employed similar practices; sometimes they were vastly crueler and their spy network was far wider. In fact, throughout the nineteenth century and for a better part of the twentieth century, the British intelligence service was acknowledged as the biggest and the best in the world. But the big difference was that they controlled the media. So they had the power of the propaganda. It had to be so, otherwise they could not have sustained such a huge empire for so long a time.

Since the more sensitive of their operations remain shrouded, we still do not know the methods they had employed in Afghanistan. One can only try and connect the dots on the basis of random clues and scraps of information that have recently come out in the open from the archives. The clinching evidence still lies buried.

Therefore, the Durand episode remains largely a mystery.

A Paranoid Amir

Talking of mysteries, it is also a well-recorded fact that Amir Abdur Rahman was cruel and suspicious. In fact, he was mortally afraid of his people, and went to extreme lengths to find what they were doing and saying. 'He was so obsessed by the possibility that his subjects might be conspiring against him that he set up an elaborate network of spies and informers modelled on the Czarist intelligence system that he had seen in operation during his exile in Tashkent.'*

Frank Martin says in his book, 'Consequently, every fourth man was a "reportchee" (spy), who sent reports to the Amir. These spies were of all classes and ranks. Every large house had one or two spies among the servants who reported all they saw and heard. That task was considerably facilitated

*David B. Edwards. 1996. *Heroes of the Age: Moral Fault Lines on the Afghan Frontier*. California: University of California Press.

by the fact that it is a custom in Afghanistan for servants to sit in the same room as their master, where they can hear all that is said at any time.

'The Amir had spies in the houses of his sons, and among the women of their harems, and spies in his own harem. Amir's obsession turned out to be infectious. His wives and his sons started having their spies among his servants, who informed them of all that concerned them.' In the end, it became a merry-go-round where rumours had no beginning and no end. All were spying and everyone seemed to know what the other was doing.

Is it then not likely that a hugely suspicious man like the Amir should have employed people to spy on his British employees and the visiting delegation? It is not known how much and to what extent the Amir's English confidant Pyne was spied upon and by whom, or whether some fly on the wall was listening to every word uttered by the visiting Durand delegation.

That the Amir was paranoid about plots against him is best illustrated by this incident. Once, one of Amir's teeth had to be extracted. Since it was going to be a painful procedure, the doctor told him that he was going to administer chloroform.

'How long would the effect last?' the Amir enquired.

'You will be unconscious for about twenty minutes,' the doctor responded.

'No. That's not possible.' The Amir decided to suffer the pain, rather than risk a coup while he was unconscious for those twenty minutes.

This was a man who was suspicious and constantly wary of plots against him. Yet we have readily accepted the British spin that this Amir had happily signed away 40,000 square miles of his territory, that too in a language that he did not know a word of.

It is, of course, possible to argue and give examples of other leaders in the world who have committed great blunders. Some took major decisions in a drunken stupor; a few others made grave errors of judgement. Examples such as these only reinforce the suspicion that all was not well with the Amir when he signed away his land.

There may have been occasional passing curiosity about the subject, but historians have not probed the issue in any great detail. British historians, in particular, have been guarded about the matter because of the fear that the entire can of worms might be split open. Lately, however, some clues have started to emerge. By piecing them together, the picture begins to emerge of a seriously sick man. It is likely that some of his psychological excesses may have been due to his imprisonment in his father's jail and the subsequent exile of eleven years in Central Asia. Both these unhappy experiences may have left him with emotional and health-related scars.

Sarfraz Khan and Noor Ul Amin write in a paper for the *Central Asia* journal that 'the Amir's immobility and worsening mental condition subjected him to hallucinations, paranoia, mania and other psychotic disorders directly affecting internal and foreign policy of Afghanistan.'

This is a long list and the illnesses they describe are serious. The Amir's physicians had also given some hints into the nature of his medical issues. Dr John Alfred Gray wrote about his severe gout and pains and delirium.

Recently, some medical experts had looked at the symptoms of the Afghan ruler's illness. Their conclusion was that he was suffering from a disease, or combination of diseases, much more acute and dangerous than previously suspected. In their opinion, his frequent illnesses may have disabled him physically and brought about a steady deterioration of his mental powers.

By the end of January 1891, his right hand was virtually paralyzed and he was unable to use it for eating. He had also stopped taking snuff because his lips were swollen. It was not until March that Dr Gray reported that the Amir had recovered to walk a little, but even then he continued to suffer from pains in the foot and had to be carried if he wished to move any distance.

In 1894, Dr Lillias Hamilton replaced Dr Gray in Kabul. She also noticed changes which would suddenly contort the Amir's features, 'That mouth, which could smile so sweetly, could be so cruel...was horrible to see; more like that of some beast than of a man made in the likeness of God.'

According to Frank Martin, the Amir had strange and violent facial contortions during fits of uncontrollable rage. This used to happen suddenly and the Amir's mood changed from perfect affability to violent and unpredictable rage. When such a mood took him, Martin records, 'his face became drawn and his teeth would show until he looked wolfish, and then he hissed his words rather than spoke them, and there were few of those before him who did not tremble when he was in that mood, for it was then that the least fault involved some horrible punishment.'

This illness had incapacitated him to such an extent that he lost the use of his hands and feet. By the middle of the 1890s, the Amir was so ill that he had to be carried everywhere in a palanquin. During the more violent and serious attacks, he was susceptible to fits and prolonged periods of unconsciousness. In order to conceal the severity of his illness and disabilities from his court and the public, Abdur Rahman used to retire to the harem, where only a few of his trusted officials were allowed to meet him. The result was virtual paralysis of state business.

The news of his ill health was known to many in the British Empire. Soon after reaching Kabul, Dr Lillias Hamilton received a letter from her former headmistress at Cheltenham Ladies' College, 'We think you have received a special call from God to prolong, perhaps save, the life of the Ameer.'*

When Lillias Hamilton left Afghanistan, she would sometimes speak about her experiences there. In a graphic passage in one of her lectures, she links the king's purges with deterioration in his mental state,

> He began to see an avenging hand wherever he turned his eyes. He recognized a poisoner in every flatterer...an usurper in every man with brains enough and independence enough to be ambitious... a possible assassin in every man brave enough to dare repay with death the death of his near relatives.

Talks Coincide with Attacks

There is strong anecdotal evidence to suggest that these several bouts of illness produced an acute psychological deterioration in the Amir. This was reflected in his increasing intolerance of political opponents, violence against citizens and erratic decisions. It also affected his decision-making capacity.

These attacks of the so called 'gout' increased during winter. Usually a period of illness was preceded by symptoms indicating he had caught either a cold or influenza. During the warmer spring and the hot summer months, he tended to recover only to succumb in the following winter. By the middle of the 1890s, these attacks were a regular feature and they happened generally between the middle of October and the end of February.

Is it just a coincidence that Mortimer Durand should have timed his

---

*Principal, Cheltenham Ladies' College, to Dr Lillias Hamilton. June 1894. *Trans-Frontier Journal.*

arrival in Kabul in such a way that he was there from October to November? Normally, such negotiations do not last for more than a couple of days. Why was it necessary for Mortimer Durand to stay for as long as seven weeks?

Was the Amir under one of his debilitating spells when the Durand mission was in Kabul? During one of the meetings the Amir developed the symptoms of a cold or flu. It was then that Pyne came over and gently placed his hand on the Amir's forehead. Pyne was an engineer, it was Dr Gray who had been treating the Amir and who would certainly have been readily available had the Amir so wished. And more importantly, what was an engineer, an untrained one at that, doing in sensitive discussions relating to diplomacy?

Salter's Sleight

There is also the related mystery about Salter Pyne's role. How could he have so enormous an influence over a hugely temperamental Amir? Why was he asked to move in with the Durand delegation during their stay in Kabul? The only reason could be their need for consulting him at all hours spiced with some conspiracy.

Pyne's opinion of the Amir must have been invaluable to the Durand delegation because he was the rare man, besides the doctor, who had constant access to the Amir. It was his advice that he trusted, even to extent of signing on the dotted line.

The report submitted by Mortimer Durand to the viceroy upon his return from Kabul has a cinematic quality to it; bringing alive his discussions and his experiences. It is elaborate and describes in detail the journey, the great welcome the delegation received in Afghanistan and the Amir's personal warmth towards them.

Durand has also referred to the cruel control the Amir exercised over the country. Besides his methods of torture, Durand writes about the peculiar satisfaction the Amir seemed to derive by humiliating his opponents; the son of a former governor was placed at his disposal as a servant. Yet, he seemed content to polish Durand's shoes. And during the delegation's discussions with Amir, the army chief was kept standing outside in the cold for hours.

Yet, a foreigner occupied a special place.

In the entire kingdom, Salter Pyne alone seemed to exercise some strange kind of hold over the Amir. Durand hints at it in his report especially when the Amir complains of fever and Pyne comes over to soothe him. Durand's report to the viceroy acknowledges unhesitatingly that Pyne played a critical role in convincing the Amir to agree to part with a huge chunk of his territory.* This was most remarkable considering the fact that the settlement of the frontier with British India did not figure in the list of objectives given to Durand. It seems that the decision to take up this issue was impromptu, based on the assessment that the Amir could be brought around. Pyne then played a critical role in persuading the Amir to sign on the dotted line. Otherwise, there was no reason why an absolute ruler like Abdur Rahman who was otherwise arguing every inch of the way on the Russian side of the boundary, should have been so malleable on this sensitive southern and more contentious side.

Pyne's input must have been vital otherwise why should the British Empire rush to give him a knighthood. The Durand Agreement was signed on 12 November 1893 and just about a month later, Pyne figures in the Queen's New Year's honours list! Isn't that remarkable speed in the age of the snail mail?

With this award, he became the youngest recipient till then of the Knight Commander of the Order of the Star of India (KCSI). The clerk from a Bombay office was now known as Sir Salter Pyne. Just playing piano and entertaining the Durand party could not have got him this honour.

In fact, the honour of the KCSI given to Salter Pyne in the New Year's honours list of 1894 was the same as the one given to Mortimer Durand! Now, Mortimer was the foreign secretary and the celebrated architect of the Durand Agreement, whereas Salter was a nobody. There is no public record of any distinguished service done by Pyne during the Durand negotiations. Yet he was given the same decoration as Mortimer! So was this a deliberate royal put down of Durand, or is there more to the entire episode than the world is aware of?

The question that has remained unasked all these years is this: what exactly was Salter's achievement? And was his contribution to the negotiations

---

*National Archives of India, Foreign Department, Secret F, Report by H.M. Durand, 193–217, January 1894.

of a level similar to Durand's? If that was so why has the British history failed to acknowledge it?

This mystery may remain unsolved because the British are unlikely to open up their archives to reveal this secret.

Pyne also knew that once the Amir had signed on the dotted line, there was no question of admitting mea culpa thereafter. The Amir could hardly retract a decision that he had taken; that admission would be lèse-majesté.

Let us also ask the rhetorical question. If he had made a mistake by signing the Durand document under duress or when he was incapacitated, why did he not retract it after he had recovered to his normal self? Well, an answer to that is available in the nature of his personality. It should suffice to give just two instances.

During his serious illness in August 1888, a proclamation was issued in the country that an oracle from Ali's shrine in Mazar-e-Sharif had prophesied that during the reign of Abdur Rahman, 'tigers and goats should drink water from the same spring.'

This bizarre proclamation was not withdrawn even after he had recovered from his illness.

There is another equally fantastic claim by which the Amir boasted that he had been given a messianic mission to transform his country. According to Dr Lillias Hamilton, the Amir was, 'absolutely convinced of his own supernatural powers,' powers which, by his own admission, led him to the conclusion that the 'ceremonial enjoined by the religion was unnecessary' as far as he was concerned, since his own mind was able to 'soar above constraints of any kind'.

How could such a man, who considered himself far above the rest, concede that he was merely human? How could he admit that he had made a mistake in signing the Durand Agreement and retract from a commitment given in his capacity as the Amir?

17

Lines in Sand

THE ENTIRE EXERCISE WAS UNDERTAKEN not because the British needed more living space or the Russian bear had to be kept away. But by pushing the British administration further up north, the Agreement was actually bringing the Russians that much closer to the British. The result was therefore in contradiction to the British objective. So was the Agreement just a huge opportunity to grab land which accidentally came Durand's way?

Perhaps it was so. And there is some evidence to support that conclusion. The British phobia of Russia had lasted through most of the nineteenth century, but it had begun to recede somewhat by the end of that century. Instead, it was the Pathan pride which pricked them now. This had to be punctured by dividing them.

This line that distinguished British India from Afghanistan was laid across the tribal lands; from the Khyber Pass to the desert town of Chaman, a dust bowl frontier post at the base of a great desert of sand and grey mountains a hundred kilometres from Kandahar. Unfortunately for Pathans, these 'lines in the sand' were in the course of time conveniently recognized by the great powers.

The traditional Pathan life had been disrupted and in many cases the line ran right through the middle of houses, dividing brother from brother. But that did not matter to Durand. His task was to advance British interests.

However, to the Pashtuns, the borders were meaningless. These tribesmen did not consider themselves Afghans or Indians, or later as Pakistanis. They were, and remain, Pashtun-speaking Pathans who believe they live in a space called 'Pashtunistan', which lies on both sides of what Durand called a Line.

Even after signing the 1893 treaty, the Afghan Amir did not cease to 'exercise interference' on the British Indian side of the Durand Line. He continued to send grants of money, arms, dresses of honour and deputations to tribal chiefs on the British side of the Line. These tribal chiefs continued to play a role in the Afghan state; they were invited to jirgas in Kabul, and participated in the choice of new Afghan Amirs. Abdur Rahman also used propaganda and agents to incite their feelings against British.

It has been a century since the Durand Agreement was signed but neither the Afghan government, nor its people or, for that matter, those who value justice in the world are convinced about the justness of this Line.

Writing for *Yale Journal of International Affairs*, Daveed Gartenstein-Ross and Tara Vassefi make this assertion,

> …Abdur Rahman was forced to agree to this border by the threat of economic embargo. He relied on British subsidies to maintain his central government's dominance, and was in particular need of it at that time… because he was then engaged in warfare against the Hazaras.

What they are alleging here is that the Amir was forced to sign on the dotted line under the threat of an economic blockade and discontinuance of subsidy. Now the issue here is not whether a nation can indulge in blackmail of this type, which unfortunately was, and, is, a fact of international life. After all, that is what sanctions are all about. If we accept the suggestion that Durand had issued such a threat, the point then to consider is this—was the threat potent enough to hurt Afghanistan seriously and disrupt its economic life?

We do not have the data to show the extent of Afghanistan's economic dependence on external sources in 1893. Nor do we know the quantum of Afghan imports then from India. Still, we can make a rough comparison with what has happened in recent years. Immediately after its creation, Pakistan began to block exports to Afghanistan. On 1 January 1950, it blockaded fuel trucks destined for Afghanistan and repeated this action in 1953, 1955 and 1961. It has carried on in this vein, blockading Afghanistan every so often. Among other things, Afghanistan is critically dependent on Pakistan for some of its daily needs. Because of that Afghanistan has been the first to blink every time there was a blockade.

But it is open to doubt if in 1893 Afghanistan was critically dependent on India for its daily needs. Moreover, if the threat of economic embargo had done the trick, then the British would not have had any reason to hide this. On the contrary, they may have quoted it as an example of successful coercive diplomacy.

It had to be something else.

Abdur Rahman had reservations about the Agreement with Durand. In a letter to Viceroy Henry Petty-Fitzmaurice, Abdur Rahman recalled that the Pashtuns in the NWFP 'being brave warriors and staunch Mohamedans, would make a very strong force to fight against any power which might invade India or Afghanistan. I will gradually make them peaceful subjects and good friends of Great Britain.'

After that he added on a cautionary note to the viceroy, 'if you should cut them out of my dominions, they will neither be of any use to you nor to me: you will always be engaged in fighting and troubles with them, and they will always go on plundering.'

From the British perspective, that was exactly the reason why they wanted the area under their control. They wished to check the plundering raids by the tribals. Moreover, the Agreement gave them the opportunity to secure high passes into India and curb Afghan interference in Balochistan.

That was the British logic. But the Amir faulted it as flawed and assessed the issue differently. He argued that the British 'had not the sense to understand that taking and keeping under British possession all these barren lands on the borders of Afghanistan was a very unwise step, by which they burdened the exchequer of India with the heavy expense of keeping an army on the spot to maintain peace in these territories.'

In fact, many Britons, from Disraeli to Lawrence, had warned of precisely these risks, but those in authority then, were jubilant. They were in no mood to see the fly in the ointment.

Abdur Rahman himself was trying to retrieve the situation as best as he could. Alas, it was too late. In any case, he did not have another option. He knew that unrest in the frontier regions would continue to undermine British authority, and his name would be dragged into the conflict one way or the other. But Abdur Rahman was also conscious of the fact that his rise to power and the maintenance of his authority within Afghanistan rested on British support.

To complicate matters, Abdur Rahman extended the practice used by rulers since Dost Mohammad of criticizing the British in public while allying with them in private and advocating jihad against the British while collecting their subsidies. He believed, however, that his action had slowed the imperial encroachment and provided the necessary stability for reforms in Afghanistan.

However, conjectures like these need to be assessed more closely. Despite the Amir's claims to have reformed the political and administrative system in Afghanistan, he had, in reality, created a centralized system of government that required his approval on the smallest issues. So centralized was the Amir's administration that governors, even of the bigger provinces like Herat and Kandahar, could not take any decision without first obtaining royal assent in Kabul, a process that could take up to two or three weeks.

There are reports to indicate that Abdur Rahman was concerned about the negative fallout of the Durand Agreement on the consolidation of power he had started a decade earlier. And he shared this worry with the viceroy, 'In your cutting away from me these frontier tribes who are people of my nationality and my religion, you will injure my prestige in the eyes of my subjects, and will make me weak, and my weakness is injurious for your Government.'

Illogical Line

In this background, what assessment can we make of the Line? Was it the best achievable under the circumstances? If for argument's sake, we concede that maybe it was, even then it had, in the words of Sir William Kerr Fraser-Tytler, 'many defects and few advantages'. It was, as he said, 'illogical from the point of view of ethnography, strategy and geography.'

Fraser-Tytler had the double advantage of having been an army officer and a diplomat in the frontier area. As someone who had seen at the ground level the fallout of the Durand Agreement between 1910 and 1941, his view should count. He gives this assessment of the Line in his book, *Afghanistan: A study of political developments in Central Asia*,

> It cuts across one of the main basins of the Indus watershed, it splits a nation in two, and it even divides tribes. It is surprising that Abdur Rahman accepted such a boundary; it is possible that in spite of Durand's careful and lucid explanations he did not really take in all

> the implications of the line drawn on the map before him, but was too conceited to say so.*

Louis Dupree, another Afghan scholar, said it was 'a classic example of an artificial political boundary cutting through a culture area.'

This strike across the Pashtun heart was the hardest part. The Line had cut tribes and tribal groups in half. The Birmal tract of Waziristan was on the Afghanistan side, with the rest of Waziristan on the Indian (or as it is now, the Pakistani) side. The Mohmand tribal areas are also cut in two. And, inevitably, because the border is generally in a very distant set of areas, it is highly porous and difficult to police, especially when family groups are on both sides. This is specially so in Waziristan, where there are many passes and paths through which it is easy to move into Afghanistan and back.

It was because of this ease of movement that the British, and later Pakistanis, did not succeed in establishing an effective administrative authority in the FATA. These included the seven semi-autonomous agencies previously created by the British (Bajaur, Khyber, Kurram, Mohmand, Orakzai, South Waziristan and North Waziristan) as well as the NWFP tribal areas adjoining Peshawar (Kohat, Bannu and Dera Ismail Khan).

The line itself, as demarcated between 1893 and 1896, was drawn all the way from the Persian frontier to the Wakhan, the little area on which the British insisted to keep a distance between the British and Russian empires. There were two exceptions which, at that time, remained undemarcated; an area in the region of Chitral and another area a little north of the routes towards Kabul, the country of the Mohmand tribe.

There were some important advantages that the Line gave to the British. Strategically, they now held positions forward of the passes and controlled the heights thus facilitating the policing of the passes; it was through these passes that the tribals used to raid trade caravans and the settlements in Punjab. By drawing this line they also managed to achieve the tripartite border, a British ambition for a long time.

The first part of the border was the buffer state of Afghanistan. The second part was the tribal areas in the hills, which the British did not try to govern, but simply garrisoned. These areas were vassal states on the Indian

---

*Fraser-Tyler explains this remark by saying that he had known Afghan officials, long after Abdur Rahman's time, who found much difficulty in reading a map.

side of the line but not under the sovereignty of British India. The third part was further back, where the real government of India started. The depth of this frontier system certainly kept the Russians away, but the corollary was that the British were now faced with the internal policing problem.

There was irony too in the situation, and the Afghans were its unfortunate victims. Almost throughout the nineteenth century, Britain's aggressive moves towards and into Afghanistan had one principal excuse—the fear of the Russian bear.

Exaggerated Fears

Every rumoured sighting of a horse-riding Russian near the Afghan border would set the telegraph wires buzzing between Simla and London. If that Russian was to be seen advancing into Afghan territory, it meant that a Rubicon had been crossed, and an alert needed to be sounded. God forbid if that exhausted Russian was to somehow limp into Kabul and worse still, if he was to be admitted into the Amir's presence. That was enough to launch British troops into Afghanistan. Sometimes, it was not even necessary that a Russian had to be seen; just the rumour of his presence was enough to wind up the British military machine into action.

The fact is that there was a vast amount of exaggeration in the British fears. Russians were actually rare visitors to Afghanistan. Just to give one example—the ostensible reason for Durand's labours was the desire to keep the Russians away. And Salter Pyne had smoothed that effort by counselling the Amir appropriately. Yet, soon after leaving the Amir's service, he admitted this to an Australian journalist, who wrote, 'Sir Salter makes light of the rumoured despatch of a Russian Mission to Kabul, and says that all the time he was in the capital, he never saw a Russian.'* And Salter Pyne was in Kabul for thirteen years.

If that was so, then what was the British hullabaloo about? Why did it waste an entire century over a phantom phobia?

*Australian newspaper, *Kalgoorlie Miner*, 19 January 1901.

18

Area of Influence

WHY WAS BRITAIN SO DEEPLY interested in the frontier area? There may have been many reasons for British concern, a principal one being the need to keep the tribal raids in check. It was then a law and order issue rather than a desire to gain more territory. Britain also knew it was futile to aim for total control over the frontier. Durand admitted as much on 23 October 1893 in negotiations with the Amir. The Amir asked Durand if he would undertake that the Government of India would not absorb Waziris, if he left them alone.

Durand replied, '...we do not regard Waziristan as British territory...'*

What did the British principals in India make of the Agreement? They were delighted by this unexpected surprise. But they were guarded in their enthusiasm as the frontier was considered an administrative beehive.

More importantly, the clear intention in Calcutta and London was that it should not be mistaken for annexation. A secret report sent by the Government of India to the secretary of state for India on 3 January 1894 sets the limit clearly, 'We...wish it to be clearly understood that nothing is further from our intentions than the annexation of tribal country on our frontier.'**

Just in case that was not clear enough, the report adds, 'We believe, however, that without annexation and without interference in the internal affairs of the tribes, it will be possible to bring them further within our influence and to induce them to regard themselves as owing allegiance to us.'

This important communication was dated 3 January 1894. It means that the viceroy considered the subject vital enough to advise London of his

*National Archives of India, Foreign Department, Secret F, Report by H.M. Durand, 193–217, January 1894.

**Ibid

cautionary note within days of receiving Durand's report. The tone of this communication is noteworthy. It is not celebratory, and it makes it a point to stress that the frontier area should be treated like a hot potato. It advised London that it was better to handle the tribes from a distance and repeatedly stressed that Britain should perish the very thought of annexation.

Clearly, therefore, the Durand Agreement was not about absorption of territory.

This note has been a matter of public record for some time. Why is it that historians have chosen to ignore it? Is it because this note contradicts the later British construct that the frontier had become a part of British India?

In this background, there is little doubt that the Durand Line was disruptive, but was it definitive? It has been 124 years since the Agreement was allegedly signed, but it continues to remain a topic of contest and debate. There are question marks about its authenticity as also its intent. Was it meant to demarcate borders or was it a temporary arrangement?

Many of the statements issued in the years following the Durand Agreement indicate that it was a temporary responsibility. And that the British interest was limited to bringing some stability to the area.

Historians have quoted Durand, who, after the negotiations, had said that,

> The tribes on the Indian side are not to be considered as within British territory. They are simply under our influence in the technical sense of the term, that is to say, so far as the Amir is concerned and as far as they submit to our influence or we exert it.

A few months later, the issue seems to have been considered by the bureaucratic machinery in India. Their recommendation to London was clear. In essence, it meant that they should dismiss the very idea of a permanent annexation of the frontier. The Government of India writing to the secretary of state for India on 10 July 1894 had recommended, 'We understand that Her Majesty's Government concur in this view...that while we emphatically repudiate all intention of annexing tribal territory we desire to bring the tribes whom this settlement concerns further within our influence.'*

Like Durand's usage, this paper too was clear in using the term 'influence',

---

*Parliamentary Papers, 1898, Vol. 63, C 8713.

rather than border. That is how it should have been because the Durand Agreement had, in reality, fixed only 'the limit of their respective spheres of influence' rather than being a demarcation of sovereignty.

A note written in 1896 by Sir Denis Fitzpatrick, the lieutenant-governor of Punjab, the senior-most official overseeing the frontier at the time, stated clearly: '...I think if the agreement between us and the Amir were treated to be anything like a partition of territory, it would have a bad effect...'

Writing in 1896, Viceroy Lord Elgin noted, 'The Durand Line was an agreement to define the respective spheres of influence of the British Government and of the Amir. Its object was to preserve and to obtain the Amir's acceptance of the status quo.'

There is a lot more that can be quoted. But these observations should be enough to raise serious doubt about how the Durand Agreement has been interpreted, or rather misinterpreted, in the period immediately before the partition of India.

Since the writers of that time found it convenient not to examine and comment on the issue, it is difficult at this stage to guess the reason for this fudge. But Sir Olaf Caroe, the last governor of Punjab and the writer of a book on the Pathans, may have put his finger on the pulse by this comment, '...the British could see a dangerous threat to their empire in the unity of the Pakhtuns.'

The *Real* Premise

That was the crux then—the British were afraid of the Pashtuns. The Durand Line has been more problematic than most because of the flimsy premise that it was drawn upon, and because of the nature of the frontier between Afghanistan and the British Raj at the time it was imposed. As Cicero said in a different context, it was a fraud which should have frightened the British.

The Line itself was based on very rough and exploratory surveys by frontier agents reflecting British expansion in the northwest frontiers rather than a concerted attempt to establish an international border. And their approach varied with the prevailing geopolitical objectives of British foreign policy vis-à-vis the perceived threat of Russian expansion.

Unlike Afghanistan's international boundaries with Russia in the north or Iran in the west that were recognized as such by all parties at the time, the status of the Durand Line remained unclear. This is because the British viewed their negotiations with the Afghans as an internal colonial issue rather than as an international one. Britain was not interested in setting Afghanistan's southeastern boundary as in reorganizing its own administration of what would later become the NWFP, and is now known as Khyber Pakhtunkhwa. With its capital in Peshawar, the NWFP was designed to provide a separate unit of administration for British India's Pashtun population. Moving outward from Peshawar, the British mapped out a concentric set of administrative territories, each under proportionately less colonial control.

The Durand Line represented the outermost limit of British control, separating its territories from those that were under the authority of the Amirs of Afghanistan.

On this basis, the Afghans have always claimed that the Agreement never constituted a formal border, but rather an agreed upon frontier between them and the British. At the time, this was a distinction without much meaning in practical terms because Pathans continued to move about freely. But whether the line constitutes a boundary or a frontier still lies at the heart of the continued legal differences between Pakistan and Afghanistan on the issue.

In legal terms, there is a difference between a boundary and a frontier.

An international boundary marks a separation (natural or artificial) between two contiguous states. A frontier is the portion of a territory that faces the border of another country, including both the boundary line itself and the land contiguous to it.

An example each of both forms was in the two documents signed by the Amir with Mortimer Durand on 12 November 1893. The words used in the Durand Agreement merely claimed to limit the states' 'respective spheres of influence'. This is to be contrasted with the agreement that Durand signed with the Afghan Amir at exactly the same moment in 1893, regarding the northern border with Russia. Here, the word used was 'boundary'.

The historic Afghan position has always been that the formal boundary to its southern frontier has yet to be set. The proponents of Pashtun unity see the Afghan nation extending well beyond Afghanistan itself right up to Indus River to create a Pushtunistan that might or might not be merged with Afghanistan.

Others draw the boundary at the limits of the settled zones of the NWFP since the Frontier Agencies were never directly administered by the British.

The contentions vary because when the British packed their bags, they left behind many unresolved issues. In fact, this was the case elsewhere too. Many of the borders that exist today, from the Middle East to India, reflect not any one plan, but a series of opportunistic proposals by competing strategists of colonial powers.

In most cases, they awarded themselves control over areas in which they had strategic and economic interests. In the case of Sykes-Picot plan for the Middle East, there was at least an attempt to account for the local ethnic, religious or cultural groups. But Durand's was an arbitrary imposition on the Pashtuns.

Interestingly, Lord Curzon addressed the scholars of Oxford on this very issue in 1907. As was his manner with others, he spoke to the students with a magnificent, late-Victorian confidence about the future of the world's frontier zones:

> It would be futile to assert that an exact Science of Frontiers has been or is ever likely to be evolved: for no one law can possibly apply to all nations or peoples, to all Governments, all territories, or all climates. The evolution of Frontiers is perhaps an art rather than a science, so plastic and malleable are its forms and manifestations.

This is a remarkable statement coming from a man of considerable authority.

Here is a man who, like Queen Victoria and the prime minister of Britain, had celebrated Durand. They had all applauded Mortimer for finalizing the Agreement. The British government, the media and the people had prided themselves on its scientific character. *The New Statesman* had eulogized Mortimer Durand as the 'strongest man of Europe' for this achievement. Yet, in a broader sweep of the subject in Oxford, Lord Curzon was dismissing the concept of scientific frontiers.

So what exactly did Curzon's celebrated and oft-quoted statement imply? Did he mean that frontiers are flexible because as he put it, 'so plastic and malleable are its forms and manifestations'. If that was so and frontiers are meant to be 'malleable', then how can a line like the one Durand scrawled casually across a small sheet of paper be regarded as set in stone?

Curzon had also asserted that 'no one law can possibly apply to all nations or peoples, to all Governments, all territories, or all climates'. Yet, long after wielding the unkind knife across Afghanistan, the British were insistent that this arbitrary cut was enforceable by law.

Capricious Interpretation

Which law were they quoting to Afghans? Was it one that had universal application? If that was not so, then a contested Agreement cannot be the foundation of a permanent border.

Or was it that they had a new and their own unique interpretation of the law? By this, there was one law for the masters, and quite another law for the colonies as per the British whims. Sadly, this seems to have been the case. Capricious interpretation became the law for the governed. Yet Britain was pragmatic enough to throw that same law into the dustbin when it met with a superior force, as in the case of Hong Kong.

But Afghanistan was, and is, a weak state.

So the question that remains unanswered is this—are frontiers scientific, or, as Curzon's celebrated comment asserts, they are malleable because there is no real law on the subject?

Either way, grave injustice has been done to the Afghans. Can a rough line drawn at the spur of the moment by a man who had no known expertise in cartography be treated as a 'scientific' border? Can such a so-called border that disregards traditions, conventions and centuries of living practice be regarded as lawful?

Alas, we have fudged the issue for the last 124 years. Perhaps that is why there is constant turmoil on that frontier.

There are other countries which were artificially carved up. Experience shows that once a line is drawn between nations, reaching across it becomes difficult. India was partitioned, and many new boundaries were made in the Middle East and Africa. More recently, countries like the Soviet Union, Yugoslavia, Sudan and Czechoslovakia have splintered to form new states.

In each of these, there was initial turmoil. In some cases, mass migration and bloodshed had followed. But after the first few bitter months, people settled down to make new lives.

Only the Pashtuns have remained unreconciled.

Is it because the Pashtuns were, and are, poor? As Henry Miller said in the American context, 'We have two American flags always: one for the rich and one for the poor. When the rich fly it, it means that things are under control; when the poor fly it, it means danger, revolution and anarchy.'

Alas, fate has handed the Pashtuns a poor flag.

To extend the argument further, one could fatalistically add that the gods are taking revenge for the imposition made by Durand on the frontier. Ever since 1893, these tribal areas have been in ferment; a people who wanted to be left to themselves are now home to multiple mutations of terror, not because they wanted to but because terrorists were imposed on them.

The question that must be asked of heavens is this—why of all the tribes in the world are only the Pathans tormented?

19

Evil Stars

THERE IS NO DOUBT THAT with this Agreement Mortimer Durand had fulfilled his ambition of 'seeing great deeds, with the chance of distinction'—just as he had written in his novel, *Helen Trevelyan or The Ruling Race*. By this single act, he had made history and inscribed his name in it.

It is, however, equally true that ever since, this claim to distinction has been questioned. What has been asked over and over again is this—does the reality of the Durand Agreement sit well with verifiable facts? Can this Agreement stand the legal scrutiny of the present times? Was the Amir fully in control of his mental faculties when he signed the Agreement? Questions like these have troubled succeeding generations of Afghans. That's why they have never reconciled to the Durand Line.

Hocus-pocus

It wasn't just the Amir who was pushed into the darker realms. Many others have had unpleasant experience. That's why there are people who believe strongly in the Durand's curse. They add by way of proof that everyone connected with this Agreement has had an unhappy life thereafter. Let us also turn believers in hocus-pocus for a while, make a blend of espionage and superstition and see the result.

Is it possible that Doctor Hamilton, Pyne and Durand conspired in this, and that the biographer of Abdur Rahman, Mir Sultan Mohammad Khan, was their co-conspirator? Was the Amir drugged, or somehow incapacitated while signing the document? Could it also have been a local affair where Durand took a spur-of-the-moment decision in anticipation of greater glory at home? It is possible that the decision was impromptu. This is what it probably was, judging by the notes to London that followed post-event from India. The underlying sentiment in almost all of them was to distance Britain from territorial responsibility. They did not want the burden of annexation to dent the empire. So the bureaucratic applause for Durand was grudging at best.

It wasn't just Mortimer who felt reduced, association with the Durand Agreement resulted in unhappy consequences for almost everyone.

Mir Sultan Mohammad Khan was said to be the only non-British present behind a purdah taking notes of the negotiations. Unlike the perception given in some accounts, he was not an Afghan; he was an Indian from Punjab who had, for some time, been in Amir's employ. After the Durand Agreement, Dr Hamilton warned him that he should leave Kabul because his life was in danger. When he reached India, he was arrested by the British as an Afghan spy. Yet, they released him shortly thereafter. Surprisingly, for a person who had been jailed by them, the British soon agreed to his appointment as the Afghan ambassador in London. Normally, countries do not accept the spies they have arrested to be appointed as ambassadors in their own land. But then strange were the ways in which Durand's curse worked. Or is it that he was arrested so that the notes he had taken of the Amir's negotiations with Durand could be seized from him? And as a reward for his collaboration, the normal rules of accreditation were waived in his favour.

Salter Pyne, once the closest confidant of the Amir, left Afghanistan for the last time in 1898. According to him, he would have returned to Kabul had it not been for the fact that an agreement which he was to have made with the Amir fell through. But, once again, according to him, he would have liked to return because the Afghan government owed him salary dues of about £20,000. Any man to whom so much money was due should have had no hesitation in going back to claim it. But the Amir's former blue-eyed boy, Sir Salter Pyne, was now afraid of returning to Kabul! He went up to Peshawar from England in November 1898, but did not dare cross the frontier. His attempts to claim his money were unsuccessful.

It seems that the Amir had finally discovered that Pyne was a British spy. Therefore, fearing for his life, Pyne had to leave Afghanistan in a hurry. Naturally then, there was no question of his return to Kabul.

Incidentally, Durand was a victim of this curse because the high honour—one much higher than a mere KCSI—which he had hoped for, did not come his way. Even his next posting as a minister in the British embassy in Iran must have been a bit of a come down for him. Later, when he was appointed the British ambassador in Washington in 1903, he had to be recalled prematurely by the British government because he was generally regarded by the Americans as too 'wooden'. Another shortcoming that he was then accused of was his inability to go horse riding with President Roosevelt. If only he had paid more attention to horse riding when he first saw his wife riding one, he might have succeeded in Washington. But in that case Durand's curse would have been ineffective.

Sahibzada Abdul Latif was not present during the negotiations, so he did not fit into the category of people directly associated with the Agreement. He was a man of impeccable lineage and one of the richest in Kabul. Besides, he was widely respected for his wisdom. He was, therefore, the Amir's choice when the physical markings of the Durand Line had to be carried out on ground by a joint Afghan–British delegation. Abdul Latif was the one who dug in the first pillar of the Durand Line, and began the formal process of dividing the Pashtun lands.

Yet, he was sentenced to death by Abdur Rahman's son and successor Amir Habibullah Khan on 14 July 1903, for blasphemy and conspiracy against the State of Afghanistan. Now if the major charge against him was blasphemy, the Chief Mullah of Kabul should have had no difficulty in casting the first stone. Yet he was reluctant. He had to be prodded repeatedly by the Amir before he threw a stone at Abdul Latif.

Abdul Latif died a slow death after he was buried alive up to his neck for the crimes of belonging to the Ahmadiyya sect and opposing jihad against British. Once again, there are questions here. Abdul Latif was not the only convert to the Ahmadiyya sect in Afghanistan. There were many others. But they were not killed. Did the death sentence have more to do with his role in the joint Anglo–Afghan mission regarding the Durand Line?

Amir Abdur Rahman too was the curse's victim. He was plagued by ill health thereafter, so much so that often he was unable to walk by himself. He was constantly in pain due to gout and his illnesses were many and more frequent after 1893.

But the biggest victims of the Durand's curse are undoubtedly the Pashtuns. They have not lived the life of peace and tranquillity ever since that Agreement was signed. And for the last few years, the bulk of them have been driven away from their homes because the Pakistani army wants to eliminate the terrorists that it had once encouraged the Pashtuns to shelter.

These tribals must be wondering if the Durand's curse has a sell-by date.

20

British Parliament Says No

THE CUNNING OLD FURY SAID in *Alice's Adventures in Wonderland*, 'I'll be judge, I'll be jury. I'll try the whole cause, and condemn you to death.'

Having taken the frontier areas through the Durand Agreement, the British Empire's treatment of tribes was arbitrary. Its governing principle was one-sided law; and that law always judged in favour of the British. This was typically the colonial manner of dispensing justice.

Occasionally though, a British parliamentarian felt the prick of his conscience. He then spoke of the pain of the native and the empire's responsibility towards the subjugated. But it was a lone voice of restraint in a chorus of the lynch mob. The mob demanded the expansion of the British Empire and they wanted it on terms that suited the empire. So having spoken and cleared his conscience that lone voice would consider his duty done and slink back into his seat. Once again, the mob would have had its way in the mother of Parliaments.

Unfortunately for the Afghans, lone voices in their favour were ignored regularly in London.

Thus, on 8 February 1898, a future prime minister of Britain, Mr Arthur James Balfour, said in the House of Commons:

> In 1894, the question came before the Indian Government and before the Secretary of State for India…as to the policy to be pursued. Now the Durand agreement had completed the delimitation between the Afghan and British spheres of influence. The question was anxiously discussed in the Council of India, and the Governor General joined the military members in favour of the proposal to occupy advance posts. The civilian members of the Council took the opposite view. They wrote a lengthy

> and most able minute expressing their dissent from the despatch of the majority…*

What Mr Balfour was conveying was clear; that the Durand Agreement was only about 'spheres of influence'. While the military brass in India wanted to pursue the Forward Policy, the civilian view based on legal and political grounds advised against such a step.

Less than a week later, on 13 February 1898, the secretary of state for India, Lord George Hamilton, informed the House of Commons, 'The main object of the Durand Agreement…was to fix the limits of the respective spheres of influence of the two Governments.'**

Is this not clear enough? The secretary of state was making it plain that the Durand Agreement was not about a boundary. It was only about the 'respective spheres of influence'. It was only later that some British officials twisted the sense of the text to suit what they thought was more suitable to British interests. And the 'sphere of influence' became 'territory' in the modified British view.

There were other voices too. One such was that of the former home secretary and future prime minister, Mr Herbert Henry Asquith. In a debate in the House of Commons on 15 February 1898, Asquith said,

> The Durand Agreement is a negative agreement. A sphere of influence is a negative conception—purely negative. What does it mean? It means this: that by contract between two Powers—which we will call A and B—A agrees to abstain from interference with a definite area, and B agrees to do the same as to a corresponding area. But that cannot affect the other Powers and nations of the world and à fortiori it cannot affect the Natives who are in occupation of the two spheres. They are not parties to the Agreement. They have never surrendered their independence to us. Because we go behind the back of a number of frontier tribes, making agreements with the Ameer that he shall not go into one place and beyond another, to say that, that affects their status is laying down a doctrine equally repugnant to international law, public justice, and common-sense.***

---

*House of Commons debate, 8 February 1898, Vol. 53, cc56-148.

**House of Commons debate, 13 February 1896, Vol. 37, cc 234-55.

***http://hansard.millbanksystems.com/commons/1898/feb/15/address-in-answer-to-her-majestys-most#S4V0053P0_18980215_HOC_96

Whatever position Mr Asquith may have taken later as the prime minister, here he was clear and clinically correct. His statement was a legally and morally sound denunciation of the Durand Agreement. And his lament was that the Pashtun people had been denied justice. They were the affected party, yet they had not been consulted before the Durand Agreement was signed.

Arbitrary Imposition

In 1893, the Pashtun peoples' destinies had been decided and their territory divided unilaterally by a stranger who had no idea of their traditions, their heritage, their way of life and their daily struggles. Pashtuns were a unified lot politically till this amputation, but this artificial division divided them. In many cases, the Durand Line passed through their lands in such a way that the land which produced their food and where their animals grazed was now on one side of the line and their house on the other side. It is this arbitrariness that Mr Asquith was bitter about.

And Mr Asquith's indictment against Durand's deceit was severe because it led to, '...laying down a doctrine equally repugnant to international law, public justice, and common-sense.'

A few years later, on 26 February 1908, the Secretary of State for Colonies Earl of Elgin, replying to Lord Curzon said:

> His Majesty's Government do not intend to make any departure from the principles of the frontier policy which were laid down by the Secretary of State ten years ago. The purport of those declarations was that there should be no extension of our responsibilities in tribal country, and no interference whatever with the tribes if it could possibly be avoided. Those principles were re-affirmed in 1904 by the then Secretary of State, and have been pursued by successive Governments since that time...

The reference to past ten years was intentional and pointed. Curzon was the viceroy then, meaning thereby that the policy, that there 'should be no extension of our responsibilities in tribal country', was pursued by Britain on a bipartisan basis.

But there was another twist in this tale.

Doubts about the Line

The British Empire wanted yet another treaty in 1919 to make the Afghan Amir's humiliation complete. Since he had been defeated in the Third Anglo–Afghan War, he hardly had any choice but to sign on the dotted line, which he did. As secretary of state for foreign affairs, Curzon (by now an Earl) informed the House of Lords,

> The previous Treaties between the Government or Sovereign of Afghanistan and ourselves were cancelled by the act of war, undertaken, as I say, without any provocation, by the Amir. I have already informed your Lordships that under the agreement the subsidy is gone; the arrears of the subsidy are forfeited; the privileges enjoyed by the late Amir in respect of the importation of arms are gone; the guarantees for the protection of the frontiers of Afghanistan against unprovoked attack are gone...*

This is categorical. Curzon says unambiguously that all previous treaties 'were cancelled'. If that was so, it means that the Durand Agreement too was cancelled.

He does not stop there. Rather, he goes on to scrap most parts of the 1893 treaty. By one stroke of their stronger pen, the British shook off all responsibility that by the treaty they had committed themselves to, since 1893.

As per the practice in international law, a bilateral agreement cannot be altered arbitrarily. There is no scope for selective pick and choose or convenient afterthoughts. A nation can either respect an agreement in full or scrap it altogether as per its provisions. If there is no provision for its revision, it cannot be tampered with whimsically. But that is exactly what was done in this case.

If the Durand Agreement was amended partially by the British, as indeed it was, then the whole thing should have stood scrapped ipso facto. A binding commitment cannot be reinterpreted. The corollary to that being that the British claim over the frontier, illegal as it was from the beginning, became even more unsustainable now.

But why take just the second part of Curzon's statement. In fact the first

*http://hansard.millbanksystems.com/lords/1919/oct/28/afghanistan

part itself says clearly that all previous treaties stand cancelled.

Let's leave for a moment the dialectics of that argument and move forward. If Asquith was bitter in the House of Commons in 1898, then twenty-five years later, in 1923, a former viceroy of India, Lord Chelmsford, struck a practical note with almost the same refrain in the House of Lords. Chelmsford was also making a more fundamental point, 'There are two possible frontier lines which can be advocated or defended on geographical, military, or strategic grounds.' He said, 'There is the line of the Indus, and there is the Durand Line.'

He was, of course, stating the obvious, but there was more to come from him, 'As regards the Indus,' he continued, 'there are those who say we ought never to have gone beyond the Indus, and that if we had not gone beyond the Indus, we should have been spared much expenditure, both in men and in money...'

What he was saying was an obvious historical fact. It was also a fact grounded in the boundaries drawn by nature. He added, 'Then we come to the Durand Line...as soon as that Treaty was made, the Amir Abdur Rahman brought the tribes on his side of the line immediately under control and subjection. We took no steps, and except at certain points—the Khyber, the Kurram, and Baluchistan—our frontier does not touch the Durand Line, and does not run up to that line.'

This was a categorical admission that the British did not try to extend their frontier towards the Durand Line. But there is more, 'There are...those who say that we ought to carry our administered territory up to that line, to disarm and control the tribes.' He continued, 'But I think it is sufficient answer...to those who advance that view that for thirty years, no Viceroy has ever found himself able to face such a policy. The expenditure in men and money which would be involved...is a reasonable explanation why every Viceroy for the past thirty years has shrunk from attempting to go forward with such a policy. There are two clear possible frontier lines then... There is the backward frontier line geographically, the Indus, and there is the possible frontier line under the Durand Treaty that present line, except at points which I named just now, runs somewhere between those two lines... No one would willingly push further into that terrible welter of hills which forms the frontier unless absolutely forced to do so.'*

As statements go, this was loaded. Chelmsford started by stating a historical fact that the Indus, the Hud-e-Sikandar, the limit of Alexander's conquest, should have been the limit of the British India's territory. This, except for certain periods in the distant past, was largely the boundary of India. It was practical, economical and it made military sense. Geographically, too, it appealed to reason because beyond Indus lay the mountains. There, the people were different; their language had more in common with Persian than Punjabi or Sind, their food was uniquely their own, their customs distinct, their ethos and history varied sharply from that of the people on the other side of the Indus.

There was also a note of caution in Chelmsford's words.

Unlike the docile Indians, these tribes were ungovernable. So his advice was to not interfere, let them be, as successive viceroys had consciously chosen to do for the previous thirty years. Finally, he was confirming that the British physical control was far short of the Durand Line, and so it should remain.

The succession of statements quoted above from the British Parliament are in line with what the Afghans themselves have been claiming throughout; that the Durand Agreement was not about borders, it was only about influence.

*House of Lords debate, 3 May 1923, Vol. 53, cc1091-112.

21

Mass Punishment and Defiance

ONE COLD MORNING IN NOVEMBER 1853, a British customs officer, Carne, and two of his aides were inspecting the area for the purpose of enforcing the British salt monopoly, when men belonging to the Hasanzai tribe shot the three dead. The archival record drafted by Sir Richard Temple notes that this murder of two British officers and an Indian was in cold blood, because 'they were infidels, defenceless travellers; with a little property about them… It was evident that the whole tribe [Hasanzais] approved of the murder, and sheltered the murderers…'

How did Temple come to the conclusion that the 'whole tribe approved of the murder'? No one asked that question, nor was any explanation volunteered. It was just not the colonial style.

Richard Temple's conclusion was accepted readily by the powers of that time. Once such a decision was made, the British did not believe in wasting time over reprisal. It was decided that a message of force could be effective only if it was delivered quickly. Ten regiments of the Indian army were mobilized, and dispatched into the hills to punish the Hasanzai tribe for what the British presumed to be their collective guilt. These regiments encountered considerable difficulty in the rough terrain.

Moreover, the tribal fighters held ground in what was a very steep and thickly wooded shoulder of the mountain, rising abruptly for nearly a thousand feet. Finding this section impassable, but also worried about routing around lest they leave their flank exposed to counter-attack, Colonel Mackeson and his men found themselves pinned down.

British forces eventually pushed their way through, when the 1st Artillery Brigade showed up with heavy artillery on 29 December. After defeating the armed resistance, the British troops set about their real work of destroying

Hasanzai settlements and property. Working twelve hours a day, the troops began to burn villages and settlements, killing livestock and laying waste to foodstuffs. After four days of such destruction, the officers decided that this 'had been sufficient punishment for the murder of the two British officers', and having delivered sufficient message to the Hasanzai tribe, they headed back to Punjab.

This punitive expedition was neither the first nor the last in the British experience on the northwest frontier. Rather, the British use of violence gained in frequency during the latter half of the nineteenth century; the military records demonstrate almost annual expeditions in the northwest frontier during this time. The twentieth century was no better either. Punishments became routine. For example, in 1907 alone, fifty-six punitive incidents took place, in 1908, ninety-nine and in 1909, 158.

This frequency points to another historical development—over time, punishment became synonymous with effective political governance. R.H. Davies, a senior civil servant in the Punjab provincial government, described punitive expeditions as 'in the nature of a judicial act'.

However, this practice was not limited to India or Afghanistan; it was the mantra of successful colonial practice everywhere. As the historian John Kaye wrote in his book *The History of the War in Afghanistan*,

> In Asia, we have pursued a career of shameless aggression in the name, not of liberal principles, 'but of civilisation'; and when this pretext has not been sufficient, the necessity of containing Russia has been put forward. The result has been to turn India from a source of wealth into a drain upon our finances, from a secure possession into our greatest danger. As our attacks upon Persia and Afghanistan have made the inhabitants of those countries our enemies, so our annexations and our assaults upon the religion and customs of the inhabitants of Hindostan have made them our enemies. From the Caspian to the Indian Ocean we are without friends.

Still, nowhere were the punishments as harsh, as frequent and as mass-scale as in the frontier. All this, while the region remained trapped in poverty and backwardness.

In Splendid Isolation

The irony is that around this time, as the nineteenth century was folding into the twentieth, 'New Liberalism' was calling for reforms in England; old age pensions, labour exchanges and workers' compensation. But in Afghanistan, they were busy dividing the country and introducing laws that were to make collective punishment a rule in the tribal areas.

However, Afghan grudges with their history go back a lot longer in time. Afghan nationalists insist that Peshawar, Afghanistan's old winter capital, was stolen from them by the Sikhs in 1834. They argue that the country's nineteenth-century Amirs were a weak lot. They were willing to compromise with the British to maintain their power and therefore allowed the Pashtun nation to become divided rather than fight to defend it. Even today, many Afghan maps do not label the territory across the border as Pakistan, but as Pashtunistan. On such maps, Pakistan (if it appears at all), begins at Punjab. A member of the Council of India, Sir Erskine Perry, records this protest against British arbitrariness, 'I will only say, as a jurist, that I have been shocked at the doctrine lately put forth by high legal authority, that the main principles of international law are not applicable to the East.'

But the British imperialists forgot that there was a higher authority too, higher than the greatest powers on earth. As the British historian Herbert Butterfield put it, 'The hardest strokes of heaven fall in history on those who imagine they can control things in a sovereign manner, playing providence...'

He may or may not have had the conduct of the British Empire in mind. But as the nineteenth century was turning into the twentieth, imperial Britain had reason to feel godlike. Its writ ran over half the world and its word was law. Yet it was in a state of 'splendid isolation'. Other nations could not defy it, but they preferred to give it a wide pass. And even as all seemed well outwardly, things began to fall apart for Britain. First, its covert support to the Jameson Raid against Transvaal in 1896 went horribly wrong. Twenty-two-year-old Churchill went to the extent of declaring that he saw in this debacle as the first downward step for the British Empire!

However, the colonial Secretary Joseph Chamberlain was not one to give up easily. If Transvaal was a failure, glory might await the British Empire elsewhere. He advised British Prime Minister Lord Salisbury, '...an act of vigour to soothe the wounded vanity of the nation was needed. It does not matter which of our many foes we defy but we ought to defy someone.'

The defiance happened sooner than Mr Chamberlain had expected, and it was not the British who defied. It was the Pathans of the frontier who rose in revolt.

In 1897, Amir Abdur Rahman convened a meeting of radical Pathan mullahs in Kabul. After the meeting, they went back with Afghan guns and ammunition.

The resentment against the British had been brewing ever since the demarcation process had started in the frontier area. In fact, the uprising of 1897 was caused by a combination of three factors. First, there was a sense of distrust and increasing uneasiness among the tribesmen over the Durand Line Agreement. When the actual demarcation process began, it was viewed by the tribesmen as annexation of their country. The second cause was the propaganda of mullahs, who incited the people against the foreigner. The third factor was the expectation of support from the Amir, which emboldened the tribesmen to rise against the British. But British authorities mainly held the mullahs and their activities responsible for this large-scale uprising.

The rebellion did not start one bad morning because some furious Pathan got up from the wrong side of the bed. The cause was the British intrusion into their territory and the British interference in their way of life. When the demarcation of the Durand Line started, the tribals saw the British officers giving bribes to their Pathan leaders, marching troops through their lands, surveying and mapping their hills and erecting boundaries of stones along the Afghan side of their hinterlands. Their natural reaction was resentment and resistance.

The Pathans did not want nosey foreigners regulating their life and imposing their laws on them. Liberalism and liberty, for them, meant the ability to live life according to their customs.

In any case, a clash was inevitable because the Forward Policy that the British started pursuing since the 1870s did result in an increase of territory, but it also brought in war. The Forward Policy, by its very nature, precluded the possibility of peace. Isolated military posts were imposed in the midst of the notoriously passionate, reckless and warlike races of the frontier. These posts were regarded as an intrusion into their society, and for the Pathans they became challenges that they were determined to remove.

There were many among the British who opposed the Forward Policy, who felt strongly that nothing should have lured the Government of India beyond the natural frontier line. They maintained that Punjab should have been the limit of Britain's outward reach.

Churchill seemed to concur with this view, 'Over the plains of India will we cast our rule. There we will place our governors and magistrates; our words shall be respected and our laws obeyed. But that region, where the land rises like the waves of a sea, shall serve us as a channel of stormy waters to divide us from our foes and rivals.'

Jihad of 1897

But the British waded into these stormy waters and sure enough, there was turbulence. In August 1897, the British government got the news that the Afridis and the Orakzais had planned a simultaneous rising in Khyber and Kurram. By this plan, Afridis were to take possession of the British posts in the Khyber Pass while the Orakzais were to attack the Sikhs and other troops in the British posts at Samana and other parts of the Kurram Valley. The rebellion of 1897 followed soon thereafter. It was a ferocious war that convulsed almost the entire northwest frontier and became the greatest challenge of that age to British arms in India.

Winston Churchill, who sent dispatches to the *Daily Telegraph* about the revolt and its crushing by the aptly named General Sir Bindon Blood, conveyed the sense of its magnitude. As he approached the front, he came upon a British supply caravan a mile-and-a-half long, and asked the officer in charge how many days it might keep the British forces going. The answer: two days.

As for the violence that followed the Pathan uprising, Churchill had this graphic description,

> …grisly apparitions of horses spouting blood, struggling on three legs, men staggering on foot, men bleeding from terrible wounds, fish-hook spears stuck right through them, arms and faces cut to pieces, bowels protruding, men gasping, crying, collapsing, expiring…

The 1897 jihad was but the start of a Pashtun challenge to the frontier that has continued with few interruptions ever since.

Pashtun children still sing verses that commemorate the battles of 1897. One of the most haunting celebrates a warrior called Beram Khan, and imagines the words of his wife:

If your body comes back with countless bullets in your chest,
I will never mind.
But I don't want to hear that you left the battlefield fearing death.
If you are martyred defending your country,
I will weave your shroud with the hair from my head

The uprising of 1897–98 was one of the most significant events in the history of frontier wars. It took the British almost a year to crush the resistance of the tribes who rose en masse. The revolt had socio-politico and religious dimensions as well; the spread of fundamentalism and extremism in the region is often traced back to the temper of that uprising. There is no doubt that it also shook the foundation of the British Empire in India. Despite that huge shock, the British admired the professionalism and the fighting spirit of the tribesmen.

Churchill acknowledged it in this manner, 'Every man is a warrior.'

The uprising and its terrible toll on men and material generated great debate in the British Parliament. They were not concerned so much about the remote frontier lands, but by the possibility that the uprising could inspire others in India and South Africa.

One immediate result of the uprising was the British decision to separate the Pakhtun land from the rest of Punjab and the formation of a new province: the North-West Frontier Province in 1901.

They also decided to introduce a separate and much harsher administrative structure for the tribal areas. The net result of all this was that thereafter, the British administration remained on tenterhooks. The British military machine may have managed to crush the resistance of the Pakhtun tribesmen for the time being, but it further deepened the animosity and hatred between the two.

When George Nathaniel Curzon became the viceroy in 1899 the British were still smarting from the wounds of the Frontier War of 1897. In his assessment of the situation, the war had not tamed the Pathans, in fact, far from it. He had then remarked famously,

> No patchwork scheme and all our present and recent schemes: blockade, allowances, etc., are mere patchwork—will settle the Waziristan problem. Not until the military steamroller has passed over the country from end to end, will there be peace. But I do not want to be the person to start that machine.

He was right to be apprehensive because when Pathans are at war they are uncontrollable. And as Afghan history shows, the question that should more appropriately be asked is this—when are they not at war? Or as Dr Theodore Leighton Pennell noted tongue-in-cheek, 'Afghans are never at peace among themselves, except when they are at war.'

If the Pathans had among them some gifted historians or prolific writers, they would have turned around and asked—when did the British leave us in peace? For that matter, and later on, they could have repeated the same question this way—when have the Americans and Pakistanis left us in peace?

Another Misinterpretation

The controversy over the Durand Line, however, got renewed after the death of Amir Abdur Rahman on 1 October 1901 and the accession of Amir Habibullah Khan, son of Abdur Rahman. The British refused to pay Amir Habibullah the subsidy which was paid to Abdur Rahman, asserting that as the deal was fixed between the Government of India and the previous Amir, it was a personal one.

But this was a mischievous interpretation.

The real British intention was to seek concessions, a more liberal commercial policy by Afghanistan, early delimitation of the Mohmand agency, and one more promise of non-interference by Afghanistan in trans-border areas. They defended their position by highlighting the use of the Government of India and the Amir as the two parties of the Agreement. The British also referred to the Treaty of Gandamak (1879), which restricted the Afghans from establishing relations with any country other than India, claiming that Amir Habibullah had violated it by accepting subsidies from Russia.

In his rejoinder, Amir Habibullah questioned the British logic, 'if the deal (with Amir Abdur Rahman) was personal then would it mean that the

Durand Line Agreement stands invalid?'

In the new Agreement that was signed eventually, Amir Habibullah defended his full rights over Bohai Dag and parts of the Mohmand territory, previously promised to Amir Abdur Rahman in a concession for an early demarcation, which the British had later seized back in 1897. Amir Habibullah also claimed his right over Smatzai in the agreement.

Third Anglo–Afghan War

No one expected the hostilities between Britain and Afghanistan to end. But the next war, when it broke out in 1919, was the briefest between the two, lasting just three months from 6 May to 8 August. It was hardly reported in the British newspapers.

Even the announcement about the beginning of hostilities appeared as a small news item on page 12 of *The Times*, 'British Enter Afghanistan. Strategic Point Seized'.

As one magazine account put it, 'So little has appeared in the newspapers about the Third Afghan War that probably most respectable citizens do not know there has been one.'

Unlike the two previous Anglo–Afghan wars (the first of which lasted the better part of three years, from 1839 to 1842, and the second for two years, from 1878 to 1880), this conflict began as the result of Afghan incursions into British-occupied territory across the border with India, rather than the other way round.

The *New Statesman* tried to find the logic of this war, but gave up the effort, 'The reasons that led the new Ameer [Amanullah Khan, the King] of Afghanistan to begin war on India are obscure, and the version of his motives given by the Indian Government make him out to be little better than a fool. One feels that there must be another and more reasonable side to the whole business.'*

One likely reason was that the Amir was trying to assert independence, both as an end in itself and due to domestic political considerations.

Though the war was short, the casualties on both sides were heavy: 1,751 killed or wounded (including over 500 deaths from cholera) on the

**New Statesman*, 16 August 1919.

British side, and an estimated 1,000 deaths among the Afghans. British tactics included what was colloquially referred to as 'butcher and bolt' operations, in which villages would be destroyed, their inhabitants killed, and thereafter troops would immediately return to their base, making no attempt to occupy any territory. During the war, Kabul and the Afghan fort at Dakka were successfully bombed using the relatively new technology of biplanes, resulting in the following editorial comment in *The Times*: 'This is the first proof that we have had of the immense military value of the aeroplanes in small wars with semi-civilized peoples.'

The war was ended by the Treaty of Rawalpindi, with both sides claiming a measure of victory; the Afghans successfully asserting their right to conduct their own foreign affairs, one of the first acts of which was to recognize the new Bolshevik government in Russia. And the British re-establishing the border as it was before the war and discontinuing their subsidy to the Amir.

The most important point was the letter written by the chief British representative at the Indo-Afghan Peace Conference to the chief Afghan representative, and attached as an Annexure to the Treaty of Rawalpindi of 1919, which clearly stated that, 'The said Treaty and this letter leave Afghanistan officially free and independent in its internal and external affairs. Moreover, this war has cancelled all previous treaties.' Did it mean that all previous treaties, including the Durand (Agreement) and others that followed, stood cancelled?

After Curzon's statement in the British Parliament, this was the second time Britain was authoritatively stating that 'all previous treaties stood cancelled.'

22

Keep a Bit of India

WHEN AN INVADER PACKS HIS bags, he leaves behind crucial issues unresolved. The Durand Line must rank very near the top of any such list. To complicate matters further, Pakistan's school of negotiations was muscular. This aggression was a carefully crafted strategy to keep Afghanistan weak and off balance. These Pakistani tactics delivered results and because of that critics blame the Afghan government. They say it did not press the Afghan case hard enough to get back the frontier territories. This criticism also maintains that Afghanistan let its case go by default by being inactive when it should have agitated vigorously.

This is unfair.

A case can get fair hearing if the judge is impartial. But what do you do if the judge is biased? Worse still, what can you do if the judge has a stake in the case? Unfortunately, that was so and Britain did not disguise the fact that it was an interested party.

It is a long story but let us begin with the immediate triggers. And who better to begin with than Winston Churchill, who, for some reason had taken an intense dislike to India and who still smarted from the rough time the Pashtuns had given to the British army in 1897.

In August 1945, Churchill, now in the opposition following Clement Attlee's victory, had a meeting with Viceroy Archibald Wavell, who was visiting London to discuss India with the new Cabinet ministers. According to Wavell, Churchill left their meeting with these parting words: 'Keep a bit of India'.

'Keep a bit of India!' Isn't that an amazing comment? As if India was a chocolate bar and Churchill wanted just one little slab of it.

Others were no better. Nor were their reasons for 'keeping a bit of India' any more solid. Foreign Secretary Ernest Bevin told the US Secretary of State George Marshall that 'the main issue was who would control the main artery leading into Central Asia.'

Middle of the Planet

Since a large country like India with leaders such as Gandhi, Nehru and Patel might refuse to accommodate Britain's strategic interests after independence, a bit that was conveniently accommodating had to be carved out of it. Therefore, Pakistan was essential to the British project because through it, the UK could control the main artery leading into Central Asia.

Britain had been bruised badly in the Second World War. Yet it was up and about again and planning part two of the Great Game. For Britain, Pakistan was, as the then Chancellor of the Exchequer Hugh Dalton put it, central to Foreign Secretary Ernest Bevin's ambition to organize 'the middle of the planet'.

Closer to the Partition, the British army's chief of staff, Field Marshal Bernard Montgomery, recommended in a top-secret memo in 1947: 'The area of Pakistan is strategically the most important in the continent of India and the majority of our strategic requirements could be met…by an agreement with Pakistan alone. We do not therefore consider the failure to obtain an agreement with India would cause us to modify any of our requirements.'

With such overwhelming endorsement, all that remained was an approving nod from the media. *The Times* provided it on the day of Partition, 15 August 1947:

> In the hour of its creation, Pakistan emerges as the leading state of the Muslim world. Since the collapse of the Turkish Empire that world, which extends across the globe from Morocco to Indonesia, has not included a state whose numbers, natural resources and place in history gave it undisputed pre-eminence. The gap is now filled. From today Karachi takes rank as a new centre of Muslim cohesion and rallying point of Muslim thought and aspirations.

Those who made such ringing endorsements in favour of Pakistan, and by implication against India and Afghanistan, are all dead. But institutions live on. Will the media at least introspect now? If *The Times* were to revisit that editorial opinion, will it wonder what happened to its grand scheme stretching from Morocco to Indonesia? Will it now repeat some of the superlatives that it had written about Pakistan?

In a manner of speaking, it could be said that the high hopes *The Times* spoke of have materialized. But they have mutated into a phenomenon called terror. Was it for this that Britain sliced India and cheated Afghanistan out of its frontier areas?

The world would certainly have been terror-free with a united India. In that case, Mahatma Gandhi may have insisted on returning the frontier areas to Afghanistan.

Alas, that was not to be. A bit had to be carved out of India and the Afghans were to remain divided. But as far as the Afghanistan government was concerned, it was not lethargic. Rather, it was quick to take up its case.

Quick on its Feet

The Partition Plan was announced by Viceroy Lord Louis Mountbatten on 3 June 1947. Afghanistan reacted almost immediately. It is important to take into account the fact that communications in that age were tentative; and in a remote area like Afghanistan the full text of the Partition Plan may have taken a day or more to reach Kabul. Once they had received the details of Mountbatten's announcement, the government machinery needed to absorb it and filter its response through the bureaucratic ladder right up to the top. That's how it is in all governments for major issues. And that's how it was in this case in Afghanistan. Yet the decision was speeded through the system and instructions were conveyed quickly to the Afghan embassy in London.

Once there, the Afghan diplomats needed to fix an appointment with someone senior enough in the British foreign office to convey their government's concern. It is creditable that within a short span of eight days, on 11 June, a senior Afghan diplomat was sitting in the British foreign office to convey his government's protest against the referendum being planned in NWFP,

> The Afghan Government was concerned at possible fate of the population of this Province if...a referendum took place and the choice were offered to them of associating themselves either with Pakistan or

> Hindustan. The Afghan Government considered that the population… should have the opportunity of deciding whether they wished to re-join Afghanistan or to form a separate State enjoying complete independence. The Afghan Government had hitherto acknowledged the necessity of treating the question of the NorthWest Frontier Province in connection with the question of partition in India. In view of recent developments, however, they considered that the moment was opportune for them to make official representations regarding the Province and to put forward proposals for its future in accordance with ethnological considerations.

This was a balanced and well-formulated approach. Afghanistan was making the point that it had waited for the change in status, and since that was happening now, they were putting forward their viewpoint. And in so far as the referendum was concerned, the only choice should be between joining Afghanistan and opting for an independent status.

This meeting was followed within two days by a note verbale by the Afghan government to Britain on 13 June 1947, '…the settlement of a matter not related to India, should on no account be dependent on the future Government or Governments of India, (if in the past such matters have ever been discussed informally with the Government of India, it has always been considered as contact with Great Britain through the British Government in India)…'

The Afghan government had, through this part of the note verbale, clarified that the issue of NWFP was a matter on which it would like to deal with Britain directly. Interestingly, it also said that 'the settlement of a matter not related to India, should on no account be dependent on the future Government or Governments of India.'

This is significant. It is a clear statement that Britain alone was Afghanistan's interlocutor all through. Since Britain was not succeeded by Pakistan, there was no question of considering the NWFP issue through the prism of a new state. It implied that Britain had a moral responsibility to respect this distinction.

Just in case this was not clear enough, the Afghan note went on to assert, 'The decision that a referendum is being arranged for the North-West Frontier Province, so that it can express its wish to join either Pakistan or

Hindustan, is in the opinion of the Royal Afghan Government incompatible with justice, as it debars them from choosing, either an obvious and natural way of forming a separate free state, or of rejoining Afghanistan their motherland.'

So, to all those who have been doubting Afghanistan's determination to make its case, these above should have been proof enough that Afghanistan had reacted quickly and registered its case strongly as per diplomatic norms. It is also worth noting that here, in this part of the note verbale, Afghanistan bluntly called the British decision to hold the referendum as 'incompatible with justice.'

Caroe's Last Act

Some Britishers were ranged against Afghanistan, the foremost among them being Olaf Caroe, the governor of NWFP. His partiality towards the Muslim League was an open secret. His actions and recommendations were biased and so one-sided that he had to be removed abruptly from his position. In his place, Rob Lockhart was appointed as acting governor of NWFP on 19 June 1947.

Unfortunately, the damage had already been done and one of Caroe's last acts was to come out openly in support of the emerging Pakistan. His recommendation to the viceroy was,

> It was inevitable that the Afghan would bring their weight to bear in this matter and raise the cry of Afghanistan irredenta, but it is interesting that they should have timed it and brought it into line with the Congress theme of Pathanistan. I do not myself think that this Afghan interference is going to be very dangerous, if (and this is the important point) the successor authority make it quite clear that the tribesmen are going to get the benefits that they enjoy at present from this side (Pakistan).

Caroe did not let the humiliation of his abrupt removal deter him. He kept espousing the Pakistani cause and, later in England, wrote extensively about Pakistan's strategic location and its role in the oil-rich Islamic world. The logic of his argument also appealed to the American power centres and he was much sought-after there for his views.

Besides Caroe's negative role, there were practical reasons for the departing British to choose the path of least resistance. The Second World War had been a huge drain on Britain financially. Its troops were exhausted and its primacy in the world was no longer what it once was. There were new power centres which had taken its place. Thus reduced, it did not want an avoidable controversy to exhaust it further. So it opted for the less-trying option by stalling Afghanistan and going ahead with the referendum as it had planned.

The decision of the British government to proceed with the referendum was unusual, and stranger still was the agreement of the (Indian National) Congress party to go along. In the case of other Indian states, no such referendum was proposed and where necessary, the decision to join either India or Pakistan was left to provincial assemblies. Had the same principle been applied to NWFP, the Congress-dominated assembly would have opted to remain with India.

This was not the only departure from the norm.

The British terms of referendum were unfair as well. By all standards of justice, the departing British should have handed the frontier areas back to Afghanistan because it was never meant to be annexed by them. Failing which, the least that they should have done was to include Afghanistan as a choice in the referendum. But the British wanted to anticipate a new Great Game. Therefore, a bespoke referendum was set in motion.

23

Nehru Had Other Ideas

JINNAH HAD PREPARED WELL FOR all contingencies. He had even arranged for storm troopers who were primed for violence. They gave an early demonstration of their capabilities when Nehru began a tour of NWFP in October 1946. Olaf Caroe was the governor of NWFP at that time. It is odd that Caroe's police should not have anticipated a gathering mob of protestors, and that his forces should not have been able to check violent demonstrations against Nehru.

The protests started from the time Nehru landed at the Peshawar airport, but he regarded the mob at the airport and its aggression towards him as an aberration. So he bravely decided to carry on with his tour. But even he had to give up when, at the next stop, a shower of glass and stones were aimed at him.

Nehru had been warned of the organized hostility, but he chose to carry on without a plan to counter it. Jinnah, on the other hand, had prepared multiple plans to achieve his objective in NWFP. As Wali Khan writes in his book *Facts are Facts: The Untold Story of India's Partition*:

> Jinnah told Iskandar Mirza that he was not going to get Pakistan unless some serious trouble was created and the best place to do this was NWFP and the adjacent tribal areas… Jinnah wanted him to resign from the [Government] service and go into the tribal areas to start a Jehad.

Unlike Jinnah, violence was never a part of Mahatma Gandhi's political lexicon, or that of the Congress leadership. Their preferred instrument was the power of speech. But at every step, Jinnah's tactics anticipated their argumentative resistance and on each major demand of the Congress party, he was able to trump them. After all, he was a celebrated lawyer and a politician with the agenda of a fundamentalist. The British, both in London and in Delhi, were generally well-inclined, even partial to his demands. Though Mountbatten disliked him and his aggressive ways, yet he allowed himself to be bullied by Jinnah repeatedly.

Consequently, the odds were loaded against the Congress leadership. Still they did not wish to give up the cause of the Pathans.

Therefore, with the encouragement of many in the Congress party and with the strong backing of Mahatma Gandhi, Khan Abdul Ghaffar Khan issued a statement on 24 June 1947,

> ...it was pointed out to the Viceroy that it would be necessary to provide an opportunity for us to vote in the referendum for a free Pathan State. The Viceroy said he was unable to change the procedure laid down except with the consent of the parties. I consulted the leaders of Congress and they assured me they were perfectly willing for this opportunity to be given to us.

Badshah Khan, as Abdul Ghaffar was popularly known, was not opposing the referendum, he was objecting to its terms. He wanted that the referendum should also have the option for people to vote for a 'free Pathan State'. His statement also clarified that the Congress party was perfectly willing for this option to be given in the referendum.

But the viceroy was unwilling to approach Jinnah in the matter. And Pandit Nehru had other ideas.

Nehru's Prejudice

The line which Nehru had decided to pursue was at variance with that of Mahatma Gandhi and his Congress colleagues. Perhaps it was the ferocity of his reception in NWFP that had worried Nehru. The British desire to settle matters quickly may also have been a factor in Nehru's choice.

Nehru was then a member and the vice president of the Viceroy's Executive Council for External Affairs in the Interim Government. He made it known that he was incensed at the Afghan propaganda. He said bluntly at a meeting of the Cabinet on 4 July, in the presence of Muslim League's Liaquat Ali Khan, that,

> ...about a month ago the press and the Radio in Afghanistan had started a campaign giving prominence to Afghanistan's interests in the North-West Frontier and the claim was made that Pathans were Afghans rather than Indians and they should have the utmost freedom to decide their own future and should not be debarred, as the proposed referendum would appear to do, from deciding either to form a separate free State or to re-join their mother-land, viz Afghanistan.

In making these remarks, Nehru was unfortunately letting his prejudice overrule his intellect. As a writer of repute, as a historian who was the author of books like *Discovery of India* and *Glimpses of World History*, did he actually mean what he had said? As a politician who took pride in his idealism and morality in politics, did his conscience not prick when he questioned the Afghan claim that 'Pathans were Afghans'?

History is proof that Pathans are Afghans. Their DNA cries out that they have nothing in common with Punjab or the rest of India. Yet, Nehru was denying them their roots.

Sadly, he went on to add,

> 'These claims had later been taken up on an official level with H.M.G. and the Government of India. The Government of India had refuted this irredentist claim of Afghanistan to the area lying between the Durand line and the Indus River, and had pointed out that the issue regarding an independent Pathan State was a matter entirely for the Government of India and the Afghan Government had no locus standi. H.M.G.'s Minister at Kabul had mentioned the possibility that the Afghan Government's object might be to divert public attention in Afghanistan from the internal economic situation which was precarious.'

Jinnah's reaction to this statement is not a matter of known record. However, it must have given him enough confidence to call off the jihad in NWFP. 'There is no need for it now.' He told Iskandar Mirza.

But Afghanistan was not to be deterred. Regardless of Nehru's views, Jinnah's machinations and British stonewalling, Afghanistan kept pressing its claim.

This time, it responded to a bureaucratically minded London with a note on 10 July 1947,

> In the Treaty of 1921 or in the previous treaties concluded between the Afghan Government and the British Government, there is no phrase or a small sentence to denote that the Afghan Government or Afghan Governments have ever recognized the Independent Frontier Belt or the Settled Districts inhabited by the Afghan race of British nationality as an integral part of India. The Treaty of 1921 was executed only between the British Government and the Afghan Government and not with any National Government in India.

Afghanistan was making a clear distinction here and pointing out that its treaty was with the British Government. And it rebutted Nehru forcefully on the role of the Government of India. It presses this aspect further in this manner,

> No National Government in India has, by force or Policy cut adrift from Afghanistan any part of the territories situated on that side of the Durand Line and stretching right up to (Rivers) Jhelum and Indus. If the British Government or the British Rule in India was a national Government or National Rule in India, then what was the significance of all these struggles put forward by the Indian nation against England, or what is the meaning of the Indian independence in these days? From the time of Lord Auckland, the Governor-General of India right up to the Third Anglo–Afghan War, it was the British Government—and not India—who constantly indulged in aggressive acts against Afghanistan.

This was the crux of the matter. Afghanistan was making the point that all along it had dealt with Britain not with India, that its argument had been with Britain not with India. If Nehru had followed the international practice and the customary law, he would have realized the enormity of the injustice he was doing to the Pakhtun cause, to Pathans and to Afghanistan.

By taking the easy way out, and for the sake of his political expediency, Pandit Nehru had consigned Pathans to a fate that they did not want.

In contrast, British diplomat, Sir William Kerr Fraser-Tytler, was fair in judgement when he pointed out, 'The British did not solve the problem of the tribes, and when in August, 1947, they handed over the control of India's North-Western defences to the untried Government of Pakistan, they handed over likewise a fluid, difficult situation, fraught with much danger.'

Did Nehru not realize that this 'difficult situation fraught with much danger' could one day become the nursery for multiple shades of terror? More importantly, was he blind to the immediate danger? How could he not anticipate the possibility that battle-hardened fighters of the Afridi and Mehsud tribes would, in 1947, cause havoc in Kashmir and succeed in grabbing a large portion of India's territory? Had the frontier areas been restored to Afghanistan, India would have been spared the tribal invasion and the loss of its territory in Kashmir.

In contrast, Jinnah had dealt himself a winning hand by inciting the Afridi and Mehsud tribals to a jihad in Kashmir.

By diverting these fierce fighters away from their home base, he had reduced the chance of a rebellion in the frontier areas against the newly independent Pakistan. Through this single stratagem, Jinnah had outwitted Badshah Khan and India as well. India, in particular, had been dealt a double blow because the tribals backed by Pakistani army succeeded in getting 78,000 square kilometres of Jammu & Kashmir territory for Pakistan.

If Durand had not forced the agreement on Amir, if Nehru had not gone to NWFP and if he had not given his opinion in the Cabinet meeting of 4 July, the history of South Asia may have been different. The conflicts that have plagued the region may not have happened.

But history is a continuing story, and there is time yet.

24

Not a Successor State

IN A DISCUSSION ABOUT SUCCESSOR states, there is usually a doubtful shake of head by the cognoscenti when it comes to Pakistan. Does Pakistan really belong to that category? If it was a successor state, who was it succeeding? Was it succeeding Britain? Or was it succeeding India?

All along, almost right up to the end of the Second World War, the official British view was that the Durand Agreement had only earmarked the area of its influence over the frontier. The British were not given the right to annex the area. Therefore, there was no question of territorial rights being transferred by Britain to Pakistan.

The Anglo–Afghan Treaty of 1921, like the other treaties before it, was executed only between British authorities and the Afghan government. If that was the case, then the axiomatic inference is that since Britain had not disintegrated as an entity in 1947, Pakistan could not have been a successor state to it.

In 1925, an official British army publication, the *Military Report on Afghanistan*, stated that,

> The [Durand] line was not described in the 1893 treaty as the boundary of India, but as the eastern and southern frontiers of the Amir's dominions and the limits of the respective sphere[s] of influence of the two governments, the object being the extension of British authority and not that of the Indian frontier.

Nothing could have been clearer than this. A British army publication has a certain stamp of authority to it and it was giving out a definitive view. Is it not obvious then that Britain could not have passed on any territory of such a frontier to Pakistan? And there was no way it could pass on 'authority', which it was carrying back with it to London.

Many British observers, in later years, were of the same opinion that the Durand Line and the administrative border between the settled districts and the tribal agencies were only delineating zones of influence and responsibility: '...the tribes between the administrative border and the Durand Line were a buffer to a buffer, and the line had none of the rigidity of other international frontiers.'

The Simon Commission repeated the same point in 1928: 'British India stops at the boundary of the administered area.'

All these statements made it clear that Britain had no intention of annexing the territory up to the Durand Line; rather its goal was to administer this territory and treat it as a sphere of influence. Its basic interest was to protect Punjab from tribal raids.

Despite this, some British politicians, for reasons of their own, supported Pakistan's point of view. Prominent among them was Noel Baker, a well-known India baiter and an equally well-known supporter of the Pakistani cause. A secret British Foreign Office document of 28 April 1949 had stated clearly, 'these areas neither belonged to Pakistan nor to Afghanistan'.

Yet a year later, Baker, as secretary of state for Commonwealth Relations, rose in the British House of Commons on 30 June 1950 to assert quite the opposite, 'In His Majesty's Government's opinion Pakistan is, in the light of international law, the successor of rights and duties of the former Government of India and His Majesty's Government towards those territories, and the Durand Line is an international boundary.'

Strange, isn't it? Noel Baker was giving an altogether new twist to a vexed question in 1950, when Britain was no longer a colonial power and had no authority over India, Pakistan or Afghanistan. In fact, he was turning the colonial British policy on its head by claiming (a) Pakistan is the successor of rights and duties of the former Government of India and His Majesty's Government towards those territories; and (b) the Durand Line is an international boundary.

How should we interpret this about-turn in the British policy? Was the secret foreign office document in error or Noel Baker? And if Noel Baker was right, then all the others starting from various viceroys, MPs and foreign secretaries to the Simon Commission must have been wrong? Suddenly, from an area of influence Noel Baker had decided to designate the Durand Line as an international boundary! The issue is not just the bias of one man, but the arbitrariness of the British.

In their whimsy, the British were going against the precedent that they had themselves set while parting from Ireland.

Moreover, Baker was also going against the opinion given by the United Nations (UN).

UN Decides against Pakistan

A legal opinion of 8 August 1947 by UN's Assistant Secretary General for Legal Affairs (and approved by the Secretary General) maintained, '…Pakistan will be a new State; it will not have the treaty rights and obligations of the old State and it will not, of course, have membership in the United Nations.'

After the Partition, Pakistan put up its case again. It claimed that as a successor state it was automatically a member of the UN. The UN Secretariat examined the Pakistani demand and expressed the following opinion rejecting Pakistan's claim:

> From the viewpoint of International Law, the situation is one in which part of an existing State breaks off and becomes a new State. On this analysis there is no change in the international status of India; it continues as a State with all treaty rights and obligations, and consequently with all rights and obligations of membership in the United Nations. The territory which breaks off—Pakistan—will be a new State. It will not have the treaty rights and obligations of the old State and will not, of course, have membership in the United Nations. In International Law the situation is analogous to the separation of the Irish Free State from Britain, and Belgium from the Netherlands. In these cases the portion which separated was considered a new State, and the remaining portion continued as an existing State with all the rights and duties which it had before.

The UN's verdict was clear; Pakistan was not a successor state. It was a new state.

By giving this opinion, the UN was also asking Britain to take a rear-view mirror look into its own history. It would have found there that it had applied an entirely different standard when Ireland separated from it. Ireland did not become Britain's successor state.

Moreover, Britain's own legal experts may have cautioned it against the course it was adopting. If it had taken the trouble to consult international experts, they too would have advised that the international custom and convention in such matters is unambiguous:

> The term succession in international law does not have its normal meaning in English, which would imply automatic inheritance by the new state of the rights and obligations of the prior state. On the contrary, a successor state is a totally new state. This is distinct from a continuing state, also known as a continuator, which despite change to its borders maintains the same legal personality and possesses all its existing rights and obligations.

Here, according to the opinion quoted above, Pakistan was not a successor state. It had not succeeded Britain in any sense of the term.

And as Farhana Razzak writes in her paper on state succession, '...it seems to be accepted that India is the same legal entity as British India and Pakistan is a totally new state. Yugoslavia was generally regarded as the successor state to Serbia, and Israel as a completely different being from British mandated Palestine.'

Moreover, if Pakistan was a successor to someone or something, it should have accepted some of that predecessor's debt, which it refused to do. As a result, India shouldered all the debt of British India. Or to put it in other words, if Pakistan was a new state, how could it be a successor state as well?

British Whims Set Rules

Now in retrospect, it seems that the entire case was a falsehood perpetrated against Afghanistan by Noel Baker and others in London. Among the reasons for this bias was the fact that by 1947, British military chiefs of staff had become enthusiastic proponents of Pakistan. They saw in its creation, several possibilities, including obtaining air bases in the new territory. 'The area of Pakistan,' the chiefs noted, 'is strategically the most important in the continent of India and the majority of our strategic requirements could be met.'

This was combined with a false hope that somehow Pakistan would ensure unhindered access for Britain and its allies to the oil riches of Arabia. On its part, Pakistan did nothing to disabuse Britain of this impression. In contrast, Afghanistan was weak and of little interest to big powers. As a result, self-interest rather than law and justice shaped Britain's view on Pakistan as a successor state. So, even as Pakistan was being rewarded for its strategic location, Afghanistan was being punished for it.

It was this arbitrariness which left Britain friendless.

For close to 200 years, the British Empire was the greatest empire and the richest country in the world. It may have continued that way, accumulating loot and wealth from its colonies. But wars had drained its men and material resources.

When this weakened, the empire packed up, but it left behind the seeds of long-term discord. The British guiding mantra throughout the nineteenth and twentieth centuries can best be summed up as, 'On principles there should be no compromise and on compromise there should be no principles.' To clarify, what it really means is this, where British interests are involved principles must be held supreme, but when it concerns the interests of others, principles could be given a wide pass by the British.

As rulers, the British whims set the rules.

25

Legally Speaking

IMPERIAL BRITAIN FIRST, AND LATER Pakistan picking up the same refrain, maintained that the 1893 Agreement was signed in perpetuity and that was that. It was the end of the argument. Still, let us examine this claim a bit closely and ask a few questions.

Every serious treaty and each important agreement has a sell-by date. Where is it written in the 1893 treaty that it had a shelf life of 'forever'?

There is serious doubt that the Durand Agreement was signed in perpetuity. Let's consider the issue differently and ask if Mortimer Durand had carried with him the authority to bind the British government in perpetuity? Could he, for instance, have parcelled out British land, or parts of India, to Afghanistan as a part of his grand bargain? And did he carry with him the Queen's or the viceroy's authority letter for the purpose? The fact is that the 1893 Agreement was legally deficient.

That's not the only Afghan complaint. There are a series of other sore points with them. The British quote the Anglo–Afghan treaty of 1921 to assert that it had validated the Durand Agreement. However, that is not the entire truth. Actually, the 1921 treaty stated that both states had the right to repudiate it within three years after a one-year notice.

How could a treaty which has a termination period written into it, validate the alleged permanence of the Durand Agreement? What is more, the 1921 treaty contained a supplementary letter specifically recognizing the Afghan interest in the trans-border tribes. This again contradicted the terms of the Durand Agreement. If all these are taken together and if you recall Curzon's statement scrapping many provisions of the Durand Agreement, then there is nothing left of that paper and its seven clauses.

Even if we regard this as a rare exception where the signatories forgot to mention the expiry date, we should take a look at what had happened in a similar case. We don't have to look far for a parallel because Britain had signed just such a deal in the case of Hong Kong.

Hong Kong's territory was acquired by Britain through three separate treaties—Treaty of Nanking in 1842, Treaty of Beijing in 1860 and the Convention for the Extension of Hong Kong Territory in 1898, which gave the UK control of Hong Kong Island, Kowloon and the New Territories.

Although Hong Kong Island and Kowloon had been ceded to the UK in perpetuity, the control on the New Territories was on a ninety-nine-year lease.

China regarded these as unequal treaties that needed to be revised by communist China as the successor state. Under pressure from it, the UK agreed to first contact on the issue in the late 1970s. Since the talks were inconclusive, matters came to a head during British Prime Minister Margaret Thatcher's visit to China in September 1982. At their meeting in Beijing, the Chinese leader Deng Xiaoping told her bluntly that China could easily take Hong Kong by force, 'I could walk in and take the whole lot this afternoon.'

It did not take long for Britain to accept the inevitable. The transfer of sovereignty over Hong Kong and Kowloon to China took place on 1 July 1997.

A principle had been established; that an unjust treaty cannot be cited as justification for sovereignty. And that 'perpetuity' is a relative term. After this example of Hong Kong, one could cynically say that force is all-important in international law.

We could still be cussed and insist that we should dig deeper. Why was the date not mentioned in the Durand Agreement? Was the omission because of Mortimer's carelessness? Or did both parties agree that it should be in perpetuity? Why was there this slip on such an important issue?

Records show that the imperial powers of the nineteenth century were extremely protocol-conscious. They could be finicky to the point of being tiresome in negotiations; each 't' in the text had to be crossed and each 'i' dotted carefully. Nothing could be left to chance, or to a vague and later interpretation. Therefore, as foreign secretary and as a professional diplomat, Durand could not pretend that he was new to the ways of writing documents. If the Durand Agreement was to be valid in perpetuity, Mortimer Durand would have made sure that a clause specifying it was inserted in the Agreement. But that was not done because the Agreement had only earmarked areas of influence, and that is a transitory arrangement.

A question that should have been asked by historians and diplomats alike is whether Britain had invariably made the validity of treaties and agreements it signed dependent upon ratification. This was the case with all important treaties it had signed with Afghanistan, before and after the one in 1893. And the Durand Agreement was certainly the most important document signed by Britain with Afghanistan. Yet, the clause for ratification or approval by the viceroy was missing here.

Why was the clause regarding the Agreement entering into force only after its approval by the viceroy not included in this particular document? Why was Mortimer Durand keen that it should come into force immediately? What was he apprehensive about? And why, when all other treaties of importance had an expiry date and an exit clause, were these elements missing in the Durand Agreement?

Let's consider the issue from another point of view. The Afghan–Russian boundary Agreement was signed at the same time. Neither Russia nor Afghanistan ever raised objection or any doubt about the boundary settled between them. Russia did not feel the need to sign a subsequent treaty to reaffirm its clauses and reconfirm the Agreement signed in 1893. But Britain felt it necessary to reaffirm the Durand Agreement repeatedly through treaties signed in 1895, 1905, 1919, 1921 and 1930. Did these five reaffirmations reflect a sense of British insecurity?

If the 1893 Agreement was to be in perpetuity, what was the need for obtaining the seal of approval from every new Amir?

Let us also look at the legal side of the argument. The first point that strikes observers is the huge confidence with which the British used to assert their view; as if whatever they had said was and had to be absolutely the last word on the subject. If they said a treaty was in perpetuity, it had to be so. If they considered a treaty immutable, there was no way anyone could argue about it. Yet, when they wanted to, they could change the terms of the treaty and cancel clauses selectively. They could also renege on commitments and interpret the same clause entirely differently. British convenience moulded the law.

Executed vs Executory

That's why there was great consternation in the British foreign office in the 1950s when a contrary opinion on the Durand Agreement reached London. The British ambassador in Afghanistan, Dan Lascelles, suggested that there was need to revisit the Durand Agreement.

The crux of his argument was that in international treaties there are two types of clauses, 'executed' and 'executory'.

The first term, 'executed', describes a clause which means that something needs to be done only once. The second term, 'executory', describes an act which is continual and requires the constant participation of both parties for its fulfilment.

Clauses related to the establishment of sovereign boundaries are 'executed', because once they are done, they are treated as a permanent feature even if one party should repudiate them. In short, an 'executed' clause cannot be revoked.

'Executory' clauses fall in a different category. They are for matters such as trade and tariff agreements which are continuous actions, which can be broken off if one of the parties should decide to do so.

Ambassador Lascelles studied the issue carefully in Kabul. In his communication to London he referred to it as the contested clause, 'The Government of India will at no time exercise interference in the territories lying beyond this line on the side of Afghanistan, and His Highness the Amir will at no time exercise interference in the territories lying beyond this line on the side of India.'

He argued that an agreement not to 'exercise interference' constitutes an action that is ongoing and continuous, requiring a constant effort from the contracting parties, rather than something which is executed once and for all. He pointed out to the foreign office in London that the clauses in the 1893 Durand Treaty had the appearance of being 'executory' rather than 'executed' and open to repudiation by either party. Hence, he reasoned, the Afghan government of President Daud Khan, which was at that time eager to repudiate the Durand Agreement and which had already denounced the frontier treaties, might well be in their rights to withdraw from any acknowledgement of the Durand Line.

He insisted that such an action by the Afghan government would stand the scrutiny of the law. It being an 'executory' clause, they would legitimately be able to cease any recognition of it.

If the matter were to be taken to an international tribunal, he argued further, Afghanistan had a good chance of winning that case against Pakistan. This would not only cause problems for Pakistan, but would cause considerable humiliation to Britain given the fact that it had, since the end of the Second World War, started asserting that the Line was legally watertight as an international boundary.

Lascelles engaged in correspondence with the foreign office's legal department, which claimed that under the international law, clauses setting up international boundaries were to be regarded as executed. The department went on to conclude; since the Durand Line was an international boundary, it could only be seen as an executed clause, and therefore, was immune to repudiation by the Afghan side.

However, the legal department was only using the privilege of being the headquarters to shut up the mission. Actually, it was treading on slushy legal grounds. Unlike what it told its Kabul mission, the reality is that the Durand Line was not an international boundary line, or a line dividing areas of sovereignty. The British parliamentary debates are proof of this.

Or to take another example, let us recall the words of Viceroy Lord Chelmsford when he was explaining the rationale for restoring to Afghanistan the right to independence in determining its foreign policy:

> We have to deal with an Afghan nation, impregnated with the world spirit of self-determination and national freedom, inordinately self-confident in its new-found emancipation from autocracy and in its supposed escape from all menace from Russia, impatient of any restraint on its absolute independence. To expect the Afghanistan of today willingly to accept a Treaty re-embodying our old control over her foreign policy is a manifest impossibility. If we were to impose it at the point of the sword, to what end? The Treaty would have to be torn to shreds the moment the point of the sword was withdrawn.

The context for this acknowledgement was the concession that the British had, at long last, agreed to give to Afghanistan in 1919. The crucial determinants in this climb down were two: first, British energies had been sapped in the First World War; second, the communistic Soviet Union was preoccupied with the issues of internal consolidation and therefore, it was no longer a threat for Afghanistan or India.

The concluding observation of Chelmsford was important too, 'The treaty would have to be torn to shreds the moment the point of the sword was withdrawn.'

This power of the sword was the essence of the empire's conquest. Sadly, violence was at the centre of the empire's story. Resistance to it, howsoever heroic, got only a marginal mention.

That difference, plus the bluster and the bluff of its representatives, was the glue that held the unfair treaties together. Force had the power of enforcement. Without the power of the sword, the British Empire could not have occupied Punjab and Sind, nor extended its reach over Peshawar and NWFP. The cruel reality is that the British claims were an artificial construct. But a weak Afghanistan was in no position to challenge them.

The same helplessness of a weak Afghanistan is now in play vis-à-vis a much stronger Pakistan.

Offer Your Blood

However, Afghanistan did not give up its efforts. It has all along refused to recognize the Durand Line. And it has consistently pressed its case with an uncaring world.

When it opposed Pakistan's membership to the UN in September 1947, Afghanistan's representative to the UN said,

> Afghanistan cannot recognize the NWFP as part of Pakistan so long as the people of the NWFP have not been given the opportunity, free from any kind of influence, to determine for themselves whether they wish to be independent or to become part of Pakistan.

Shocked by this development, Pakistan took the initiative in December 1947 to discuss the issue with Afghanistan in Karachi. The Afghan representative, Najibullah Khan, took the stand at this meeting that his country wanted 'the Durand Line to be seen as null and void and also wanted Pakistan to allow the establishment of Pashtunistan.'

Afghanistan kept up its efforts consistently. In an appeal to 'Pakhtoon Brethren' on 22 December 1952, Kabul Radio gave out this message,

> ...freedom cannot be achieved through begging, it will have to be courted and wooed with red, fresh blood. Offer your blood at the altar of freedom and she is yours. If you hesitate, others will snatch her away from you and you will ever afterwards curse your cowardice.

In 1960, Afghan Prime Minister Daoud sent about 1,000 Afghan soldiers disguised as nomads to Bajaur district for acts of disruption against Pakistan. Later, in the 1970s, Daoud's government established camps on Afghan territory where thousands of Pathan and Baloch tribesmen were trained for guerrilla war against Pakistan.

In its turn, Pakistan resorted to force by surreptitious means.

The common and mistaken impression is that armed opposition to the government in Kabul started with the occupation of the capital by Soviet troops. That is not so. Actually, jihadi activities long predated the arrival of Soviet troops in December 1979. Every one of the Pakistan-based Afghan mujahideen leaders who became famous during the 1980s as the Peshawar Seven were helped by the United States, Pakistan, Saudi Arabia and China. Pakistan had sheltered and financed their activities to blunt Daoud's aggressive posture on the Pashtunistan issue.

After the fall of the last communist regime, Pakistan hoped that the Islamist leaders, whom it had supported in their fight against the Soviets, would settle the issue of the Durand Line to its satisfaction. However, to Pakistan's disappointment, the Islamic leaders, Burhanuddin Rabbani and Ahmad Shah Massoud, refused to accept the Durand Line as the international border between Afghanistan and Pakistan.

It was the same when by 1996 the Taliban had established its control over 90 per cent of Afghanistan's territory to form the Islamic Emirate of Afghanistan. Much to Pakistan's disappointment, even the Taliban refused to recognize the Durand Line. It may have been because of their firm stand on Durand Line that Major General Mahmud Ali Durrani said at a seminar at the Pakistan embassy in Washington, 'I hope the Taliban and Pashtun nationalism don't merge. If that happens, we've had it, and we're on the verge of that.'

In view of the uniformity of the stand taken by successive Afghan governments post 1947, it would be fair to say that they had no doubt at all that the Durand Agreement was unfair and unjust.

In an impartial court of justice, Afghanistan will have a solid case to argue. If and when the world community wakes up to the historical inequity imposed on Pashtuns, and views the issue as its 'Responsibility to Protect', then, and only then, the frontier lands that belong to Afghanistan may be restored to it. But before that, the world community will have to contend with an aggressive Pakistan.

26

Pleasure Was Outlawed

As THUCYDIDES SAID, 'THE STRONG do what they want and the weak suffer what they must.' The challenge for Pashtuns has been whether they must tolerate those who are murderously intolerant of them.

For a moment let us suspend belief, because torture of the kind the Pashtuns have gone through is beyond belief. Let us simply recall the horrors they have suffered generation after generation from different oppressors. Let us start with the British. As Winston Churchill wrote to a friend in September 1897, 'After today, we begin to burn villages. Every one. And all who resist will be killed without quarter. The Mohmands need a lesson, and there is no doubt we are a very cruel people.'

He noted matter-of-factly in his autobiography, *My Early Life,* how the British went about their business: 'We proceeded systematically, village by village, and we destroyed the houses, filled up the wells, blew down the towers, cut down the great shady trees, burned the crops and broke the reservoirs in punitive devastation.'

Churchill's letter was written when he was just 23, so his enthusiastic support to British methods could be blamed to his youth. But the gleeful record that he wrote in his autobiography was in the autumn of his life. Even then, there was neither remorse nor a feeling of regret at the cruel treatment of Afghans by the British.

These punitive expeditions were not questioned in historical literature either. There were some imperial-era justifications for the mass punishments, but none of them were satisfactory. In any case, the results of these expeditions were meagre. As Viceroy Lansdowne admitted in a private letter in 1889, 'punitive expeditions have been frequent, but have been attended with very few permanent results.'

If that was so, why kill so many for the fault of a few? But the powerful want quick results, not debate. And the tribes continued to be punished.

The British atrocities against Afghans did not end in the nineteenth century. As the new century dawned, so did the new forms of mass punishment.

As the century progressed, the methods of suppression multiplied. In 1932, in a series of Guernica-like atrocities, the British used poison gas in Waziristan. The disarmament convention of the same year sought a ban against the aerial bombardment of civilians, but Lloyd George, who had been the British prime minister during World War I, gloated: 'We insisted on reserving the right to bomb niggers.'

Unfortunately, his view prevailed.

Kabul Must Burn

Did this attitude or methods change in the modern age? Alas, no. Atrocities against the Pashtuns did not stop after the British left in 1947. Only the baton changed hands.

There is an oft-quoted comment in this regard by the cricketer-turned-politician Imran Khan. He told *The Daily Star* newspaper of Bangladesh about his experience as an 18-year-old on tour in Dacca in 1971. 'These ears heard people saying: "Small and dark. Kill them. Teach them (Bengalis) a lesson,"' he said. 'I heard it with my own ears.'

Many years later, as the leader of the political party Pakistan Tehreek-e-Insaf (PTI), Imran said he now hears similar commands being given in Pakistan. 'It is exactly the same language which I hear this time,' he said, adding that today it is the Pashtuns who are ill-treated. 'In Pindi, in Lahore, in Karachi, they've been picked up and thrown into jail because they are Pashtun. This is a sad legacy.'*

Pashtuns have been targeted under every Pakistani regime. To compound their misery, they were tortured by their own, too, when the Taliban were in government in Afghanistan. They wanted to bind the people in a tight fundamentalist leash. As a former torturer of the Taliban, Hafiz Sadiqulla

---

**The Daily Star*, 15 January 2012, 'Pakistan learnt no lesson from 1971', http://www.thedailystar.net/news-detail-218441

Hassani admitted to *The Telegraph*, his indoctrination into methods of torture began with this instruction, 'I want your unit to find new ways of torture so terrible that the screams will frighten even crows from their nests and if the person survives he will never again have a night's sleep.'

These were the words of the commandant of Taliban's secret police to his new recruits.

'Pleasure was outlawed,' Hassani added, 'if we found people doing any of these things we would beat them with staves soaked in water—like a knife cutting through meat—until the room ran with their blood or their spines snapped. Then we would leave them with no food or water in rooms filled with insects until they died.'*

It is a matter of conjecture if the Taliban's torture was being encouraged by their mentors across the border. But it is a fact that the attitude of the Pakistani Generals towards Afghans and Afghanistan has been nothing short of tyrannical. General Akhtar Rahman was the director general of Inter-Services Intelligence (ISI) during the period of Pakistan-sponsored Taliban resistance to the Soviet occupation of Afghanistan. In that phase, General Rahman had remarked that when the Taliban take over, 'Kabul must burn.'

No one questioned him or tried to impede his venom or asked why innocent men, women and children must burn?

This heartlessness is best exemplified in an excerpt from Mohsin Hamid's short story, 'Terminator: Attack of the Drone'. Mohsin imagines life in Pakistan's tribal areas bordering Afghanistan under constant attack from US drone bombings. His narrator is one of the two boys who go out one night to try to attack a drone.

> 'The machines (drones) are huntin' tonight,' the narrator says. 'There ain't many of us left. Humans I mean. Most people who could do already escaped. Or tried to escape anyways. I don't know what happened to 'em. But we couldn't. Ma lost her leg to a landmine and can't walk. Sometimes she gets outside the cabin with a stick. Mostly she stays in and crawls. The girls do the work. I'm the man now.

**The Telegraph*, 30 September 2001, 'I was one of the Taliban's torturers: I crucified people', http://www.telegraph.co.uk/news/worldnews/asia/afghanistan/1358063/I-was-one-of-the-Talibans-torturers-I-crucified-people.html

'Pa's gone. The machines got him. I didn't see it happen but my uncle came back for me. Took me to see Pa gettin' buried in the ground. There wasn't anythin' of Pa I could see that let me know it was Pa. When the machines (drones) get you there ain't much left. Just gristle mixed with rocks, covered in dust.'

Pakistan not only gave a conspiring nod to such drone attacks by the US, it has also been carrying out aerial bombardment of its own. In October 2007, Pakistani aircraft bombed a village bazaar packed with shoppers near the Afghan border killing 250 of them. Major General Waheed Arshad, making light of the incident, said the airstrikes might have killed some civilians who were living in the areas! Since then, there have been more attacks, and many more civilians have been killed. Technology has added a touch of perfection to killing.

The sad fact is that no place on earth has seen more drone strikes than this northwestern corner between Pakistan and Afghanistan. More than 350 drone strikes have hit the Waziristan region alone. A recent report of Amnesty International also accuses the Pakistan army of rampant summary detentions with no due process, torture and deaths in custody.*

The unfortunate reality is that an independent Pakistan did not abandon the imperial British tradition of mass punishment. It simply carried on from where the British had left it. But Britain was a colonizer; Pakistan is punishing its own. Still, mass punishments continue to be practised by it routinely, as are mass displacements.

A recent case exemplifies this. Five days after the Pakistani army launched a major offensive in the summer of 2014, the people of North Waziristan received a notice of evacuation. All residents surrounding the towns of Miram Shah, Mir Ali, Datta Khel and others were given three days to leave, after which all roads leading out of North Waziristan were going to be closed. Anyone who stayed behind would be considered hostile to the state, said the evacuation notice.**

Pakistani army was not satisfied with simply pushing out close to a million people from their homes. The military suspected that terrorists could

---

*'Amnesty International-Annual Report-Pakistan, 2016/2017', The Bureau of Investigative Journalism, 19 December 2012.

** Maham Javaid, 'Pakistan's Neocolonial War', *The Nation*, 11 June 2015.

find shelter in these vacant homes. So, it removed the roofs of all the houses in the area to have a better aerial view and stop the militants from taking refuge inside the houses!

Meanwhile, the displaced Pashtuns have been living like nomads in open, inhospitable spaces. Some are known to wonder in deep winter if the world is immune to their pain.

27
Obama's Error

IN HIS ADDRESS TO THE nation on Afghanistan and Pakistan in December 2009, US President Barack Obama said: 'We will act with the full recognition that our success in Afghanistan is inextricably linked to our partnership with Pakistan...'

No one pressed the pause button to stop Mr Obama there and ask, 'Why should America's success in Afghanistan be linked to its partnership with Pakistan?' Did anyone ask the otherwise morally upright Barack Obama, 'Did you actually mean what you just said?' Because what he said really meant this, 'American success in Afghanistan was dependant on Pakistani whims.'

Did he say it to propitiate Pakistan? After all, Pakistan has, on many occasions, choked the American supply line to its troops in Afghanistan. And every time the US had to climb down. Or was Obama fearful of the terrorists that Pakistan breeds as in a hatchery? Unless of course, we have misread Obama completely and missed the point he was making. Perhaps, he had genuinely meant that Pakistan's partnership was vital for the American success in Afghanistan.

If that was how the American president viewed it, then there was a major disconnect with the way the leaders of the region assess the situation.

The day after 9/11, I happened to be in Central Asia. Now, in retrospect, it seems like a leaf out of the Great Game that soon after a cataclysmic event an Indian diplomat should be in Central Asia consulting with its leadership. But this happened just by chance.

Inevitably, the conversation turned to the horror of that attack and the likely retribution from the US. It could not have been mere coincidence that every Central Asian leader that I talked to conveyed the same message;

if America targets terrorists in Afghanistan, it will only be trimming the branches. If it wants to strike out terror once and for all, it must destroy the roots of terror in Pakistan.

Yet, after eight frustrating years of bombing Afghanistan and achieving very little because of Pakistani perfidy, Barack Obama was serenading Pakistan as America's partner!

If that was meant to encourage Pakistan to carry on with its disruptive acts in Afghanistan, then Obama had chosen just the right words. And if he wanted the larger international community to pay attention, the occasion was perfect. An address to the nation by the US president is a global event and the message is followed widely. But did the US, or for that matter Afghanistan, gain as a result of Obama's soothing words to Pakistan?

If the reality on the ground is the test of Pakistani sincerity to American concerns, then the harsh fact is that even as Obama was making that address, Pakistan was giving shelter to Mullah Omar and his Quetta Shura, besides hiding Osama bin Laden.

But the US propitiation of Pakistan did not end there. Seymour Hersh, an American journalist, wrote in his book, *The Killing of Osama bin Laden*, that under President Obama, Pakistan's ISI secured 'a commitment from the US to give Pakistan "a freer hand" in Afghanistan as it began its military draw-down there.'

Once it had received that nod the ISI got busy pushing even more terrorists across the Durand Line into Afghanistan. And this time, they terrorized and slaughtered Afghans (mainly Hazaras) under a new brand name: the Islamic State.

One of the most persistent myths of recent wars in Afghanistan is Pakistan's decisive role. It is accepted unthinkingly as part of the conventional narrative of the war. And Pakistan does nothing to discourage it. Some Pakistanis go as far as to say that the alleged Soviet defeat in Afghanistan helped to cause the collapse of the Soviet Union itself. Some claim they destroyed one superpower in Afghanistan and are on their way to destroying another.

The reality is different. The US and Pakistan-backed mujahideen did not defeat the Soviets on the battlefield. They won some important encounters, notably in Panjshir valley, but lost others. The Soviets could have stayed on in Afghanistan for several more years, but they decided to leave when Gorbachev calculated that the war was no longer worth the high price in men, money and international prestige.

In private, US officials came to the same conclusion. Morton Abramowitz, of the State Department's Bureau of Intelligence and Research said: 'In 1985, there was real concern that mujahideen were losing, that they were sort of being diminished, falling apart. Losses were high and their impact on the Soviets was not great.'

If that was so, why is the US worried? Surely it can defeat the Taliban. It can also summon courage to keep Pakistan in check, or at least check its potential for mischief in Afghanistan.

Helpless America

Pakistan is vulnerable because it is not without multiple challenges. It is on a slippery slope on many measures ranging from its uncertain economic condition to its poor international standing. But the US hesitates, and Pakistan remains steadfast on what it feels should be its strategic goals. And it is convinced that its path to that strategic Valhalla lies through the terrorist networks.

There is no magic bullet that will deter it from following that path. If the carrots and sticks of the past sixteen years have failed to convince Pakistan to change course, nothing will.

For the world, however, that poses a dilemma. Does it have a viable and enforceable option other than the propitiation of Pakistan and hoping for the best? It is an indication of the debilitating grip Pakistan has on matters concerning Afghanistan, that despite knowing about its negative role, a super power like the US finds itself helpless.

In 2014, Barack Obama told then Afghan President Hamid Karzai that Pakistan is a strategic 'ally' in the War on Terror, and while already fighting a war in Afghanistan, his administration 'cannot open another front against Pakistan'. He repeatedly urged his Afghan counterpart to address Pakistan's 'concerns' about the Indian influence in Afghanistan. Encouraged by Pakistan, the US President even suggested that Karzai find a 'resolution of differences' on the Durand Line with Pakistan. He proposed that 'any issues concerning the border must come through mutual agreement between the parties concerned'.

Karzai is said to have responded that Afghanistan cannot accommodate

Pakistan's desire to control Kabul's foreign policy, nor can it be expected to recognize the imposed Durand Line.*

Former US Vice President Joseph R. Biden did not have Afghanistan in mind when he said in 2016 that the 'Middle East's problems stem from artificial lines, creating artificial states made up of totally distinct ethnic, religious, cultural groups.'

But his diagnosis fitted the Afghan ailment as well. He could have extended his argument to add that 'Western imperialism had a malignant influence on the course of Afghan history.'

Sir Sherard Cowper-Coles, a former British ambassador to Afghanistan, writes in his book, *Cables from Kabul*, 'Sometimes President Karzai would become emotional about…the need to reunite the Pashtuns/Pathans on both sides of the Durand Line.' He goes on to add, 'Like all his predecessors, Karzai believed that for him officially to recognise the border would amount to committing political suicide with his Pashtun base.'

An Old Map

I met Hamid Karzai in the quiet of a Delhi hotel. But the ring of security around him was a reminder that unquiet follows Afghans even when they are away in relative safety. We were talking about a past that continues to shackle Afghanistan's destiny; the past that goes about with the name called the Durand Line.

I expressed my surprise that an Amir who had systematically expanded the territory of Afghanistan should have agreed so readily to parcel out a large slice of his land to the British. For me, this was one of those historical mysteries that remain unsolved after 124 years.

'Will that historical wrong ever be corrected?' I asked Mr Karzai, 'What did your American interlocutors think about it?'

He was hesitant at first. But when I pressed him to give at least one instance from his discussions, his eyes sparkled, 'In the last year of my presidency, I was meeting CIA Chief John Brennan at his office in Washington,' Karzai said opening up. 'We were discussing the issue of the Durand Line and my anguish over its historical inequity. At one point,

*'An Afghan agenda for Trump', *The Hindu*, 18 January 2017.

he went into one of the adjoining rooms and came back with a map of South Asia. It was a two-century-old map drawn much before the Durand Agreement was signed. There was naturally no Pakistan then. The CIA Chief smiled as he handed over the map to me.'

Karzai too had smiled as he recalled that incident. I left our meeting wondering whether Obama and his CIA chief were playing good cop, bad cop. While one was massaging the Pakistani ego, the other was hinting at its demise. Otherwise, what was that two-century-old map about?

It is contradictions like this which make America's partnership with Pakistan complicated.

President Barack Obama was expected to bring in change and introduce more transparency in the relationship. The award of Nobel Peace Prize at the beginning of his first term was about morality in decision-making. It is a pity that he could not live up to those high expectations.

As time goes by, Obama's record will be subjected to greater public scrutiny. But even during his term in office, critics had wondered whether the hope that he would bring peace to the world was justified?

Afghans, at least, continue to suffer from a virtual war.

28

Lust for Land

A PATHAN'S LUST FOR ZAMEEN CAN turn him into a trickster. Churchill had said so bluntly,

> Truth is unknown among them. A single typical incident displays the standpoint from which they regard an oath. In any dispute about a field boundary, it is customary for both claimants to walk round the boundary he claims, with a Koran in his hand, swearing that all the time he is walking on his own land. To meet the difficulty of a false oath, while he is walking over his neighbour's land, he puts a little dust from his own field into his shoes. As both sides are acquainted with the trick, the dismal farce of swearing is usually soon abandoned, in favour of an appeal to force.

However, it is not just the Pathan who tries tricks to grab land. And it is not only a Pathan who seeks to gobble up that land by force. Nations do it as well, but there are exceptions too.

India is one such exception, and so is Afghanistan. Like India, and unlike its Pashtuns, Afghanistan as a nation is docile and hesitant on matters concerning zameen.

Pakistan, in contrast, has been revisionist from day one. It grabbed Gilgit and Baltistan illegally. Then it occupied a large portion of Jammu & Kashmir. Its quest for strategic depth in Afghanistan is yet another sign of its hunger for more land.

China, too, has been consistently revisionist in its conduct. The most serious trouble to flare up in East Asia in recent decades was that between China and Vietnam. There have also been stand-offs between China and the Philippines besides those between China and Japan. The list of China's transgressions is large, but by way of illustrating the point it should suffice to mention the following incidents:

In 1974, China seized the Paracel Islands from Vietnam, killing more than seventy Vietnamese troops. This was followed in 1988 by another clash between the two sides in the Spratly Islands, with Vietnam again coming off worse, losing about sixty sailors.

In early 2012, China and the Philippines engaged in a lengthy maritime stand-off, accusing each other of intrusions in the Scarborough Shoal.

In 2013, the Philippines sought international arbitration through the UN Convention on the Law of the Sea. Giving its verdict in July 2016, the tribunal backed the Philippines' case, saying China had violated the Philippines' sovereign rights.

China knew it had a weak case so it decided to boycott the proceedings. When the ruling went against it, China brazenly called it 'ill-founded' and insisted that it would not be bound by it. The world community has not been able to tell China that it should abide by the rules of the Convention to which it is a party.

In contrast, look at India's record. We have lost territory in almost all the arbitrations that we have participated in. But because of our pride in being a good global citizen, we have never considered the Chinese option.

Why do we lose in arbitration is an issue that will require critical and lengthier examination of our decision-making process, the extent of preparation for the case and the presentation of arguments by our legal teams. But to give one instance of our failure, let this sorry story of the arbitration after the Battle of Bets in 1965 be a case in point.

The British Prime Minister Harold Wilson suggested ceasefire by both sides, India and Pakistan (it came into effect on 30 June), followed by talks between the two adversaries and a return to the status quo on ground pending a decision by an international tribunal. India nominated Ales Bebler, a Yugoslav jurist. Pakistan made its choice shrewdly by nominating Nasrollah Entezam, former foreign minister of the friendly Iran. The UN secretary general nominated a Swede, Gunnar Lagergren, as the presiding judge. Bebler kept a low profile during the proceedings and Lagergren went largely by the opinion of the Iranian judge, who was clearly inclined to take Pakistan's side.

As C.S. Jha, the then foreign secretary of India, records, 'The award was not in conformity with the agreement that it would be based solely on facts and evidence; it was close to a political award...'

The verdict of the Kutch Tribunal was given on 19 February 1968 and it went against India. Despite the bias in the verdict, we accepted it meekly and handed over 802 square kilometres of our territory to Pakistan, which included Kanjarkot and Chand Bet.

India had found itself friendless in 1962, now it had been outwitted on the legal-diplomatic front. In both cases India had lost territory.

It is a pity that our collective memory is like that of a goldfish. How many of us remember the loss of territory in Kutch? Did we learn any lesson from this award in favour of Pakistan; that it was a mistake to choose a non-aligned Yugoslav as our representative, and that we should have lobbied our case more vigorously? Or for that matter, how many in India can recall instantly where Gilgit and Baltistan lie? More importantly, how many know why and how we lost these large land parcels to Pakistan?

Another characteristic that others brand us by is our fickle stand. What historical claim can a questionably created new state have over the territory of Gilgit and Baltistan? Yet, Pakistan grabbed these two provinces and went on to occupy more land in Jammu & Kashmir (J&K) during 1947–48. But that did not satisfy it. Pakistan claims that India has unfairly denied it the remaining two thirds of J&K!

In contrast, we stumble. We confuse the world by our apologetic explanations. This, despite the fact that the Indian Parliament had voted unanimously in 1994 to assert that the entire J&K is Indian territory. Now, how does this assertion balance with our readiness to talk to Pakistan about the Kashmir issue? No one has ever paused to ask what exactly we propose to talk about? Pakistanis, on their part, are clear about their strategy and call it the 'unfinished agenda of Partition'; they are brazen in their lust for the rest of zameen in Kashmir.

And what about the 40,000 kilometres of Aksai Chin grabbed by China? That too is a part of J&K. Do we hope to get that back too?

But a goldfish-like memory and a fickle stand is not the end of the story. We must be the unique country in the world which has lost territory in multiple ways and to almost every neighbour of ours.

Some we lost to China in the 1962 war. In some other cases, we gave up territory in a fit of generosity. There is no satisfactory explanation for

India's decision to gift away the Coco Island to Burma.

Later, in the seventies, we turned generous again and decided to hand over the Katchatheevu Island to Sri Lanka. But having done that, we have been strangely reluctant to face the Parliament; the formal ratification has yet to pass that test.

Talking of our respect for arbitration awards, there is also the recent decision of an arbitration court where we have lost 106,613 square kilometres of the sea area to Bangladesh.

There are many questions that arise. Why are we such happy losers? Is it that we fight shy of scenes and therefore avoid quarrels or is it that we have more than enough land and do not mind parcelling out some to our more needy neighbours? Or is it that as the bigger country we must be generous with others who are smaller?

If that last argument is to hold true then it can very well be asked as to why China is not equally generous with its smaller neighbours. Rather, it has taken land from every one of its neighbours, including India. Each one of China's neighbours is smaller in size than it.

China may turn out to be the most expansionist power of this age but there are others too. When Mauritius was still a British colony, one of the Chagos islands in the Indian Ocean, the Diego Garcia, was leased out by Britain to the US for its military base in 1966 for fifty years (this was just two years before Mauritius's independence in 1968). Nearly 2,000 islanders were forced out of their homes by the UK and settled in Mauritius and the Seychelles. Though that fifty-year lease expired in 2016, it was renewed by the UK until 20 December 2036, much to the horror of Mauritius.

Since then, Mauritius has threatened to take Britain to the International Court of Justice on the issue. But Britain's excuse is a post-colonial lie. It says that the island has been taken for defence purposes which contribute significantly towards global security!

Why do countries, with the notable exceptions of India and Afghanistan, resort to every trick known to man to grab other people's territory? On the other hand, will a revisionist regional power like Pakistan ever give up the frontier areas?

We will discuss this issue in greater detail elsewhere in this book, but for the moment, let this authoritatively delivered verdict by Lord Curzon suffice,

> Frontiers are indeed the razor's edge on which hang suspended the modern issues of war and peace, of life and death to nations.

Some nations are possessive; they are assertive about their land. They zealously guard every inch of it. They are ready to interpret and remould history to suit their case. Curzon must have had such nations in mind when he spoke of frontiers determining 'war and peace, of life and death to nations'.

There is also another category of nations; the well behaved global citizens. As in human behaviour, so at the national level, these nice guys end up as losers. They are few in number, but like India and Afghanistan, they wait and watch as others pinch yet another 'bit' of their 'zameen'.

29

Razor's Edge

THERE IS NO DOUBT THAT geography is a big temptation for the powerful, but there are other factors as well which make a country great. Yet, the greatest of empires have regarded geography as destiny. In the age of sea power that lasted 400 years, from 1602 to the beginning of twentieth century, the great powers competed to control the Eurasian world via the surrounding sea lanes that stretched for 15,000 miles from London to Tokyo.

At the peak of its imperial power near 1900, Great Britain ruled the waves with a fleet of 300 ships and thirty naval bases that ringed the world from the North Atlantic to Hong Kong. Just as the Roman Empire enclosed the Mediterranean, making it *Mare Nostrum* ('Our Sea'), Britain made the Indian Ocean its 'closed sea'.

However, history shows that world orders collapse, and when they do, it is often unexpected, rapid and violent.

One January morning in 1904, Sir Halford Mackinder, the director of London School of Economics, challenged the assumption that sea power would continue to be the basis of great power. No one felt the freezing cold outside as he kept the audience at the Royal Geographical Society entranced with his paper titled 'The Geographical Pivot of History'. At the presentation's conclusion, the society's president termed it 'a brilliancy of description…we have seldom had equalled in this room'.

Mackinder had argued that the future of global power lay not, as most British then imagined, in controlling the global sea lanes, but in controlling a vast land mass he called 'EuroAsia'.

More than a century has passed since then. The world has seen great convulsions in between. In many of them, the regions of Central Asia and Afghanistan have been the chessboard and through them all power has passed steadily to those who control land.

One such convulsion began in 1979 when Zbigniew Brzezinski, the then US national security adviser, persuaded his president, Jimmy Carter, to launch 'Operation Cyclone' with an annual kitty of $500 million. Its aim was to mobilize Islamic militants to attack the Soviet Union in its Central Asian states and defeat the Red Army in Afghanistan.

'We didn't push the Russians to intervene in Afghanistan,' Brzezinski said in 1998, 'but we increased the probability that they would... That secret operation was an excellent idea. Its effect was to draw the Russians into the Afghan trap.'

The US officials were quick to follow up on this political decision. They saw advantage in the mujahideen rebellion which grew after a pro-Moscow government toppled Afghanistan's Daoud Khan government in April 1978. In his memoirs, Robert Gates, then a CIA official and later defence secretary under presidents Bush and Obama, recounts a staff meeting in March 1979 where CIA officials asked whether they should keep the mujahideen going, thereby 'sucking the Soviets into a Vietnamese quagmire'. The meeting agreed to fund them to buy weapons.

Asked about this operation's legacy when it came to creating a militant Islam hostile to the US, Brzezinski was unapologetic. 'What is most important to the history of the world?' he asked. 'The Taliban or the collapse of the Soviet empire?'

Today, not many would subscribe to that view. The Taliban are a continuing menace and Afghanistan remains central to the great power projects. What we are witnessing there is a Hobbesian-type rage of 'all against all'. No one is sure any longer if geography is the issue at all in this state of permanent convulsion in Afghanistan.

There is an even more fundamental shift that is taking place, slowly but surely. The second half of the twentieth century marked a moment in history when there was a global order based on a mix of American idealism and the European concept of 'Balance of Power'. The period from 1991 to 2008 was an 'Age of Optimism' because the Western economies were booming and all the world's major powers had reason to be satisfied with the way the globalized world system was working for them.

However, over the past couple of years, as the US economy began to falter, China's has been growing. A world dominated by the West is giving way to a new order in which economic and political power is much more contested.

In this time of change, the US is engaged in self-doubt. Its interventions in Afghanistan and Iraq have drained American resources and taken its attention away from larger foreign policy issues. There is, therefore, a fundamental tension in the US foreign policy. Must it take the responsibility to intervene in every conflict abroad or keep its focus on preserving the post-World War global structure?

In the space thus created, conflict and tensions are rising. Will America's role in this uncertain world draw on its tradition of exceptionalism? Can the US keep its focus on its military intervention as it did in the past? This seems to be the current American doubt because of a sense of fatigue and disappointment with poor outcomes from recent interventions.

Therefore, neo-isolationism could be the new American norm.

American Architecture

This was not the case earlier. In the post-World War-II period, the US had built two basic architectures to support its international engagement. First was anchored in the global institutions it created. The UN served the US well on political and strategic issues. It endorsed all its major demands; from operations in Iraq to those in Libya.

The Bretton Woods twins of World Bank and International Monetary Fund (IMF) for economy besides the General Agreement on Tariffs and Trade (GATT) for trade ensured that the US was the prima donna on global bread and butter issues.

The US, in the post-War world, was thus in a very happy position. It was the shaper and preserver of a global order presided over by it. And to ensure that this carefully crafted arrangement stayed in place, it had set up a variety of alliances. This was the second part of the two basic architectures it had created. This American pillar was principally grounded in the Western defence system of NATO. But there were other regional military alliances as well.

Therefore, except for the Eastern bloc, the world ticked to the American clock. And when things seemed to fall apart in one part or the other of the world, the US stepped in to rearrange them militarily. This was evident in the resistance organized by the US and Pakistan against the Soviet occupation in Afghanistan. This was also the case when it intervened directly in Afghanistan post 9/11.

That is beginning to change now.

'Post-West World Order'

Over the last few years, the Western world has lost the swagger it once had. It is not a sufficient economic force any longer; its defence budgets have reduced as has the appetite for sending forces to fight other peoples' battles. NATO can still maintain the territorial defence of Europe, but it may not be in a position any longer to sustain financially a long engagement beyond the European borders. In the space vacated by the West, Russia and China are squeezing in, using economic and political pressure to reshape the domestic politics of their neighbours.

The Russian Foreign Minister Sergey Lavrov has gleefully termed the coming change, 'Post-West World Order'.

Lavrov may have been hasty in that pronouncement, but there is no denying the fact that the West is no longer the undisputed leader of the world. In this evolving picture, power and influence are not likely to stem from economic strength alone.

Decisive leadership and the ability to grab strategic opportunity quickly will decide the winners in this new game. Both Russia and China are becoming increasingly more assertive at the global high table. Russian intervention in Syria is one such defining moment. China is setting new rules of engagement through its enormous economic power.

Within the region, the picture is becoming increasingly complex and intense; more players are crowding into the Afghan arena. Pakistan continues to play all sides and all roles with equal ease. Russia is back again courting the Taliban, Pakistan, China and Afghanistan. The US is now at the receiving end of the Islamic militants' violence. And Russia hopes to do to the US in Afghanistan what the Americans had done to the Soviet Union there.

However, it is China that is positioning itself to take the lead role in the region stretching from the furthest steppes of Central Asia to Afghanistan and Pakistan. Its ability to capitalize on resentment of centuries of Western domination should not be underestimated.

It has completed a breathtaking project by laying down an elaborate and enormously expensive network of high-speed, high-volume railroads as well as oil and natural gas pipelines across the vast breadth of Eurasia. And for the first time in history, rapid transcontinental movement of oil, minerals and manufactured goods will be possible on a massive scale. Thereby, Beijing hopes to shift geopolitical power from the maritime periphery deep into the Asian continent's heartland.

As if that was not enough, China is now constructing a massive road-rail-pipeline corridor from western China to the Gwadar Port in Pakistan, creating the logistics for future naval deployments in the energy-rich Arabian Sea.

Where will all this frantic Chinese activity lead to? Will it mean transfer of global power from the US to it?

Despite some speculation by strategy pundits, this is unlikely to happen any time soon. The global system set up by the West in the post-War world is too large and too intricate to be either replaced or taken over easily.

It is true that America's current dilemmas are largely similar to those of Britain when it was the sole global player. But there is one important difference; when Britain was trying to maintain its superpower status its challenge was economic, whereas for the US it is still mainly political. Therefore, the US will continue to play a necessary, perhaps not indispensable, role in carrying a large portion of the burden of creating and maintaining order at the regional and global level. The US is and will remain the most powerful country in the world for decades to come, and no other country has either the capacity or the mindset to build an alternative global order.

But what about the land mass of EuroAsia as Mackinder put it? It is this nerve centre of the world that the Russia-China combine is already dominating. Will the US stand by and watch as these two build their strategic architecture on this foundation? And where does Afghanistan, that 'Graveyard of Empires', fit in this evolving shape? If you look at the map and consider geography as destiny, then Afghanistan, more than Pakistan, seems to hold the strategic key to the Eurasian landmass.

Emerging Dynamics

Undoubtedly, one way or the other, these developments are going to affect

Afghanistan, the frontier areas as also Pakistan. China's role in all three might increase further.

And where does India figure in this picture? Can it make a critical difference in Afghanistan's strategic portrait?

Even if Afghans may want it to, and even though India might wish to play a purposeful role in this 'heart of Asia', as the poet Iqbal once called it, the fact is that the life-giving blood to this heart can only flow through the arteries. In so far as India's trade with Afghanistan is concerned, Pakistan controls these arteries, and it has simply squeezed them shut. In the absence of a land corridor between India and Afghanistan, there are limits to what India can do. In military terms, it means that India cannot put boots on the ground, nor can it be a major arms supplier to Afghanistan.

Pakistan, on the other hand, feels that it is now poised better than at any other time in the past to determine the shape of things in Afghanistan. And it may just be close to the mark this time.

Another factor working in Pakistan's favour is the fact that China is on the verge of reordering Halford Mackinder's assumption that land power should replace sea power.

China specializes in borrowing ideas and bettering them. It is now doing that in the strategic sphere by concentrating both on the sea and land power domination. The Chinese string of pearls on the sea coasts are designed to complement its rail and road networks on land. In both these, Pakistan has a major role. First through its Gwadar Port; from there China can keep a naval eye on freight and war ships passing by. In case of a war or warlike situation in future, India may find this area a difficult passage for its oil supplies from the Gulf.

Second, China is developing economic interests in Afghanistan for its mineral wealth and its strategic location. Pakistan can smoothen its path there in a variety of ways; particularly by keeping the Taliban on a tight leash. Therefore, even as it checks the Taliban against China it will keep unleashing them on the US forces in Afghanistan.

All this will gladden Russia in its desire for *badal* against the US in Afghanistan.

Is there another way of arranging the dynamics in this region—one that keeps the Taliban out of the picture and makes the region secure? The chance for that happening seems bleak, but one way of strengthening Afghanistan will be to correct the historical wrong and restore the frontier areas to it. A reduced Pakistan will not be the global menace that it is now. That changed picture is the only hope for tranquillity in the region. And it is this change that could give the US a lead say in the evolving Eurasia. Otherwise, the US faces a shrinking strategic space as Russia and China wiggle to increase their roles steadily.

How close are these trend lines to the intersection point where China's desire for absolute control will clash with the American denial to it of that complete space? Which way will Russia finally turn—towards mercurial Trump who allegedly wishes to woo it or towards China which has been cosying up to it despite some basic differences? There are other players as well; the Taliban, the Pakistani proxies who are inching towards Kabul yet again.

All this is an incendiary mix. A mix that is made even more dangerous by the fact that the US, Russia, China, India and Pakistan are all nuclear-armed. Moreover, the Taliban and the other terror networks in the Af-Pak region may only be one lucky grab away from acquiring a nuclear weapon.

Are we, therefore, three, five or ten years away from a major crisis in the Pak–Afghan–Central Asia region? That we are somewhere on that path, is unmistakable. Sadly, geography, that big temptation of the powerful, was and remains a curse for Afghanistan. This means that the Pashtuns might remain suspended in the middle of a geostrategic storm. If in this turbulence, they find some moments of calm; those precious few interludes will be balanced on razor's edge.

30

All Pashtuns Are Afghans

MONSTERS DO NOT REFLECT IN mirrors. But if by some miracle they did, Afghans would find reflected a whole line-up of their tormentors. From Alexander to Soviets, Americans and Pakistanis, each one of them has treated Afghanistan and its people shabbily.

In every case, Afghans have fought them stoically. And from each invading force, they have earned the greatest praise for their grit. As a Russian General said in 1987, 'Pashtuns are the bravest people ever born on the earth; these people can't be defeated by force.'

This sentiment was echoed by an American General in 2004, 'We are fighting a meaningless war against the rocks.'

All this praise may sound very heroic, but it has condemned Afghans to a perpetual state of war even in the few moments they are at peace. The result is one long carnival of blood.

This Afghan saga makes sad but fascinating history. It is a pity, however, that Afghans do not have a strong tradition of writing. The few books and other accounts that were written have suffered from the ravages of war and loot. As a result, surmises, rather than certainty, provide rough sketches of its past. To ensure reasonable accuracy, history needs continuity, preservation of records and a seamless chain. But how do you ensure continuity when a land is incessantly punctured by wars? If writers and narrators get killed regularly, history, even oral history, suffers and becomes a jumble of assumptions.

The Afghan historical accounts, such as they are, lack both continuity and proof. In contrast, the British records of the events are many and copious; every major event is covered in great detail, their victories as well as their defeats in Afghanistan. But on seminal issues, like the Durand Agreement, there are no details at all in British writing. Suddenly, their descriptive powers suffer cramps; the detail vanishes, writers flip over the event as if there is an officially sanctioned code of omertà. This amnesia, however, has not blurred the Pathan pain. They have not forgotten that a line drawn casually over a small map divided their people and lands. Pathans have been unable to de-install the injustices of the British Empire from their collective memory because Durand's division continues to bleed them. This was not the case with India, South Africa and many other countries that were divided. They have moved on. But the Afghan hurt simmers; they have not forgiven the collective punishments by the British or those that are now being imposed by Pakistan.

The Pathan response has mostly been emotional and knee-jerk; the code of 'Pashtunwali', the 'way of the Pathan' being their guide. The chief among its aspects is the need for *badal*, revenge, the tribal vendettas that can last generations. *Badal* wreaks its malign curse against foreigners too. It is, therefore, no coincidence that the Waziristan villages that were bombed by the RAF in the 1930s in an attempt to curb jihadist revolt proved readiest to take in al-Qaeda fighters fleeing Afghanistan in 2001. The Haqqani network is among the Afghan Taliban's deadliest elements, but its headquarters have for long been in North Waziristan, on the Pakistani side of the Durand Line.

Yet, despite the strength of their *badal*, the fact is that the tribals have suffered far more. Since Alexander and most other conquerors after him were birds of passage who did not stay long, let us jump straight in time to the nineteenth century and the British interest in the country. In fact, if Mortimer Durand had followed this secret communication of 1892 by the viceroy's office to London, he may not have caused the havoc of his agreement,

> All the Pushtu speaking tribes consider themselves Afghans whether they reside in what is now distinctly the Amir's territory or what is now British territory, or in the intervening hills now occupied by what we call border tribes...they were politically part of Afghanistan till Sikhs annexed them; the fact that these border tribes are independent or semi-independent is nothing new; they were so when the Afghan boundary extended to the Indus, and then there were Governors of the Amir of Kabul in Peshawar and Kohat, and they were so still earlier when the whole of Afghanistan was part of the Mughal Empire. And in

> fact, not only these border tribes which are semi-independent; the same position has generally been held by the mountain tribes in most parts of Afghanistan... These mountain tribes, including those we call border tribes used to say that they were Afghans, and the Amir of Kabul their Amir...*

But Durand and his colleagues refused to recognize the basic truth that all *the Pushtu speaking tribes consider themselves Afghans.*

Greater Afghanistan

They wanted to impose their will on an independent-minded people. The colonial view of Pathan tribals became 'justification for conquest, repression, and, often, the indiscriminate destruction of villages and communities'. British writers, too, often confused nationalist opposition with frenzy. They did not want to acknowledge that the major cause of Pashtun resistance was a desire to preserve their old tribal independence.

These tribal areas were under the influence of British India rather than India and thus did not become a part of either India or Pakistan at independence. As a matter of fact, in the months before the Partition, British officials in a secret note had determined that, 'Pakistan would not have been able to raise any legal objection if the tribes had placed themselves under the protection of Afghanistan or if, with the consent of the tribes, the tribal areas had been annexed by Afghanistan.'

Even after they had left India, the British were not sure as to how to interpret the issue. An illustration of their confusion is a secret document, dated 28 April 1949, which stated that in the light of law, the situation was not clear as to the status of the tribal areas. According to this document, these areas neither belonged to Pakistan nor to Afghanistan, but at the same time, this new situation did not give Afghanistan any rights to extend its territory up to tribal areas without the approval of the latter's population, and the same applied to Pakistan.

However, Afghanistan has been consistent in its stand. Its opposition to the Durand Line has been continuous post-1893, despite regime changes and

*National Archives of India, Foreign Department, secret F, Memo on Afghan Affairs—20 June 1892, 199, August 1892.

revolutions. Selig Harrison mentions in his book, *In Afghanistan's Shadow*, that despite the internal turmoil various Afghan regimes post-1947 have not forgotten to register their claim, 'At various times, Zahir Shah's monarchy, Muhammad Daoud's republic and post-1978 Communist governments in Kabul have all challenged Pakistan's right to rule over its Pashtun areas, alternatively espousing the goal of an autonomous Pashtun state to be created within Pakistan, an independent Pashtunistan to be carved out of Pakistan or a 'Greater Afghanistan', directly annexing the lost territories.'

Soviet support in relation to the Pashtunistan case was also very important for Kabul. On 15 December 1955, Soviet Prime Minister Nikolay Bulganin stated that the Soviet Union supported the Afghan point of view and that a plebiscite should be conducted in the area where the Pashtuns live, '...The demand of Afghanistan that the population of neighbouring Pakhtunistan should be given an opportunity of freely expressing their will is justified... The people of this region have the same right of self-determination as any other people.'

At different points in time, the leaders of the Soviet Union have publicly stated that, 'Pushtuns should decide in a free referendum if they wish to stay in Pakistan, to create a new and independent state, or to unite with Afghanistan.'

US Demurs

However, the American attitude was ambivalent. During the sixties, it pretended that the best solution of the issue was to brush it under the carpet. When President Dwight Eisenhower tried to understand the issue from President Ayub Khan, the latter treated it as a bit of a joke. At their meeting in Karachi on 8 December 1959, Ayub told him, '...it (the frontier issue) went back to the eighteenth century when an Afghan dynasty controlled parts of Pakistan. The British took over the area and later relinquished it to independent Pakistan, and the Afghans claimed that it should revert to them.'*

For good measure, the Field Marshal added that when Afghans had tried to occupy the area by force, Pakistan had killed 300 of their soldiers. That was the end of the matter for Ayub Khan. But the pity is that Eisenhower

*Memorandum of a conversation, US Embassy, Karachi, 8 December 1959.

did not think it fit to probe further. Had he enquired, he would have found that British came close to that area only in 1839, not the eighteenth century as Ayub Khan had said.

Had Eisenhower been impartial in the matter he would have also wondered if Ayub Khan had got his history right when he said, 'it...went back to the eighteenth century when an Afghan dynasty controlled parts of Pakistan.'

However, the US was not interested in probing. It wished to be in the good books of Pakistan because it had promised to fight by its side as an ally.

Afghanistan understood the game. Put in simple terms, Afghans were aware that they were weak and remote and of insignificant strategic importance to the Americans. Pakistan, on the other hand, was the supposed strategic partner. It is another matter that Pakistan duped the US at every turn and on each occasion. It could hardly intercede on America's behalf with the Arabs; it had too many favours of its own to seek. And it turned its face the other way when America asked for its army to be sent to Vietnam. In recent years its role in Afghanistan has aided the Taliban and irritated the US consistently.

Afghanistan, on the other hand, may have proved a steadier and more reliable strategic ally for the US. It was located next to Iran, China and the Soviet Union. Moreover, it would have provided ample manpower for the US military engagements. But the US had decided to court Pakistan.

Therefore, as far as Afghanistan was concerned, the US was in no mood to act as an honest broker or even to give it a patient hearing.

On 27 October 1960, a frustrated Afghan Foreign Minister Naim Khan told the US ambassador bluntly, 'He (Naim) felt there was really no need to again give me (US Ambassador) detailed explanation of their feelings as regards Pushtunistan issue. He felt that there were "too many ready ears" in the US who automatically sympathized with Pakistan. He felt that every premeditated move of Pakistan was made with view to the propaganda it would receive, particularly in America. He felt that as a nation we were "somewhat unilateral" in our thinking on this problem and he supposed this not surprising as we and Pakistan were allies.'*

Could there be greater indictment than this of a country that claimed

*Telegram, US embassy in Afghanistan to the Department of State, 27 October 1960.

to be the moral leader of the world?

The US did not wish to sour its relations with Pakistan, so it just about listened to Afghanistan's complaints. The only reason why it even cared to listen was the fear of pushing Afghanistan into Soviet embrace. It was the same colonial logic looping all over again, though this time in a democratic garb.

However, the Soviets were interested. They came into Afghanistan; first via aid offers and then militarily. It was during this phase that Afghan President Hafizullah Amin was encouraged to claim '...unity for all Afghans from the Oxus to the Indus.' In his opinion, Pushtunistan belonged to 'Great Afghanistan'.

Similarly, Amin's successor Babrak Karmal called for the re-unification of all Pashtuns. He said the NWFP, was 'the sacred land'.

However, the US was still not convinced. It had been pampering Pakistan with arms and money from the very beginning. It was Jinnah who first suggested a transactional relationship based on Pakistan's strategic geographical location and its presumed role in the Islamic world. Soon after the creation of Pakistan, Jinnah asked the US for $2 billion in military and financial aid. The US considered the request and gave Pakistan $10 million.

Ever since, the US has kept its side of the bargain in the vain hope that its trust will one day be reciprocated. But Pakistan has consistently fallen short of America's expectations. It did not send its soldiers to fight in America's wars. And the guns that the US supplied to Pakistan in this millennium were not used to eliminate terrorists, but were trained via the Taliban at the American soldiers. Sometimes, ISI agents themselves got into the fray as in Kunduz.

But Pakistan joined in enthusiastically when American drones targeted areas in the frontier. It wanted the terrorists hiding there to be eliminated because they were fighting against the Pakistani army. If civilians died in the process, Pakistan readily agreed with the US that such collateral damage was unintentional.

It may have been so, but once again the victims were the Pathans.

31

An Incomplete State

THE FRONTIER THAT MORTIMER CARVED for the British Empire remains a live, unresolved problem. Pakistan claims the Durand Line constitutes a natural border; Afghanistan sees it as an illegitimate colonial imposition.

Given these two diametrically opposite positions, what does the future hold for Afghanistan, and more particularly for the Pashtuns? Will the scrapping of the Durand Line remain the unfinished agenda of the Pathan complaint against Pakistan?

A lot will depend on the jostling among foreign powers. If that be the case and if we assume the result of that tussle among the Taliban, the US, Russia, China, Pakistan, Iran and India would be extended conflict over many years, then the chance of peace or some form of normality coming to the region is slim.

Meanwhile, the country has undergone some change.

Unlike in the previous two centuries, Pashtuns have not remained rooted to their soil in recent decades. They have fled during wars in large numbers. Two of the largest exodus happened during the Soviet occupation of Afghanistan and during the Taliban rule over it.

Over the course of the last forty years, they have scattered like autumn leaves wherever they were granted refuge. As a result, Afghans have been dispersed so far and wide that they belong everywhere and nowhere. They live there indifferently and uncertainly at the whims of their local hosts. The greatest majority have migrated to different parts of Pakistan. There they live in slums; where they are increasingly being racially profiled and hounded by the security agencies.

Every bomb blast in Pakistan becomes an excuse for police raids on Afghan homes. Even the Pathans from the frontier and Khyber are under search and suspicion.

To add to their woes, Afghans living in Pakistan are now being repatriated en masse back to Afghanistan. There, they face the grim prospect of starting life all over again.

In a single lifetime, they would have lived twice the life of exile; first away from their homes and a second time upon return to a land that no longer seems like their home, because others may have taken it over in the meanwhile. This carries the risk of mass anger bursting over.

So the future remains uncertain for Pashtuns and for the powers that seek to decide their destiny.

But do these powers have a standard formula to control the region? In the past the British had one. A Pakistani commentator Rafia Zakaria writes, 'Amid the details of negotiations and agreements, and the complications of competing interests, it is easy to forget that the demarcation of borders was seen as a central instrument of colonial control… In this sense, the co-option of the "barbaric" tribesmen presented a final frontier in the act of colonial domination… Like the British of old, the Americans today consider Afghanistan as a moral evil that must be fought in order to proclaim their global power.'

This observation must have carried great validity when America was the sole superpower and seemed to be winning in Afghanistan, but times have changed since then. The US is no longer the sole superpower. Its will is being challenged like never before, and it is in a defensive mode already in Afghanistan. How can it alone set the rules if there are other powers in almost equal play?

Moreover, when there is more than one power competing for the same space, truth becomes the first casualty. Fact and fiction merge to create a landscape of smoke and mirrors. A word given by a nation may not always mean what it was supposed to.

Even as a great power is engaged in the act of gobbling up a state, it window dresses its narrow self-interest as global good. The unfortunate reality is that in the great power rivalry it is the smaller states that suffer. But it can also happen that an angry people may succeed in making the bigger power retreat. It happened to the US in Vietnam and to the Soviet Union in Afghanistan. It could happen to any of the powers now in fray in Afghanistan.

Fundamentalism Takes Hold

But the interference of powers can have unintended consequences as well. Once the frontier area was placid and its people welcoming of the foreigner. Since then, they have been scarred repeatedly by foreigners. Yet, despite their tragedies, they remain hospitable because Pashtuns are a trusting lot essentially. That's why the Islam practised by Pashtun tribes in the earlier centuries was predominantly mystical, Sufi and pacific. In the works of the seventeenth century writers such as Rahman Baba, it spawned not bloodshed, but an intense lyric poetry.

How did this tradition mutate?

It was a long and complex process, the foundation of which was the division of Pashtun lands and the resentment against mass punishments. To compensate for their weakness against a superior force, the tribals turned to religion. Since the softer Sufi versions would not do, the import of Wahhabi theology via the madrasah at Deoband came in handy. But underlying it and making that possible was resistance to colonialism in general, and the Durand Line in particular. The shift to a more militant version of Islam provided the tribal leaders with their vocabulary and their ideological rallying point.

The fostering of jihadist militancy was not the sole end of the Durand Line's consequences. It also went on to foster the 'Pashtunistan' movement—a political campaign to reunite the Pashtuns on either side of the border.

On a national scale, wars, foreign interference and occupation—first by the Soviet Union and then by the US—provided Afghans with a cause; the hatred of the occupier and the need for unity.

The Soviet occupation led to mass incubation of the the Taliban and sundry other variants of extremism. After 9/11, the al-Qaeda and Taliban simply shifted their bases and bided their time. As Karzai said, 'The fact is that the US presence in Afghanistan has not brought security to us. It has caused more extremism.'*

Afghanistan today can be described as a strong nation but a weak state, while Pakistan is a strong state with no strong sense of nationhood. Each, therefore, has different sets of vulnerabilities and different constituencies to satisfy. Afghanistan's current central government is institutionally fragile, but this weakness is counterbalanced by a strong sense of national unity that has

---

**The Wall Street Journal*, 27 January 2017.

developed among its people over the past thirty years.

Even in the absence of a state administration in Kabul, Afghans never feared that their country might disintegrate. By contrast, Pakistan never developed a secure national identity. It has been preoccupied throughout its short history by fears of internal disintegration.

Are we then facing a crossroads where one or the other may lose direction? Well, the path ahead certainly seems to be fraught and it has a lot to do with the recent past. As a Pakistani commentator said, 'Afghanistan does not see Pakistan as a friend—it never has and, perhaps, it never will. More than the realities of international relations, this fact is rooted in how Afghans define their identity. Ever since Pakistan was created, Afghanistan has defined its identity in opposition to its neighbour.'*

Therefore, far more than the games that the big powers decide to play in Afghanistan, its future may be hinged to the convulsions that shape Pakistan.

---

*Zaigham Khan, 'Afghanistan reloaded', *The News*; 13 March 2017.

32

Nobody Fishes in the Middle

IN ONE OF HIS MANY prescriptions for the region, Rudyard Kipling wrote, 'Asia is not going to be civilized after the methods of the West. There is too much Asia and she is too old.'

Kipling was right to stress that Asia needs Asian solutions. This logic could be extended to say that Afghanistan needs Afghan solutions. Any external influence will sooner or later result in some form of imposition. And habitually Afghans resist imposition.

Had Pakistan wished, it had many opportunities to press Afghanistan to recognize the Durand Line. It could have pressed the issue as part of the Agreement in 1988 which ended the Soviet occupation of Afghanistan. But it did not. Nor did it press the Taliban regime sufficiently to sign on the dotted line.

Ahmed Rashid writes in his book, *Descent into Chaos*, that maintaining ambiguity was a deliberate choice of the Pakistan army. It was a part of President Zia-ul-Haq's vision to achieve strategic depth vis-à-vis India. Zia's strategic plan embraced a Pakistani reach right up to and including Central Asia. Had he been successful, he would have outdone the British Empire.

However, the key to his strategy was to leave the issue of the Durand Line unsettled. That would give the flexibility to avoid international scrutiny if and when he needed to send his forces across the line. A recognized border, on the other hand, would have entailed respecting international law.

Unfortunately, like the British, the Pakistani view of the frontier area has been informed by its military considerations. Territory rather than the people living there are of primary consequence. But the Pakistani idea of strategic depth is untested and ephemeral.

Can a fragile state provide long-term stability to a region many times larger than it? Can a state that has lived on foreign funding throughout its existence provide the billions needed for running the poor countries of Central Asia besides Afghanistan? Strategic depth also presumes that Pakistan will enforce strategic calm over these unruly lands. Does Pakistan have the military wherewithal and vast amounts of spare cash to sustain a force of occupation, because essentially strategic depth would involve occupation.

Moreover, as occupiers, Pakistan would have to face unbridled Afghan hostility of the sort that no previous conqueror has faced before. Simply put, Afghans consider Pakistan an enemy state.

Ahmed Rashid also talks of discussions among ISI officers to create a broad 'Talibanized belt' in FATA. To their military mind, the scheme promises multiple benefits. It will keep pressure on Afghanistan to bend to Pakistani wishes, keep the US forces under threat while maintaining their dependence on Pakistani goodwill, and create a buffer zone between Afghan and Pakistani Pashtuns. According to this ISI calculation, such a Talibanized Pashtun population along the border would pose a threat to Afghan government and the US, but no threat to Pakistan!

Recent events have, however, proved that this ISI arithmetic was wrong. To paraphrase Hillary Clinton's famous rebuke to Pakistan, a snake bites whoever crosses its path. And Pakistan learnt this to its bitter cost when it carried out military operations one after the other, first in South and then in the North Waziristan.

Hillary Clinton was not the only American leader to talk of snakes and mistakes.

In 1957, a few years after heavy US military and financial involvement in Pakistan began, President Eisenhower remarked that the military commitment to Pakistan was 'perhaps the worst kind of a plan and decision we could have made. It was a terrible error, but we now seem hopelessly involved in it.'

Sixty years later, little has changed. Successive US administrations and Congresses have colluded with the Pakistani army and intelligence services to maintain their oversized, dysfunctional roles in Pakistan and South Asia. In all these years, US governments have acknowledged that they have been double crossed repeatedly by Pakistanis, yet they remain drawn to it like moths to a flame. It is this certainty of US support which makes the likes of ISI agents, the type that Rashid talks about, feel confident that one day Pakistan will have the strategic depth in Afghanistan that it chases.

It is still not clear whether after years of military bombardment, the frontier areas have been cleared of terrorists and cleansed of the 'Talibanized belt' that the Pakistani military once wanted to create there. But what is obvious is the hardship and privations that ordinary residents have had to go through. They have been driven away from their homes and there are complaints already that the Pakistani army is trying to change the demographic complexion by settling Punjabis in some of the tribal areas. This would be a sure recipe for further strife as and when the tribals return in their full strength to reclaim their lands.

Recasting FATA

When they return, they will find some other changes too. They would see hectic construction activity aimed at shutting them out from their Afghan kin. In contrast to Zia's policy, the Pakistani government is now building a wall along the Durand Line, permanently dividing the fifty million Pashtuns who had so far criss-crossed freely.

They may also find that FATA, as they had been used to calling the conglomeration of their seven agencies, is no longer the same and has been merged with Khyber Pakhtunkhwa (KPK) in their absence.

This KPK was once called NWFP. Interestingly, NWFP had originally included the districts of Multan, Mianwali, Bahawalpur and Dera Ghazi Khan as well, as these areas had formed part of Afghanistan from 1747 until the 1820s, when Maharaja Ranjit Singh took possession of them. It was a consequence of the Durand Line that the British carved out the new province of NWFP in 1901 from out of the areas that had been wrested from Afghanistan (from the foothills to the Line).

In 1955, Pakistan decided to abolish the provinces and introduce the 'one unit' system (in West Pakistan) comprising Punjab, NWFP, Sind and Balochistan. However, this proved to be an unpopular move and in 1970 the 'one unit' system was dissolved. Once again, the previous system of old provinces was revived. But in this new arrangement the four districts mentioned above were excluded from NWFP. Instead they were included in Punjab, resulting in a reduced NWFP. This was another blow to Pashtuns.

Had the four districts remained with NWFP, then it, rather than Punjab, would have been the dominant force in Pakistan.

Though all this is a bit complicated, the Pathans remember it all; from the time Durand duped the Amir to the different incarnations of their land. But one thing has remained constant through all these changes; and that is their misery.

Ninety-seven per cent of FATA's 3.5 million people live in rural areas. Sixty per cent of them fall below the poverty line and their literacy rate is only 17 per cent. The employment rate is just about 20 per cent. These dismal statistics are bound to be so because the state views them with suspicion. As *The Guardian* wrote in 2009, 'Bodies have been dumped throughout the valley—bloated corpses have been found floating down the rivers while others dangle from electricity poles with notes warning of dire consequences... According to eyewitnesses and the Human Rights Commission of Pakistan, the army and state paramilitaries have carried out reprisal killings on a mass scale.'*

It is, of course, true that the history of such mass punishment in the Pakhtun areas goes back to the British times. The Murderous Outrages Regulation was enacted in 1867 to give the government additional powers to prosecute serious crimes such as murder. It was re-enacted with minor changes in 1877 as the Ghazi Act for its use in the Pashtun-inhabited frontier districts.

But this Regulation was found to be inadequate to contain Pashtun opposition to British rule, so new acts were added to it from time to time. The regulation took its present form primarily through the Frontier Crimes Regulation of 1901. In 1947, Pakistan added the clause that residents can be arrested without specifying the crime. By this addition, the Regulation permits collective punishment of the family or tribe members for crimes of individuals.

These mass punishments continue to be practised even now. When an army major was killed in Miranshah Bazaar in 2016, the entire bazaar was bombed out by the Pakistani army.

That apart, the larger question that the international community needs

*Mustafa Qadri, 'Spectre of tribal punishment haunts Swat', *The Guardian*; 3 October 2009.

to face is whether it has a responsibility to protect the tribals and their way of life. Must Pashtunwali be trampled upon by external impositions; first by the British and now by the Pakistan army's jackboot?

An Incomplete State

W.K. Fraser-Tytler had spent thirty-one years between 1910 and 1941 in the frontier area as a British administrator and diplomat. He is generally credited with a balanced view, which is largely reflected in his book, *Afghanistan: A Study of Political Developments in Central Asia.* As the book was published in 1950, Fraser-Tytler had the double benefit of having viewed the region before, during and after the creation of Pakistan. His remarks about the future of Pathans in the concluding chapter of his book are pertinent:

> Unfortunately the Pathan races, which make up the ruling portion of the Afghan nation, have spilled over their mountain boundaries and spread down into the plains, so that in large areas of Pakistan dwell a people whose affinities are with Kabul, so far as they are with anybody, and not with Karachi (incidentally Karachi was then the capital of Pakistan. Tytler's allusion here is to the country and not to the city of Karachi). As it stands at present behind the artificial boundary of the Durand line, Afghanistan is ethnographically, economically and geographically an incomplete state.

More recently, in 2007, a conference by the American Institute of Afghanistan Studies and the Hollings Center in Istanbul reached a similar consensus. It acknowledged that,

> No Afghan government ever accepted the Durand Line as an international border. This refusal has continued for more than a century under regimes of all political stripes, some of which called for the reincorporation of the territory into Afghanistan or the creation of a new state of Pashtunistan.

In an article written in April 2008 for the magazine *ARI,* Selig Harrison mentions, 'If history is a reliable guide, the prospects for the survival of the Pakistani state in its present form, with its existing configuration of constituent ethno-linguistic groups, cannot be taken for granted.'

As one example in support of his claim, he says, 'The ideologues of Pakistani nationalism exalt the historical memory of Akbar and Aurangzeb as the symbols of a lost Islamic grandeur in South Asia. By contrast, for the Baluchis, Sindhis and Pashtuns, the Moghuls are remembered primarily as the symbols of past oppression.'

Pakistan may or may not be a broken project, but the world handles it gingerly as a neighbourhood drunk. Therefore, logic is unlikely to help with this irrational state, and Pakistan will continue its aggression against Afghanistan to keep it weak.

However, Afghanistan presents a different picture. Despite the collapse of central authority and the rise of ethnically based militias in the 1990s during the Afghan civil war, the country never experienced the threat of partition because none of the factions saw this as a useful outcome. Each wanted a stronger position within the Afghan polity, rather than independence from the Afghan state or amalgamation with co-ethnics in neighbouring states. This was because Afghans' sense of national unity, particularly after their success in the anti-Soviet war, was rooted less in ethnicity than in the will to persist together, united by common experience.

Therefore, the question regarding Afghanistan's future has to be nuanced differently. It is not a matter of the Afghan desire or will, because they will want to stay together. It is more a question of how fierce is the foreign ill wind? Will it scatter yet another generation of Afghans across the world?

Global Environment

There the prognosis is uncertain. In recent years, the democratic order in the world has weakened. Economic conditions are hardly encouraging, nationalism and protectionism are on the rise, and generally speaking, the political leadership is either weak or authoritarian.

This is the type of global environment where revisionist powers sense advantage. Moreover, such powers with large military capabilities make use of them when they believe the possible gains outweigh the risks and costs.

Russia has invaded two neighbouring states—Georgia in 2008 and Ukraine in 2014—and in both cases it hived off portions of those two nations' territory. China has settled its land boundary with most of its neighbours to its advantage, gaining thousands of square kilometres of territory in each case. It is now expanding its claim in the South China Sea.

Strategically, another opportunity beckons both Russia and China. But they should also remember what Osama bin Laden said in a video message in 2004, 'All we have to do is send two mujahideen...and raise a piece of cloth on which is written al-Qaeda... It is enough to cause America human, economic & political losses.' The same al-Qaeda tactic was the cause of grief for the Soviets in Afghanistan. And it could very well happen to Russia-China combine if one or both decide to send in forces there. However, there is also the chance that the dice might fall in their favour. If Afghanistan comes into their sphere of influence, as Durand might have termed it and with Iran and Pakistan as their allies, we might then be seeing the *grand finale* of the Great Game part II.

Perhaps, we might even see a replay of what Sir Walter Bullivant, head of British intelligence, said to Sir Richard Hannay, the hero of *Greenmantle*, before despatching him to prevent the spark: 'There is a dry wind blowing through the East, the parched grasses wait the spark. And the wind is blowing towards the Indian frontier...'

That was fiction. Alas, the reality on the northwest frontier could be stranger than fiction. As a Russian General of nineteenth century put it, 'Of the twenty-one attempted invasions of India over the centuries from the north and the west, eighteen were successful.'

The Great Game was about preventing the nineteenth successful invasion of India. Are we in a better position today to prevent that feared nineteenth? Alas, the answer to that is slightly iffy. A bit like, perhaps we can. The reason for that hesitation is the nature of threats. Unlike in the past, the dangers now are many, and they could come singly, in a combination of two states or a state supported by non-state actors. And they need not all come through Afghanistan as was mostly the case in the past. Therefore, the prospects for India in this Great Game part II are a proportion of multiple external factors.

Or to give another, more concrete example, India might get the great power largesse once in a while to mollify it on one ground or the other and also to spur us into some action. Philip Zelikow, former State Department official and the then adviser to Secretary of State Condoleezza Rice, recently disclosed that the initial motivation for the timing of the Indo-US nuclear deal was the US decision to supply F-16s to Pakistan. 'What's the side thing we can do with India that will mitigate the impact or the decision to go ahead with F-16s to Pakistan?' This was the question that the state department asked itself.

Zelikow provides this answer. A decision was taken to cut the 'Gordian knot' and 'take the nuclear issue head on'. From the US perspective, the nuclear deal was at one level about deflecting recurring Indian concerns and political backlash to its Pakistan policy, and, at a more ambitious level about shaping India's rise, the texture and future geopolitical direction of its regional and global roles.

Again, to quote Zelikow, the deal was a 'long-term geopolitical bet' on India 'becoming a great power' that would 'shape the future of the Eurasian landmass in a positive direction'.

The follow-up question that the state department forgot to ask itself could have been along these lines. How can India shape the future of the Eurasian landmass without having connectivity with it?

India's hope for access to Afghanistan and beyond through the Iranian route has its limitations. Chahbahar is unlikely to be India's strategic promise that it once was hoped to be. Besides Iran's own distractions, Gwadar's operation as Sino-Pak naval base has affected these strategic calculations. India's access to and from Chahbahar and even for its trade with Gulf will now have to contend with Gwadar's naval watch. Moreover, in the past during critical times, Iran has always sided with Pakistan. Therefore, Pakistan holds the key to India's land connectivity with Afghanistan.

But it has defied all pressure so far and has refused to give transit rights to Indian goods being shipped to Afghanistan or further to Central Asia. It is least likely now to facilitate any project that gives India a major strategic role in Afghanistan or in the Eurasian landmass. And Pakistan is unlikely ever to allow Indian arms to be carried across its territory to Afghanistan. Even if Pakistan were to magically change its character and approve the transit of harmless non-military goods, it takes years for a long-term, viable economic relationship to be built up between countries. Alas, that luxury of time may not be available.

On the Brink of Eternity

Regardless of the shape that the global economy takes, and irrespective of the temper of the world leaders, the prospects for peace and quiet in Afghanistan remain slim. The next invasion there or the next takeover of Kabul by the Taliban is not beyond the realm of the possible.

So to limit our crystal ball to a single outcome will be unwise. Many futures beckon Afghanistan; most of them leading to trick lanes. Perhaps that is the Afghan destiny. As Lord Ronaldshay wrote once, 'The life of a frontiersman is hard. He treads daily on the brink of eternity...'

Sadly, that's how it is likely to remain.

But let's give the last word to an American. Milt Bearden, a former CIA agent, described the Afghan predicament in this manner, 'There is a lake near Webster, Massachusetts called Chargoggagoggmanchauggagoggchaubunagungamaugg. Translated from the original Nipmuck, it lays down this thoughtful code for keeping peace: "You fish on your side, I fish on my side, nobody fishes in the middle."'*

He goes on to add, 'Halfway around the globe, there is a place called the Federally Administered Tribal Areas (FATA) of Pakistan, seven so-called tribal "agencies" along the border between Pakistan and Afghanistan where about six million of the most independent humans on the planet live on 27,000 square kilometres of rugged and inhospitable terrain.

'They are the Pashtuns, and they have lived on their lands without interruption or major migration for about 20,000 years. They know their neighbourhood very well, and their men have been armed to the teeth since the first bow was strung. Their ancient code involves a commitment to hospitality, revenge and the honour of the tribe. They are invariably described as your best friend or worst enemy.'

The former CIA agent has summed up the frontier people well. He is also right in believing that the tribes there would like to live life on their own terms, just like the people of Webster. But, will the world allow them to live by that thoughtful code for keeping peace?

**International Herald Tribune*, 31 March 2004.

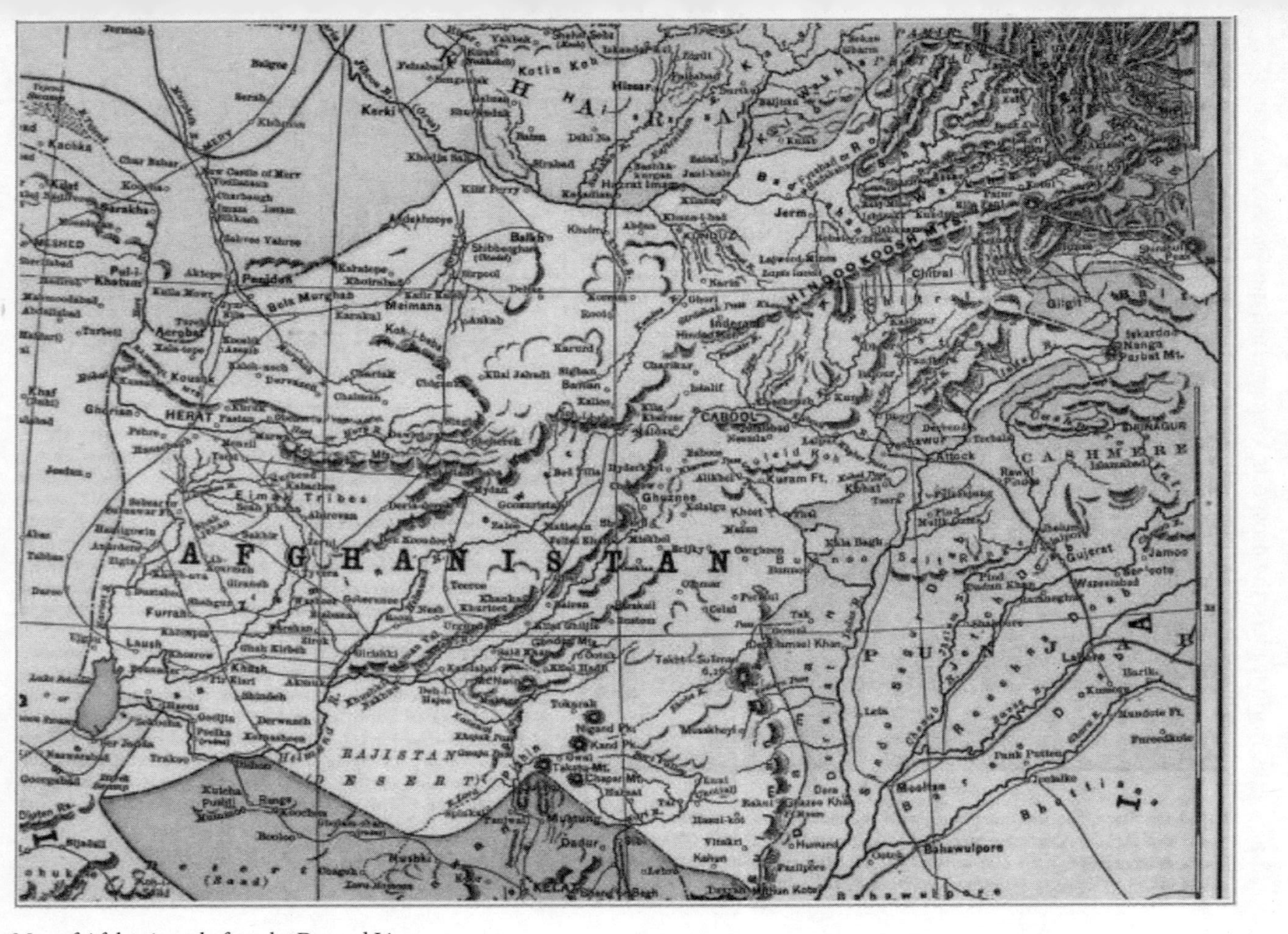

Map of Afghanistan before the Durand Line

Source: Library of Congress, http://memory.loc.gov/cgi-bin/map_item.pl?data=/home/www/data/gmd/gmd7/g7630/g7630/ct001040.jp2&itemLink=

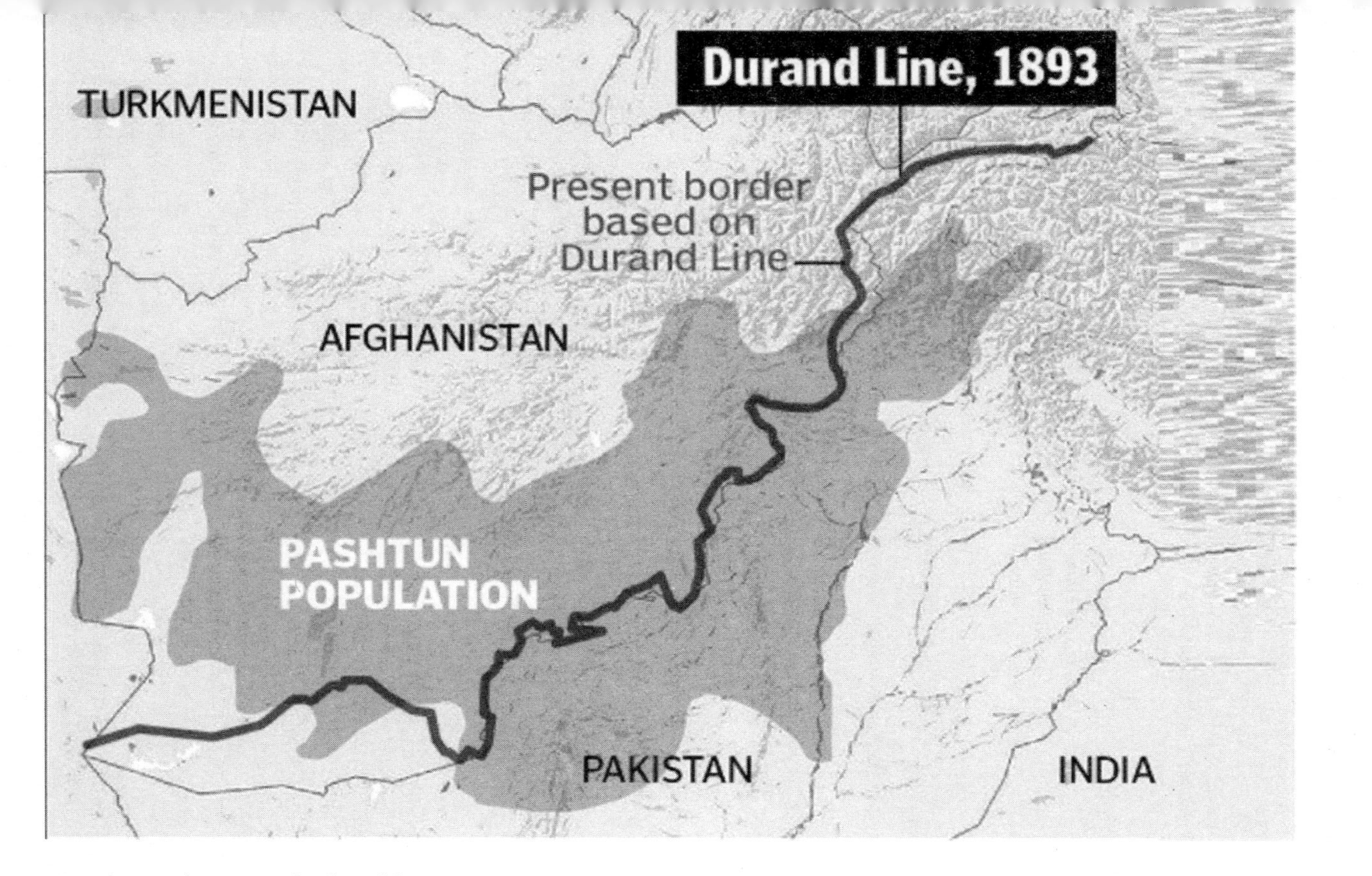

Map of Durand Line as it divides Afghanistan

Source: 'Sensational book on Durand Line coming soon', Afghanistan Times, 15 February 2017, http://afghanistantimes.af/sensational-book-on-durand-line-coming-soon/

Annexure-I

Agreement Demarcating Northern Part of Afghan Boundary with Russia*

Whereas the British Government has represented to His Highness the Amir that the Russian Government presses for the literal fulfillment of the Agreement of 1873 between Russia and England by which it was decided that the river Oxus should form the northern boundary of Afghanistan from Lake Victoria (Wood's Lake) or Sarikul on the east to the junction of the Kokcha with the Oxus, and where as the British Government considers itself bound to abide by the terms of this agreement, if the Russian Government equally abides by them, His Highness Amir Abdur Rahman Khan, G.C.S.I., Amir of Afghanistan and its Dependencies, wishing to show his friendship to the British Government and his readiness to accept their advice in matters affecting his relations with Foreign Powers, hereby agrees that he will evacuate all the districts held by him to the north of this portion of the Oxus on the clear understanding that all the districts lying to the south of this portion of the Oxus and not now in his possession, be handed over to him in exchange. And Sir Henry Mortimer Durand, K.C.I.E., C.S.I., Foreign Secretary to the Government of India, hereby declares on the part of the British Government that the transfer to His Highness the Amir of the said districts lying to the south of Oxus is an essential part of this transaction, and undertakes that arrangements will be made with the Russian Government to carry out the transfer of the said lands to the north and south of the Oxus.

**Source:* National Archives of India, Foreign Department, Secret F, Report by H.M. Durand, 1894, 37–38.

Annexure-II

Durand Line Agreement, 12 November 1893*

Agreement between Amir Abdur Rahman Khan, G.C.S.I., and Sir Henry Mortimer Durand, K.C.I.E., C.S.I.

Whereas certain questions have arisen regarding the frontier of Afghanistan on the side of India, and whereas both His Highness the Amir and the Government of India are desirous of settling these questions by friendly understanding, and of fixing the limit of their respective spheres of influence, so that for the future there may be no difference of opinion on the subject between the allied Governments, it is hereby agreed as follows:

1. The eastern and southern frontier of his Highness's dominions, from Wakhan to the Persian border, shall follow the line shown in the map attached to this agreement.
2. The Government of India will at no time exercise interference in the territories lying beyond this line on the side of Afghanistan, and His Highness the Amir will at no time exercise interference in the territories lying beyond this line on the side of India.
3. The British Government thus agrees to His Highness the Amir retaining Asmar and the valley above it, as far as Chanak. His Highness agrees, on the other hand, that he will at no time exercise interference in Swat, Bajaur, or Chitral, including the Arnawai or Bashgal valley. The British Government also agrees to leave to His Highness the Birmal tract as shown in the detailed map already given to his Highness, who

*_Source:_ National Archives of India, Foreign Department, Secret F, Report by H.M. Durand, 1894, 37–38.

relinquishes his claim to the rest of the Waziri country and Dawar. His Highness also relinquishes his claim to Chageh.

4. The frontier line will hereafter be laid down in detail and demarcated, wherever this may be practicable and desirable, by joint British and Afghan commissioners, whose object will be to arrive by mutual understanding at a boundary which shall adhere with the greatest possible exactness to the line shown in the map attached to this agreement, having due regard to the existing local rights of villages adjoining the frontier.
5. With reference to the question of Chaman, the Amir withdraws his objection to the new British cantonment and concedes to the British Government the rights purchased by him in the Sirkai Tilerai water. At this part of the frontier the line will be drawn as follows: From the crest of the Khwaja Amran range near the Psha Kotal, which remains in British territory, the line will run in such a direction as to leave Murgha Chaman and the Sharobo spring to Afghanistan, and to pass half-way between the New Chaman Fort and the Afghan outpost known locally as Lashkar Dand. The line will then pass half-way between the railway station and the hill known as the Mian Baldak, and, turning southwards, will rejoin the Khwaja Amran range, leaving the Gwasha Post in British territory, and the road to Shorawak to the west and south of Gwasha in Afghanistan. The British Government will not exercise any interference within half a mile of the road.
6. The above articles of agreement are regarded by the Government of India and His Highness the Amir of Afghanistan as a full and satisfactory settlement of all the principal differences of opinion which have arisen between them in regard to the frontier; and both the Government of India and His Highness the Amir undertake that any differences of detail, such as those which will have to be considered hereafter by the officers appointed to demarcate the boundary line, shall be settled in a friendly spirit, so as to remove for the future as far as possible all causes of doubt and misunderstanding between the two Governments.
7. Being fully satisfied of His Highness's goodwill to the British Government, and wishing to see Afghanistan independent and strong, the Government of India will raise no objection to the purchase and import by His Highness of munitions of war, and they will themselves grant him some help in this respect. Further, in order to mark their sense

of the friendly spirit in which His Highness the Amir has entered into these negotiations, the Government of India undertake to increase by the sum of six lakhs of rupees a year the subsidy of twelve lakhs now granted to His Highness.

H.M. Durand,
Amir Abdur Rahman Khan
Kabul, November 12, 1893

Acknowledgements

My mother was my first teacher. It was just two simple words that she repeated to me over and over again. She had faith in them because she and her larger family had used them as Guru Mantra to shake off the dust of the Partition. For me, it became a tough act to follow because 'Self Respect' isn't easy to practice when shortcuts tempt. It also means working harder than everyone else with uncertain results. And it made me reach out for more, when good could have been enough.

But 'life experience' need not be the monopoly of the old. Kapish Mehra, the Managing Director of Rupa, is an example of grace and dignity. Both he and Yamini Chowdhury, the cheerful and competent Senior Commissioning Editor of Rupa, overwhelmed me with their faith. It is their persistence and constant encouragement that led to *Durand's Curse*. Otherwise, I thought I had done my bit for non-fiction by writing *Where Borders Bleed*, and that it was time for me to turn to writing fiction again. Kapish and Yamini have been the supportive muses one can only dream of. This book owes its existence to their confidence that it must be written.

Bibliography

While care has been taken to give attribution in the text to the source, any omission is inadvertent.

A.C. Yate. 1887. *England and Russia Face to Face in Asia: Travels with the Afghan Boundary Commission*. Edinburgh: William Blackwood and Sons.

A.H. McMahon. 1909. *Letters on the Baluch-Afghan Boundary Commission 1896*. Calcutta: Baptist Mission Press. http://digitalcommons.unl.edu/cgi/viewcontent.cgi?article=1011&context=afghanenglish

A.Z. Hilali. 2005. *U.S.-Pakistan Relationship: Soviet Invasion of Afghanistan*. Hampshire, UK: Ashgate Publishing Limited.

Abdul Samad Ghaus. 1988. *The Fall of Afghanistan: An Insider's Account*. Washington, D.C.: Pergamon-Brassey's International Defense Publishers.

Ahmed Rashid. 2008. *Descent into Chaos*. London: Allen Lane.

Alfred C. Lyall, 'British Frontiers and Protectorates', *The Review of Reviews*, August 1891.

Amin Tarzi. 2006. 'Historical Relationship Between State and Non-State Judicial Sectors in Afghanistan', Washington, D.C.: United States Institute of Peace.

Arif Hussain. 1966. *Pakistan: Its Ideology and Foreign Policy*. London: Cass.

Arnold Fletcher. 1965. *Afghanistan: A Highway of Conquest*. Ithaca, New York: Cornell University Press.

Benjamin Hopkins. 2008. *The Making of Modern Afghanistan*. New York: Palgrave Macmillan.

Bijan Omrani, Frank Ledwidge, 'Rethinking the Durand Line. The Legality of the Afghani-Pakistani Frontier', *RUSI Journal*, Vol. 154, No. 5, October 2009.

Brad L. Brasseur. 2011. 'Recognizing the Durand Line. A Way Forward for Afghanistan and Pakistan', The East West Institute Report, New York.

C.E. Yate. 1888. *Northern Afghanistan; or, Letters From the Afghan Boundary Commission*. Edinburgh: William Blackwood and Sons.

C.M. MacGregor. 1873. *Central Asia, Vol. 1: A Contribution towards the Better Knowledge of the Topography, Ethnography, Statistics and History of the North-West Frontier of British India*. Calcutta, India: Government Central Branch Press.

C.S. Jha. 1983. *From Bandung to Tashkent: Glimpses of Indian Foreign Policy*. New Delhi: Sangam Books.

Charles Allen. 2000. *Plain Tales From The Raj: Images of British India in the 20th Century (New Edition)*. London: Little Brown Book Group.

Christian Tripodi. 2011. *Edge of Empire: the British Political Officer and Tribal Administration on the North-West Frontier, 1877-1947*. Farnham: Ashgate.

Christine Noelle. 1997. *State and Tribe in Nineteenth-Century Afghanistan: The Reign of Amir Dost Muhammad Khan (1826-1863)*. Padstow, Cornwall: Curzon Press.

D.C. Fosbery, 'The Umbeyla Expedition', *RUSI Journal*, Vol. 11, 1868.

D.S. Richards. 1990. *The Savage Frontier: A History of the Anglo-Afghan Wars*. London: Macmillan.

E.G. Hastings. 1880. *Genealogical Tree of the Peshawari Tree of the Kandahari Sardars of the Barakzai Family*. Lahore: Government Printing and Stationery Office.

Edgar O'Ballance. 2003. *Afghan Wars: Battles in a Hostile Land: 1839 to the Present*. New York: Oxford University Press.

Eliza Griswold, 'In the Hiding Zone', *The New Yorker*, 26 July 2004.

Farzana Shaikh. 2009. *Making sense of Pakistan*. London: Columbia University Press.

Frances Stevenson. 1971. *Lloyd George: A Diary by Frances Stevenson*. New York: Harper & Row (1st U.S. ed.).

Frank Clements. 2003. *Conflict in Afghanistan: A Historical Encyclopedia*. Santa Barbara, CA: ABC-CLIO, Inc.

Frank Martin. 1907. *Under an Absolute Ruler*. London: Harper & Brothers.

Frederic Grare. 2006. 'Pakistan-Afghanistan Relations in the Post-9/11 Era'. Washington, D.C.: Carnegie Endowment for International Peace. http://www.carnegieendowment.org/files/cp72_grare_final.pdf

G.J. Younghusband, 'The Permanent Pacification of the Indian Frontier',

The Nineteenth Century: A Quarterly Review, Vol. 43, No. 252, February 1898.

Georg Wilhelm Friedrich Hegel. *Lectures on the Philosophy of World History (1822-28)*. Reprinted in Eze.

Greg Miller, Greg Jaffe, 'Petraeus would helm an increasingly militarized CIA', *The Washington Post*, 27 April 2011.

H.C. Wylly. 1912. *From the Black Mountain to Waziristan*. London: Macmillan.

Hafizullah Emadi, 'Durand Line and Afghan-Pak Relations', *Economic and Political Weekly*, 14 July 1990.

Hassan Abbas. 2005. *Pakistan's Drift into Extremism: Allah, the Army, and America's War on Terror*. Armonk, NY: M.E. Sharpe.

Herodotus. 1954. *The Histories*. London: Penguin Group.

Husain Haqqani. 2010. 'Pakistan. Between Mosque and Military'. Washington, D.C.: Carnegie Endowment for International Peace.

Ian Cameron. 1980. *To the Farthest Ends of the Earth: 150 Years of World Exploration by the Royal Geographical Society*. New York: E.P. Dutton.

Ian Stephen. 1964. *Pakistan: Old Country, New Nation*. London: Penguin.

J. Eliott. 1968. *The Frontier 1839-1947*. London, Cassell.

J.R. Seeley. 1883. *The Expansion of England: Two Courses of Lectures*. Boston: Roberts Brothers.

James Crawford. 2006. *The Creation of States in International Law*. UK: Clarendon Press.

James Spain, 'The Pathan Borderlands', *Middle East Journal*, Vol. 15, No. 2, 1961.

Jennifer Siegel. 2002. *Endgame: Britain, Russia, and the Final Struggle for Central Asia*. New York: I.B. Tauris & Co Ltd.

John Adye. 1867. *Sitana: A Mountain Campaign on the Borders of Afghanistan in 1863*. London: Richard Bentley.

John Alfred Gray. 1895. *At the Court of the Amir*. London: Richard Bentley and Son.

John Wood. 1874. *Journey to the Source of the River Oxus*. London: John Murray.

Jonathan L. Lee. 1996. *The 'Ancient Supremacy': Bukhara, Afghanistan, and the Battle for Balkh, 1731-1901*. Leiden, Netherlands: Brill.

Karl E. Meyer, Shareen Blair Brysac. 1999. *Tournament of Shadows: The Great Game and the Race for Empire in Central Asia*. Washington, D.C.: Counterpoint.

Kenneth Roberts-Wray. 1966. *Commonwealth and Colonial Law*. London: Stevens.

Khan Azmat Hayat, M.Y. Effendi. 2000. *The Durand Line: Its Geo-Strategic Importance*. University of Peshawar.

Khan Abdul Wali Khan. 1987. *Facts are facts: The Untold Story of India's Partition*. New Delhi: Vikas Publishing House.

Khurshid Hasan, 'Pakistan-Afghanistan Relations', *Asian Survey*, Vol. 2, No. 7, 1962.

Kux Dennis. 2000. *The United States and Pakistan, 1947-2000: Disenchantment Allies*. Washington, D.C.: Woodrow Wilson Center Press.

Lord Curzon. 1907. *Frontier, the Romanes Lecture*. Oxford: Clarendon Press.

Louis Dupree. 1973. *Afghanistan*. Princeton, New Jersey: Princeton University Press.

M. Hasan Kakar. 2006. *A Political and Diplomatic History of Afghanistan 1863-1901*. Leiden, Netherlands: Brill.

Malcolm Yapp. 1980. *Strategies of British India: Britain, Iran and Afghanistan, 1798-1850*. Oxford: Clarendon Press.

Martin Ewans. 2002. *Afghanistan: A Short History of Its People and Politics*. New York: HarperCollins.

Martin Ewans. 2002. *Afghanistan: A New History*. New Delhi: Routledge.

Marvin Weinbaum, Jonathan B. Harder, 'Pakistan's Afghan policies and their consequences', *Contemporary South Asia*, Vol. 16, No. 1, March 2008.

Mary Louise Pratt. 1992. *Imperial Eyes: Travel Writing and Transculturation*. London and New York: Routledge.

Mohan Lal. 1846. *Life of Dost Mohammad*. London: Longman, Brown, Green, and Longmans.

Mohan Lal. 1846. *Travels in the Punjab and Afghanistan and Turistan to Balkh, Bikhara and Herat and a Visit to Great Britain, Germany*. Reprinted Lahore: Al Biruni, 1979.

Mountstuart Elphinstone. 1969. *An Account of the Kingdom of Caubul and Its*

Dependencies in Persia, Tartary, and India. Graz, Austria: Akademische Druck u. Verlagsanstalt.

Muhammad Husain (ed. [parts I and II from Shuja, part III from Herati]. 1954. *Waqiat-e Shah Shuja—Herati*. Kabul: Afghan Historical Society.

Narendra Singh Sarila. 2005. *The Shadow of the Great Game: The Untold Story of India's Partition*. New Delhi: HarperCollins.

Olaf Caroe. 1965. *The Pathan*. London: Macmillan & Co Ltd.

Olaf Caroe. 1967. *Soviet Empire: The Turks of Central Asia and Stalinism*. London: Macmillan, p. 353.

Olivier Roy, 'The Taliban: A Strategic Tool for Pakistan', in Christophe Jaffrelot (ed.). 2002. *Pakistan: Nationalism without a Nation?* London: Zed Books.

Olivier Weber, Reza. 2002. *Eternal Afghanistan*. Paris: UNESCO Publishing.

Omar Khan. 2002. *From Kashmir to Kabul*. Ahmedabad, India: Mapin Publishing. '

'Pakistan: The Taliban's Godfather', National Security Archive, Electronic Briefing Book No. 227. 2007.

Patrick Dumberry, Daniel Turp. 2013. 'State Succession with Respect to Multilateral Treaties in the Context of Secession: From the Principle of Tabula Rasa to the Emergence of a Presumption of Continuity of Treaties'. *Baltic Yearbook of International Law*.

Percival Sykes, 'The Right Hon. Sir Mortimer Durand, A Biography', *Journal of the Royal Asiatic Society of Great Britain and Ireland*, Vol. 2, 1927.

Percival Sykes. 1940. *A History of Afghanistan*. London: Macmillan.

Peter Hopkirk. 1990. *The Great Game: The Struggle for Empire in Central Asia*. New York: Kodansha International.

Raj Moon Penderel. 1989. *The British Conquest and Domination of India*. London: Duckworth Publishers.

Ralph H. Magnus. 1985. *Afghan Alternatives: Issues, Options, and Polices*. New Jersey, Transaction Inc.

Rana Muhammed Amir, Safdar Sial, Abdul Basit. 2010. *Dynamics of Taliban Insurgency in FATA*. Islamabad, Pakistan: Shah M Book Co.

Rashid Ahmed. 2000. *Taliban: Islam, oil and the new great game in Central Asia*. London, I.B. Tauris & Co Ltd.

Rasul Bakhash Rais. 2009. *Recovering the Frontier State: War, Ethnicity, and State in Afghanistan*. Lanham, Maryland: Lexington Books.

Richard F. Nyrop, Donald M. Seekins. 1986. *Afghanistan Country Studies*. Washington, D.C.: American University Press.

Rifaat Hussein, 'Pakistan's relation with Afghanistan: Continuity and Change', *Strategic Studies*, Vol. XXII, 2002.

Rizwan Hussain. 2005. *Pakistan and the Emergence of Islamic Militancy in Afghanistan*. Burlington, VT: Ashgate Publishing Company.

Robert Boggs, 'Pakistan's Pashtun Challenge: Moving from Confrontation to Integration', *Strategic Analysis*, March 2012.

S. Fida Yunus (ed.). 2005. *The Durand Line Border Agreement 1893*. Area Study Centre, University of Peshawar, pp. 45–69.

S.A. Mousavi. 1998. *The Hazaras of Afghanistan: An Historical, Cultural, Economic and Political Study*. Surrey: Curzon.

S.M. Burke, Lawrence Ziring. 1990. *Pakistan's Foreign Policy: An Historical Analysis*. Karachi: Oxford University Press.

S.M.M. Qureshi, 'Pakhtunistan: The Frontier Dispute between Afghanistan and Pakistan', *Pacific Affairs*, Vol. 39, 1966.

Sarah Chayes. 2006. *The Punishment of Virtue*. London: Penguin.

Sarfraz Khan, Noor Ul Amin, 'Mir Munshi Aala Sultan Muhammad Khan and His Services to Afghanistan', *Central Asia*, No. 72, Summer 2013.

Selig S. Harrison. 2009. *Pakistan: The State of the Union*. Washington, D.C.: Center for International Policy.

Selig H. Harrison. 1981. *In Afghanistan's shadow: Baluch nationalism and Soviet temptations*. Washington, D.C.: Carnegie Endowment for International Peace.

Seymour M. Hersh. 2016. *The Killing of Osama bin Laden*. New York: Verso.

Shah Mahmoud Hanifi. 2008. *Connecting Histories in Afghanistan:*

Market Relations and State Formation on a Colonial Frontier. Stanford, California: Stanford University Press.

Sherard Cowper-Coles. 2011. *Cables from Kabul: The Inside Story of the West's Afghanistan Campaign*. London: Harper Press.

Shireen Mazari, 'The Durand Line: Evolution of an International Frontier', *Strategic Studies*, Vol. II, No. 2, Autumn 1978.

Shuja Nawaz. 2009. 'FATA—A most dangerous place: meeting the challenges of militancy and terror in the Federally Administered Tribal Areas of Pakistan', CSIS Report. Washingon, D.C.: Center for Strategic and International Studies.

Sir Charles Woleseley, 'The Negro as Soldier', *Fortnightly Review*, Vol. 44, No. 264, December 1888.

Sir James Douie. 1916. *The Panjab, North-West Frontier Province, and Kashmir.* Cambridge: Cambridge University Press.

Sultan Mahomed Khan. 1900. *The Life of Abdur Rahman, Amir of Afghanistan.* London: John Murray.

Susan Pedersen. 2015. *The Guardians: the League of Nations and the Crisis of Empire.* Oxford: Oxford University Press.

T.L. Pennell. 1909. *Among the Wild Tribes of the Afghan Frontier: A Record of Sixteen Years' Close Intercourse with the Natives of the Indian Marches.* London: Seeley & Co. Ltd.

T.R. Moreman. 1998. *The Army in India and the Development of Frontier Warfare, 1849-1947.* London: Macmillan in association with King's College, London.

Thomas Barfield. 'The Durand Line: History, Consequences, and Future', report of a conference held in Istanbul, Turkey in 2007 by American Institute of Afghanistan Studies and The Hollings Center for International Dialogue.

Thomas Holdich, 'The Use of Practical Geography Illustrated by Recent Frontier Operations,' *The Geographical Journal*, Vol. 6, 1899.

Thomas Martin. 2008. *Empires of Intelligence: Security Services and Colonial Disorder after 1914.* Berkeley: University of California Press.

Thomas Simpson, 'Bordering and Frontier-Making in Nineteenth-Century British India', *The Historical Journal*, Vol. 58, No. 2, June 2015.

Timothy Mitchell, 'Orientalism and the Exhibitionary Order', in Nicholas Dirks (ed.). 1992. *Colonialism and Culture.* Ann Arbor, Michigan: University of Michigan Press.

Vazira Fazila-Yacoobali Zamindar, 'Altitudes of Imperialism', *The Caravan: A Journal of Politics and Culture*, 1 August 2014.

Victor Kiernan. 1969. *The lords of human kind: European attitude towards the outside world in the Imperial Age.* London: Weidenfeld and Nicolson.

Victoria Schofield. 2003. *Afghan Frontier: Feuding and Fighting and Central Asia.* New York: Tauris Parke Paperbacks.

W.K. Fraser-Tytler. 1967. *Afghanistan: A Study of Political Developments in Central and Southern Asia.* London: Oxford University Press.

William Paget. 1874. *A Record of the Expeditions Undertaken against the North-West Frontier Tribes.* Calcutta: Government of India.

Willem Vogelsang. 2008. *The Afghans.* Chichester, West Sussex, UK: John Wiley & Sons Ltd.

William Henry Paget. 1908. *Frontier and Overseas Expeditions from India, Volume II: North-West Frontier Tribes between the Kabul and Gamul Rivers.* Simla, India: Government Monotype Press.

Zak Leonard, 'Colonial Ethnography on India's North-West Frontier, 1850-1910', *The Historical Journal*, Vol. 59, 2016. 'While care has been taken to give attribution in the text to the source, any omission is inadvertent.'

Index